SYSTEMS PERSPECTIVES ON RESOURCES, CAPABILITIES, AND MANAGEMENT PROCESSES

ADVANCED SERIES IN MANAGEMENT

Series Editor:
Professor Ron Sanchez
IMD, Lausanne, Switzerland

The intent of the Advanced Series in Management is to produce foundational books for a new era of management theory that will be long-lived in serving future generations of management researchers and practitioners. To this end, the Advanced Series in Management has three goals:

(i)   publishing volumes that develop new conceptual foundations for management theory;
(ii)   countering the trend towards increasing fragmentation in management theory and research by developing a new theory base for management that is interconnected and integrative;
(iii) developing new management theory that has clear, direct usefulness for the practice of management.

The volumes in the Advanced Series in Management are intended collectively to elaborate a broadened and more integrated theory base for understanding and addressing the challenges facing contemporary managers. Volumes in the Advanced Series in Management therefore seek to stimulate and shape the development of management thought in ways and directions that reach beyond the content and perspectives of established management theory. The Advanced Series in Management intends to be, in effect, the series of academic management books that is willing to break away from the pack and to publish titles that advance new frameworks for management thinking.

Forthcoming titles include:

SKÖLDBERG
Tracks and Frames: The Economy of Symbolic Forms in Organizations

HEDBERG, BAUMARD & YAKHLEF
Investigating Imaginary Organizations

MAULA
Knowledge-Intensive Service Companies as Living, Learning and Evolving Systems

MITLETON-KELLY
Complex Systems and Evolutionary Perspectives on Organisations

Related Elsevier journals:
Business Horizons
European Management Journal
Journal of Management
Leadership Quarterly
Long Range Planning
Organizational Dynamics
Scandinavian Journal of Management

SYSTEMS PERSPECTIVES ON RESOURCES, CAPABILITIES, AND MANAGEMENT PROCESSES

EDITED BY

JOHN MORECROFT

London Business School, London, UK

RON SANCHEZ

IMD — International Institute for Management Development, Lausanne, Switzerland

AIMÉ HEENE

University of Gent, Gent, Belgium

2002

Pergamon
An Imprint of Elsevier Science

Amsterdam – London – New York – Oxford – Paris – Shannon – Tokyo

ELSEVIER SCIENCE Ltd
The Boulevard, Langford Lane
Kidlington, Oxford OX5 1GB, UK

First edition 2002

Library of Congress Cataloging in Publication Data
A catalog record from the Library of Congress has been applied for.

British Library Cataloguing in Publication Data
A catalog record from the Library of Congress has been applied for.

ISBN 0-08-043778-8

∞ The paper used in this publication meets the requirements of ANSI/NISO Z39.48-1992 (Permanence of Paper).
Printed in The Netherlands.

Contents

Part III: Systems Concepts and Models for Improving Management Decision Making

Part IV: Systems Concepts for Self-Managing Organizations

Contributors

John Harald Aadne

Institute of Management
University of St. Gallen
St. Gallen, Switzerland

Michael D. Boehlje

Department of Agricultural Economics
Purdue University
West Lafayette, Indiana, USA

L. Martin Cloutier

Department of Management and Technology
School of Management
University of Quebec at Montreal
Montreal, QC, Canada

Pål I. Davidsen

Department of Information Science
University of Bergen
Bergen, Norway

Aimé Heene

University of Gent
Gent, Belgium

Philippe Lorino

ESSEC
Cergy-Pontoise, France

Volker Mahnke

Copenhagen Business School
Frederiksberg, Denmark

Edoardo Mollona

Istituto di Economia Aziendale "Gino Zappa"
Area for Organisational Modelling
Universita' Commerciale "Luigi Bocconi"
Milano, Italy

John Morecroft

London Business School
Sussex Place
London, UK

Ron Sanchez

IMD – International Institute for
Management Development
Lausanne, Switzerland

J. Michael Spector

Department of Information Science
University of Bergen
Bergen, Norway

Jean-Claude Tarondeau

ESSEC
Cergy-Pontoise, France

Kim Warren

London Business School
Sussex Place
London, UK

Jenshou Yang

Department of Business Administration
National Yunlin University of Science and Technology
Touliu, Yunlin, Taiwan

Introduction to the Advanced Series in Management

The intent of the Advanced Series in Management is to produce foundational books for a new era of management theory that will be long-lived in serving future generations of management researchers and practitioners. To this end, the Advanced Series in Management has three goals:

(i) publishing volumes that develop new conceptual foundations for management theory;
(ii) countering the trend towards increasing fragmentation in management theory and research by developing a new theory base for management that is interconnected and integrative;
(iii) developing new management theory that has clear, direct usefulness for the practice of management.

The volumes in the Advanced Series in Management are intended collectively to elaborate a broadened and more integrated theory base for understanding and addressing the challenges facing contemporary managers. Volumes in the Advanced Series in Management therefore seek to stimulate and shape the development of management thought in ways and directions that reach beyond the content and perspectives of established management theory. The Advanced Series in Management intends to be, in effect, the series of academic management books that is willing to break away from the pack and to publish titles that advance new frameworks for management thinking.

The Series introduces new conceptualizations for management theory that rise above any single or dominant theoretical perspective. In essence, the defining theoretical sensibility of the Series is a new perspective on management that includes essential dynamic, systemic, cognitive, and holistic aspects of managing organizations and that seeks to treat these aspects theoretically as an interconnected whole. A key focus in this new approach to building management theory is therefore elaborating the dynamics of the interactions between the multiple aspects of the management processes that thus far have not been — and indeed cannot be — adequately addressed through the theoretical lens of a single discipline.

The Advanced Series in Management takes as a given that *change* is the normal state of the world that managers face — and that management theory must therefore address adequately the dynamics of markets, technologies, organizations, and society that managers need to contend with. Understanding the disequilibria in the environments of contemporary organizations and how managers can respond to them is thus a central concern of the Series.

The Series also holds firmly to a view of organizations as *human systems* in which the multiple interactions and interdependencies of all participants must be explicitly recognized and reconciled in theory as well as in practice. The systemic view of organizations and the management process is intended to provide a conceptual framework that is receptive to inputs from both established theory and new theoretical perspectives and that is capable of more balanced and thus more realistic representations of organizations in theory.

The Series also advances a cognitive perspective in which imperfect information, bounded rationality, and the resulting cognitive limits of managers are not assumed away for the sake of building elegant theory, but rather are seen as "core constraints" in the management process that must be directly addressed by new management theory. In plain language, the Advanced Series in Management is not an outlet for yet more management theory that pretends that managers — or observers of managers — have information and understanding that no one can actually have in the complex and uncertain environments managers actually work in. Rather, the Series intends to establish new management theory that is consistent with the actual cognitive processes and limitations of human managers and researchers.

A final sensibility of the Series is the belief that management theory must recognize the full set of interrelated stakeholder interests (employees, suppliers, customers, communities, debt holders, and shareholders) that interact in organizations. New theory developed in the Series will recognize and explore the identification, weighing, and balancing of multiple stakeholder interests that is fundamental to the management process.

Our expectation is that this volume and the other volumes in the Series will form a collection of foundational books that will be long-lived in providing theoretical impetus to both current and future generations of management academics and practitioners.

Each volume in the Series must meet the dual requirements of achieving conceptual clarity and theoretical coherence, while yielding useful recommendations for improving management practice. Each volume in the Series has the mission of advancing our thinking about management in ways that

- connect management theory with management practice by refocusing management theory and research on the actual problems and concerns of contemporary managers;
- link together the currently fragmented areas of management theory by elaborating new concepts that can connect and integrate the theory bases of relevant disciplines — and do so in ways that more effectively address the real concerns of managers;
- introduce new theory that is not currently established in the management disciplines, but that can be used to represent management problems more fully and realistically.

To meet these criteria, development of volumes for the Series is guided by the four principles of inclusiveness, connectedness, theoretical grounding, and applicability.

Inclusiveness means that the volumes in the Series include many disciplines, perspectives, and approaches, both established and new, that offer useful improvements in our understanding of the problems and processes of managing. What the Series will not do, however, is proliferate volumes that apply a single theoretical perspective to a wide range of management issues and topics — i.e., a single theoretical hammer treating every management problem as if it were a nail. Thus, the Advanced Series in Management is not just another collection of "the usual suspects" — a marketing perspective, an operations title, an advanced organization behavior perspective, etc. — that have no evident theoretical connection with each other. While conceived as a collection of volumes that is intendedly broad in its theoretical scope, the Series nevertheless requires each volume to make a definable, significant, and coherent contribution to developing management theory that embraces and integrates multiple perspectives on managing.

Connectedness means that each volume in the Series must develop clear conceptual connections to other perspectives developed in existing or planned volumes in the Series. While each volume must develop well an approach to studying management that is distinctive in its own emphases, it must also establish theoretical connections with the themes developed in other volumes. In this way, the volumes in the Series are intended to weave a web of interconnected concepts and theories that will in time collectively define a new theory base for management. What we want to achieve through connectedness is nexus of ideas — each volume not only bringing its own useful ideas for understanding management, but also linking its ideas to ideas in other volumes in the Series to compose an interconnected view of the multiple aspects of the management process.

Theoretical grounding means that each volume must develop a perspective that is carefully grounded in actual management processes and built up from a well defined and carefully elaborated conceptual framework for representing and analyzing those processes. What we wish to avoid in the Series is theoretical rigidities and narrowness that make us blind to important management realities. What we wish to achieve in the Series is the progressive development of concepts and theories that are understandable to both academics and managers. Thus each volume starts with a statement of fundamental concepts and basic presumptions and then moves on to comprehensible theoretical propositions, clear applications to important management contexts, and useful suggestions for both practice and further theory development.

Applicability means that each volume in the Series must meet a test of clear applicability to actual — not imagined or posited — management problems and concerns. To meet the criterion of applicability, each volume must have a well stated, theoretically developed set of ideas that it applies directly to a well defined and important set of management concerns. What the Series will avoid is volumes that are laden with theory but short on useful applications, on the one hand, and volumes that approach important management problems with inadequately developed concepts or flawed logic, on the other. In essence, what the Series intends to achieve is volumes that advance ideas about managing that have both theoretical clarity and demonstrable usefulness to managers.

If successful in meeting these goals and norms, the Advanced Series in Management will play an important role in shaping the direction of management theory and practice in the next decade — and in the decades to follow as well.

The Advanced Series in Management was conceived in present form in 1996 and published its first volumes in 2001. I would like to thank Tony Seward, Sammye Haigh, Tom Clark, David Lamkin, and many others at Elsevier for their support for the Series during its long and still ongoing incubation.

Ron Sanchez, Series Editor
Lausanne, Switzerland

Series Editor's Introduction to This Volume

A view of organizations as human systems is an integral element in the philosophical foundation of the Advanced Series in Management. It is appropriate therefore that one of the first volumes to appear in the Series develops systems perspectives on the resources, capabilities, and management processes that collectively make up organizations as human systems.

This volume unites leading scholars and core ideas from a number of fields — systems, strategy, competence-based management, information science, accounting and control, operations management, and technology management — that share a common interest in understanding the internal dynamics and aggregate behaviors of organizations as systems, but that have previously not worked together in a concerted way. The present volume is an effort to interrelate and integrate concepts and methods from these essential perspectives to develop a more multidimensional, strategic, and robust framework for studying and managing organizations as human systems.

Contemporary management thinking is increasingly concerned with designing management processes that can be more effective in building and leveraging both an organization's own resources and capabilities and the resources and capabilities it can access beyond its own boundaries. The cross-pollination of systems, competence, and other concepts in this volume has produced new insights into the requirements for designing organizations as effective systems for building and leveraging resources and capabilities, as well as useful suggestions for improving the management of these key processes.

As the growing complexity and accelerating dynamics of organizations and their environments make it increasingly problematic to derive useful prescriptions for managers from traditional methods of analysis and optimization, the role of dynamic modeling and simulation in management research and practice is certain to grow. The system dynamics models used in several of the papers in this volume illustrate how organizational processes for building and leveraging resources and capabilities can be dynamically modeled and simulated — often in rather straightforward and accessible ways — to develop deeper understanding of those processes and to devise more effective management policies for guiding those processes.

The present volume thus meets the goal of the Advanced Series in management to advance new ideas that are theoretically inclusive, interconnected, well grounded in the realities of organizations, and directly applicable in the practice of management.

Ron Sanchez, Series Editor
Lausanne, Switzerland

Introduction

Systems Thinking and Competence Concepts

Chapter 1

Integrating Systems Thinking and Competence Concepts in a New View of Resources, Capabilities, and Management Processes

John Morecroft, Ron Sanchez and Aimé Heene

Introduction

Management theory and practice advance through three kinds of evolutions. From time to time there are fundamental theoretical renewals that lead to development of important new concepts for managing organizations. At other times there is rediscovery and renewed appreciation of the relevance and usefulness of concepts developed in earlier years. A third form of advance occurs when new ideas and pre-existing ideas are integrated in ways that lead to new perspectives on organizations, to deeper understanding of the challenges that managers of organizations face, and to new, more effective approaches to meeting those challenges.

In this volume, we aspire to contribute to the third form of advance of management theory and practice. The papers in this volume seek to integrate essential insights into the systemic behaviors of organizations[1] with important new ideas about managing organizations recently developed under the banners of the resource-based view, the dynamic capabilities perspective, and competence-based management theory.[2] Our specific objective in bringing together the papers in this volume is to show how contemporary systems thinking can illuminate and extend some central competence-based management concepts about the nature and use of *resources, capabilities, and management processes* in effective organizations.

We focus here on the resources organizations use, the capabilities organizations develop in using resources, and the management processes organizations adopt to coordinate their resources and capabilities, because these are recognized as the essential elements of organization in both the systems and competence perspectives. What we try to accomplish

---

[1]See, for example: Forrester (1961), Senge (1990), Richardson (1991), and Sterman (2000).
[2]For an introduction to competence-based management theory, see Hamel & Heene, 1993; Sanchez, Heene, & Thomas, 1996; Sanchez & Heene, 1997a, 1997b; Heene & Sanchez, 1996; and Sanchez, 2001a. For a survey of how earlier strategy perspectives like the resource-based view (e.g., Wernerfelt, 1984, Dierickx & Cool, 1989, Barney, 1991) and dynamic capabilities (Teece, Pisano, & Shuen, 1997) have been incorporated into competence-based management theory, see Sanchez, 2001b.

Systems Perspectives on Resources, Capabilities, and Management Processes, pages 3–16.
Copyright © 2002 by Elsevier Science Ltd.
All rights of reproduction in any form reserved.
ISBN: 0-08-043778-8

through this focus is a broadening and deepening of our understanding of the critical systemic interrelationships between resources, capabilities, and management processes that must be recognized and managed in building and leveraging organizational competences. The ideas developed by the authors in this volume offer a fundamentally important theoretical perspective on the nature of the management task and the practical challenges involved in carrying out that task. Taken together, the ideas herein suggest important new directions for management research and practice that can lead to better approaches to managing organizations as human systems (Sanchez, 1997).

The volume presents papers by systems-and-strategy scholars (John Morecroft, Kim Warren) and researchers in competence-based management theory (Ron Sanchez, Aimé Heene, Volker Mahnke, John Harald Aadne). Importantly, the volume also includes work by researchers from several management disciplines who offer innovative integrations and applications of systems and competence ideas in addressing specific issues of broad management concern. These contributors are Edoardo Mollona from strategic management, Michael Spector and Pål Davidsen from information science, Philippe Lorino from accounting and control, Jean-Claude Tarondeau from operations management, Martin Cloutier in technology management, Michael Boehlje in agribusiness, and Jenshou Yang in general management.

Collectively, the papers in this volume have taken two essential steps in developing a unified view and coherent understanding of the systemic interrelationships of resources, capabilities, and management processes in a competent organization. First, the authors have adopted a common set of meanings for the terms "resources," "capabilities," and "management processes." Second, the authors ground their analyses directly on the four conceptual "cornerstones" of competence-based management theory. Let us briefly consider each of these critical steps.

The Concepts of Resources, Capabilities, and Management Processes

Linguists have proposed that words are introduced into a language whenever it becomes desirable to make functionally important distinctions in a given context of human endeavor (Bickerton, 1993). In the context of management theory and practice, we are endeavoring to understand:

● Why and how organizations form;
● How organizations survive, develop, and evolve over time;
● Why some organizations prosper and grow, while others struggle and fail;
● How managers can improve an organization's ability to survive, prosper, and grow.

To develop and communicate our understanding of these phenomena, both researchers and practitioners must have a conceptually consistent terminology for describing and analyzing organizations and their behaviors. In this volume, the terms *resources, capabilities, and management processes* provide the essential vocabulary and concepts for describing and analyzing the "building blocks" of organizations and the important interactions of those building blocks in the behaviors of organizations as systems (Sanchez, Heene & Thomas, 1996).

Assets include anything tangible or intangible that could be used to help an organization achieve its goals. *Resources* are defined as anyone (human assets) and anything (tangible or intangible assets) that are available and useful in any activities an organization undertakes in pursuing its goals. Resources can be firm-specific (i.e., under the legal control of a firm and thus residing "within the boundaries" of a firm) or firm-addressable (beyond the legal control of a firm and thus residing "outside the boundaries" of a firm, but accessible to it).

Capabilities are an organization's repeatable patterns of action in the use of resources, again usually in the context of activities that the organization undertakes in pursuit of its goals. Organizational capabilities result from the coordinated application of the knowledge and skills of individuals in person-to-person interactions and in the interactions of people with non-human tangible assets (e.g., production machines, computers, etc).

Management processes refer to the data gathering and interpreting, goal setting, decision making, resource allocating, and coordinating activities that managers undertake in acquiring, developing, and deploying an organization's resources and capabilities. An organization's management processes determine the specific goals an organization sets for itself, the activities the organization undertakes in pursuing those goals, and the stocks and flows of resources and capabilities available to the organization in its goal-seeking activities. Management processes lead to the building up through acquisition or internal development of an organization's resources and capabilities, to their use (leveraging) and maintenance, and to their replacement or retirement.

The "Four Cornerstones" of Competence-Based Management Theory

Competence-based management theory (Sanchez & Heene, 1997a,b; Heene & Sanchez, 1996; Sanchez, 1997) intends to recognize and address the real issues managers face in the task of managing organizations. These issues are represented as being intrinsically complex because of:

- the *dynamic* nature of an organization's environment;
- the *systemic* interrelationships of the resources and capabilities in an organization;
- the need to develop a *holistic* view of the intersecting interests of all providers of essential resources and capabilities in an organization;
- the *cognitive* challenge in trying to understand the changing environment an organization faces, in coordinating the varied interactions that must take place between an organization's resources and capabilities, and in balancing the many interests of people in an organization as a human system as it defines and pursues its goals in a changing environment.

A *competent organization* is one that "can sustain coordinated deployments of resources and capabilities in ways that enable an organization to achieve its goals" (Sanchez, Heene, & Thomas, 1996). Building and managing a competent organization demands that managers successfully cope with these four fundamental aspects of the management task, which are referred to as the "four cornerstones" of competence-based management theory. Let us look briefly at each.

The first cornerstone of competence-based management theory is that the environment of a contemporary organization is *dynamic*. Market needs and preferences, the technological means for serving markets, and the legal and social contexts in which an organization uses its technologies and serves its markets will be changing, both incrementally and sometimes radically. The sources of environmental changes will often be complexly inter-related and will therefore result in an environment that defies reliable prediction and that may even tend to the chaotic. Analysis of an organization's environment at any point in time is likely to suggest both multiple opportunities for creating value and multiple threats to any value-creating processes the organization may undertake. Moreover, the opportunities and threats that can be identified will be changing, often in significant but imperfectly predictable ways. In the competence perspective, coping with change and uncertainty is a defining feature of the management task.

The second cornerstone of competence theory is that organizations are essentially *goal-seeking open systems*. As a human system, an organization must provide something of value to its members in exchange for the resources and capabilities they provide to it. Thus, an organization must pursue (and at least to an acceptable extent *achieve*) a goal or set of goals for creating value in ways that can be shared with, and will be appreciated by, providers of the resources and capabilities it needs. To sustain its goal-seeking activities, an organization must behave like an open system that not only uses the resources and capabilities of its own members, but also draws on resources and capabilities of people and entities external to the organization. An organization's interactions with various external providers of resources — as well as its interactions with other organizations competing to attract the same resources — embeds an organization in larger economic, social, techno-logical, and legal systems.

The third cornerstone of competence theory is the necessity for taking a *holistic* view of an organization's goal-seeking and value-creating activities. Managers must mediate the diverse and sometimes conflicting interests of various stakeholders as providers of resources and capabilities the organization needs, so that each essential provider feels he or she is being adequately compensated (in all essential respects) for their contribution to the organization. Thus, within the competence perspective, managers must do more than perceive and respond to opportunities to *create* value through the organization's interactions with its product markets. Managers must also be able to *distribute* the value an organization creates so as to assure the continued participation of all essential resource providers in the organization's value creation activities.

The fourth cornerstone of the competence perspective recognizes the daunting *cognitive* challenges that managers face in trying to understand changing environments, to coordinate many kinds of resources and capabilities, and to balance diverse human interests in defining and pursuing an organization's goals. In the competence perspective, the cognitive tasks of sensemaking, analyzing, imagining, designing, and other challenging intellectual activities are regarded as fundamental to the management task. Strategic competition between organizations is therefore in important measure a "contest between managers' cognitive processes" in different organizations. As a consequence, managers face the unique challenge of *managing their own cognitive processes* as an integral, enabling, and sometimes constraining part of the overall sensemaking and action-taking capabilities of an organization.

Systems Perspectives on Resources, Capabilities, and Management Processes

We now introduce some central concepts developed over the last three decades in the study of systems and their dynamic behaviors. We consider both some general characteristics of systems and, more specifically, some important ways in which the resources, capabilities, and management processes in an organization collectively behave like a system. Our objective in this section is not to provide a comprehensive systems analysis of resources, capabilities, and management processes. Rather we introduce some key systems concepts that help to frame a general systems perspective on resources, capabilities, and management processes in organizations. These concepts will subsequently play important roles in the analyses developed in the papers in this volume.

We first consider the fundamental property of *interdependency* among the elements of a system, and the ways that interdependency occurs as an organization uses its resources and capabilities. We then introduce the notion of the *boundary* of a system, and consider why organizations will virtually always be *open systems* with relatively "porous" boundaries. We then examine more closely the nature of the interactions between system elements. We explain the potential for system elements to have either "positive" or "negative" influences on each other that may combine to form either *reinforcing* or *balancing feedback loops* that largely determine an organization's dynamic behaviors and greatly affect its performance over time.

Interdependency of System Elements

A *system* is a collection of interacting elements. In the example illustrated in Figure 1, element A both affects and is affected by element B, and the same is true of elements A and C. Thus, elements A-B-C form a system of interacting elements. (Note that elements B and C also indirectly interact with each other through their respective effects on element A.) The elements that make up a system may be animate or inanimate, tangible or intangible, and the possible kinds of interactions among the elements of a system are virtually inexhaustible in their variety. The essential meaning of *interactions* between system

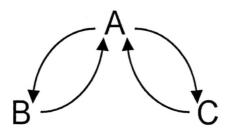

Figure 1: Interacting Elements A, B, and C in the System A-B-C.

elements, however, is that a change in one system element causes, induces, or otherwise leads to a change in one or more other system elements. As a result, the current state of any given element of a system will always depend in some way and to some extent on the state of one or more other elements in the system. This *interdependence* of elements is therefore the defining characteristic of a system, while the dynamic behavior exhibited by a system depends on the nature of the interactions between system elements and the speed and intensity with which the interdependent elements interact.

The Boundaries of a System

Strictly speaking, given the above definition of a system, the entire social and business world may be viewed as one large system. As a practical matter, however, we are usually interested in understanding some more limited part of the world, such as a given economy, industry, organization, or unit within an organization. To focus on some subset (or more precisely, on some *subsystem*) of the business world, we commonly place *boundaries* around a collection of people and things of interest, and then refer to that bounded collection as a system. If correctly placed, the boundaries of a system demarcate the elements that have relatively intense and frequent interactions (those that are "inside" the boundary of the system) from elements that have relatively less intense or frequent interactions (those elements that are then regarded as being "outside" the system). As suggested in Figure 2, the boundary around the relatively intense interactions among A, B, C, and D distinguish the system A-B-C-D from the external element X, which has a relatively less intense or frequent interaction with A. Although we may place boundaries around a system for some purpose of analysis or management, all systems nevertheless remain *open systems* in the sense that there will always be some form and level of interactions between the elements "inside" a system with some elements "outside" the system.[3] Thus, to some extent, the boundaries of a system are inevitably artificial and somewhat arbitrary in their placement and are always "porous" to some degree.

Feedback Loops

A feedback loop exists in a system when a change in one system element precipitates a chain reaction of changes in other system elements that eventually induces a further change in the first system element. The interactions between A and B and between A and C in Figure 1 and the interactions between A, B, C, and D in Figure 2 are examples of feedback loops in systems. Feedback loops have two characteristics that directly affect the dynamic behavior of a system in fundamentally important ways.

---

[3]Competence-based management theory reflects the inherent "porosity" of the boundaries of a system by characterizing an organization as an open system that depends on many kinds of resource flows. New resources (people, technology, information, revenues) are obtained from entities in the external environment of an organization, while other resources (products, knowledge, people) are exported or retired from the organization and usually absorbed by entities in the external environment of the organization.

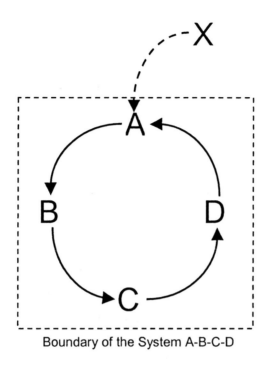

Boundary of the System A-B-C-D

Figure 2: Setting a Boundary Around the System A-B-C-D.

Time delays are usually encountered in the effects that interdependent system elements have on each other as they interact. Significant delays may occur, for example, between the time a firm changes its goals and the time the firm actually achieves those goals. Delays in the effects that increased resources have on output and productivity are also likely. As papers in this volume by both Morecroft and Warren demonstrate, such delays can greatly affect both the speed and steadiness of a firm's overall growth process.

Systems theory also recognizes that the interactions between elements may be of two basic types, each of which has a very different impact on the internal dynamics of a system. When an increase or decrease in a system element leads to a *corresponding* increase or decrease in another system element, the first element is said to have a "positive" influence on the second element. When a change in one system element leads to an *opposite* change in another system element, the first is said to have a "negative" influence on the second. If some interacting elements of a system have an overall positive influence on each other, they form a positive or "reinforcing" feedback loop, as illustrated by the reinforcing feedback loop A-B-C in Figure 3. When some interacting elements of a system have an overall negative influence on each other, they form a negative or "balancing" feedback loop, as illustrated by the balancing feedback loop A-D in Figure 3.

Reinforcing feedback loops tend to create "positive-gain systems," in the sense that a change in one direction in one system element will eventually (and sometimes quickly)

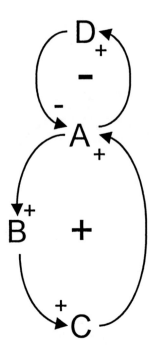

Figure 3: Positive Feedback Loop A-B-C and Negative Feedback Loop A-D in System
A-B-C-D.

precipitate a "chain reaction" of changes in other interacting elements that ultimately
cause even further change in the same direction by the first system element. Thus, reinforcing loops tend to drive systems increasingly upward or downward in potentially
destabilizing explosive growth or implosive collapse unless restrained by the moder-
ating influence of one or more balancing feedback loops. In Figure 3, for example, an
upward change in A leads to a corresponding upward change in B, which in turn leads
to an upward change in C, which returns to drive further upward change in A, which
would then precipitate further positive gain cycles through the loop. However, in the
balancing loop A-D, an upward change in A leads to a corresponding upward change in
D, but an upward change in D leads to an opposite, downward change in A. Thus, the
negative influence of D on A through the balancing feedback loop A-D tends to
moderate or stabilize the positive-gain influence of B and C on A through the reinforcing feedback loop A-B-C. Given appropriate relative intensities of these positive
and negative feedback loops, the overall system A-B-C-D has the potential to be a *self-
regulating system* that is capable of steady, controlled adaptation when, for example, an
external influence X causes a change in system element A. If the feedback loops A-B-C
and A-D are not appropriately "balanced" in their influences on their respective system
elements, the system A-B-C-D may experience unstable, uncontrollable behavior if an

environmental change in X causes a change in A (e.g., the cross-boundary interaction X-A).

Applying Competence and Systems Concepts to Resources, Capabilities, and Management Processes

In combining competence and systems concepts in various ways, the papers in this volume can help meet one of the central challenges in managing organizations today — the need to design organizations as human systems whose internal dynamics for building and leveraging resources and capabilities are aligned effectively with the dynamics of their competitive environments. The papers in this volume develop a number of management perspectives, policies, and practices that can help create organizations with appropriate *strategic flexibilities* to respond to a changing array of environmental demands and opportunities. In essence, these papers explain key aspects of "systems thinking" — and acting — that are essential skills for managers pursuing Hamel and Prahalad's (1993) notion of "strategy as stretch and leverage."

A second perspective developed in this volume is that the complexities confronted in trying to manage large organizations and their environments are likely to overwhelm the cognitive capabilities of even the most brilliant managers. Thus, from a systems perspective on competence, creating the organizational strategic flexibilities needed to sustain value creation processes in a dynamic environment requires organization designs with high levels of distributed intelligence, as well as management processes that enable an organization to function as a largely *self-managing human system.*

Each of the papers in this volume examines important aspects of the systemic nature and behavior of the competent organization. The papers are grouped in sections of the volume in the following way:

The first section includes papers by John Morecroft, Kim Warren, Martin Cloutier, and Michael Boehlje that explain and apply some fundamental systems concepts and modeling techniques to the analysis of organizations as dynamic resource systems.

In his paper "Resource management under dynamic complexity," John Morecroft investigates the impact of a firm's resource management policies on the firm's performance in a dynamic environment. Focusing on the management of human resources, Morecroft shows how feedback effects and their associated time delays can generate complex and puzzling dynamic behaviors in even a simple business model as specific management policies are applied to selecting staffing levels, assessing labor productivity, and setting performance goals. Morecroft also shows how applying management policies based on alternative strategic logics leads to significant differences in patterns of resource accumulation, productivity levels, goal attainment, and performance. He then illustrates these effects by modeling management policies for resource building and leveraging in the dramatic rise and then precipitous decline of People Express airline in the 1980s. The case study illustrates the power of system dynamics models as vehicles for improving policies for resource building and leveraging in dynamic, complex, competitive environments.

Kim Warren's paper "Operationalizing the impact of competence-building on the performance of firms' resource systems" looks further into the processes of accumulating and depleting resources in organizations as systems of resources. Warren explores ways in which interdependencies between resources within an organization create the need for careful balancing of resource building processes. He uses a simple model of resource flows in an organization to show that small initial differences in firm capabilities can, over time, lead to large accumulated differences in its stocks of interdependent resources and capabilities. As a result, small (and seemingly insignificant) variations in a firm's policies for managing resource accumulations can actually lead to large differences in a firm's available capabilities, its organizational effectiveness, its competitive advantages, and thus its performance in responding to environmental exigencies.

Cloutier and Boehlje's paper "Innovation management under uncertainty: A system dynamics model of R&D investments in biotechnology" uses systems modeling to explore alternative strategies for developing and commercializing a new biotechnology product. They use dynamic simulations to discover the impacts of time delays and uncertainties encountered in using various development and commercialization resources on the economic value of a biotech innovation. By using dynamic systems models to investigate alternative development strategies, Cloutier and Boehlje demonstrate how systems models can help decision makers make better investment decisions in complex management situations.

Section 2 includes papers by Sanchez and Heene, by Mollona, and by Lorino and Tarondeau that identify and explore some key concerns in managing flows of resources, creating and applying new capabilities, and developing effective management processes for identifying, building, and leveraging organizational competences.

Sanchez and Heene's paper "Managing strategic change: A systems view of strategic organizational change and strategic flexibility" introduces a model of *organizations as open systems* and uses their open systems model to investigate key challenges in managing the dynamics of organizational change and in improving an organization's strategic flexibility. Sanchez and Heene investigate how the flexibilities of an organization's resources and of its managers in coordinating its resources combine in various ways to create five essential forms of organizational flexibility referred to as five *competence modes*. They discuss some key interdependencies between the competence modes that must be managed in an effective, adaptive organization. They also consider the different impacts that "bottom-up" and "top-down" processes of data gathering and interpretation have on managers' ability to develop effective policies for improving an organization's five competence modes and its resulting strategic flexibility and capacity for organizational change.

Edoardo Mollona's paper "A competence view of firms as resource accumulation systems: A synthesis of resource-based and evolutionary models of strategy making" develops an "ecological" systems perspective on an organization's resource building processes. Mollona develops a model of a firm in which its resource building and allocation strategies evolve through essentially Darwinian processes of variation, selection, and retention. In this model, a firm will tend to use the resources and capabilities that have a history of succeeding in the firm's competitive environment, but will from time to time acquire and deploy new (but usually not too different) variations and combinations of resources and capabilities, especially when current patterns in deploying resources and capabilities appear to be losing their ability to compete effectively. Mollona elaborates the critical role of an organization's informational feedback loops both in precipitating a willingness to try new resources and capabilities and in shaping a firm's decisions to commit current resources to building new resources and capabilities.

Lorino and Tarondeau's paper "From resources to processes in competence-based strategic management" elaborates on the fundamental theoretical premise in the competence perspective that resources and capabilities can only become strategically valuable contributors to an organization's competences when they are deployed and coordinated through the processes an organization undertakes. Accordingly, Lorino and Tarondeau develop the concept of strategic processes as the unit of analysis for both designing and researching effective systems. Through an extended case analysis, they illustrate the ways in which strategic processes become the focal point for strategically aligning a firm's internal resources and capabilities with the threats and opportunities in its environment, while also providing an arena for strategic learning by managers when they experiment by deploying new combinations of resources and capabilities.

Section 3 includes papers by Spector and Davidsen, by Mahnke and Aadne, and by Yang that explore a number of critical cognitive issues in managerial decision making and that suggest a number of ways that systems concepts and models can improve management decision processes.

Spector and Davidsen's paper "Cognitive complexity in decision making and policy formation: A system dynamics perspective" argues that complexity in managerial decision environments results both from the multiplicity of factors that managers may recognize as potentially relevant to a decision situation and from uncertainties of managers about underlying cause-and-effect relationships among those factors. Spector and Davidsen discuss the design of system dynamics-based decision-support models that can help managers cope with both of these sources of complexity. They argue that effective decision making depends on reducing the complexity of decision situations through processes of categorizing factors and events and then establishing matching patterns of appropriate responses — i.e., discovering categories of actions that appear to be effective in dealing with specific categories of events. Spector and Davidsen propose that system dynamics models can help managers in both complexity-reduction processes by clarifying internal feedback mechanisms, time delays in feedback effects, nonlinear forms of behavior in interactions among factors, and uncertainties about interactions among factors, as well as changes in the foregoing.

Mahnke and Aadne's paper "Managing speed in competence-driven strategic renewal" represents a firm as a complex, co-adaptive, open system that must undergo periodic strategic renewal. Mahnke and Aadne characterize strategic renewal as a three-step progression from strategic imagination to new coordinated strategic actions. The critical middle step in the renewal process is the development of a new "common ground" for an organization as a human — and thus cognitive — system. The building of an adequate new common ground requires creating a shared language for describing the organization's current and future contexts, building a strategic agenda of new goals and objectives, and defining an alignment of the organization's past, present, and future representations of itself. Mahnke and Aadne identify several ways in which the processes of building common ground and achieving coordinated action can break down, and they propose ways of avoiding and overcoming such breakdowns.

Yang's paper "Systems thinking in managerial decision making" investigates some of the cognitive challenges to managers in managing organizations as systems in environments of growing complexity. Yang's particular interest is in understanding why people not only have difficulty making good decisions in complex situations, but also often fail to improve their decision making. Yang reports the results of a laboratory experiment to investigate the effects of varying levels of guidance in systems thinking under alternative incentive schemes on the ability of decision makers to improve their performance in a simulated management decision situation. The results of Yang's experiments suggest that training in systems thinking can improve managers' decision making in specific ways, but that incentives must also be designed to encourage systems thinking to achieve improvements in decision making and longer-term performance.

Section 4 presents a paper by Sanchez titled "Strategic management at the point of inflection: Systems, complexity, and competence theory." Sanchez discusses the common conceptual foundations of systems theory and complexity theory and explains how those concepts have been incorporated in competence-based management theory. He then argues that contemporary forms of organization reflect those concepts in their increasing use of organization designs based on self-managing processes. Self-managing processes help an organization to reduce the cognitive challenge of managing in a complex dynamic environment and improve the strategic flexibility and adaptive capability of an organization. Sanchez proposes that strategic management is now at an historic "point of inflection" in which its conceptual foundations are shifting from an emphasis on "content" variables to "process" variables, from a focus on industry structures to the study of managers' cognitive processes, from asserting the primacy of making strategic commitments to recognizing the value of increasing strategic flexibility, and from hierarchical "decide and control" models of organizations to designs of organizations as systems with extensive reliance on self-managing groups and processes.

Contribution to Building New Management Theory and Practice

The ideas developed in this volume should be of considerable value to management theorists, researchers, and practitioners.

From the theory-building point of view, all the chapters in the volume suggest useful integrations of competence-based mangement theory and systems theory — two fields of theory that share much in common conceptually, but that have not previously collaborated professionally in theory building. The systems concepts developed in the volume provide new approaches to identifying, analyzing, and designing processes of resource building, resource leveraging, and capability development. These systems concepts also bring to the competence perspective new tools and techniques that can enable more precise scientific understanding of key aspects of an organization's processes of competence building and leveraging.

From a research point of view, several papers in this volume suggest practical, accessible approaches to using computer modeling to simulate organizational behaviors in dynamically complex organizations and environments. Computer modeling and simulation are now being recognized as an important, perhaps even necessary research methodology in further developing competence-based management theory (McKelvey, 1998). These papers demonstrate the usefulness of simple computer models in investigating the dynamics of competence building and leveraging processes, thereby contributing to both the empirical grounding of competence-based management theory and the integration of systems modeling into mainstream strategy and management research.

Almost all chapters in the volume also include real-world examples and cases that illustrate how the systems and competence concepts presented play out the "reality" of daily managerial practice. Thus, managers who read the papers in this volume will find more than just a set of ideas about more systematic approaches to building, leveraging, and maintaining organization's competences. Most of the papers also show how those ideas have been put into practice by other managers. Careful reading of the case studies can alert managers in similar circumstances to key systemic aspects of competence building and leveraging processes that are likely require close attention and informed intervention.

References

Barney, J. (1991). Firm resources and sustained competitive advantage. *Journal of Management, 17(1)*, 99–120.

Bickerton, D. (1990). *Language and Species*. Chicago: University of Chicago Press.

Dierickx, I., & Cool, K. (1989). Asset stock accumulation and sustainability of competitive advantage. *Management Science, 35(12)*, 1504–1510.

Forrester, J. (1961). *Industrial Dynamics*. Cambridge, MA: MIT Press (currently available from Pegasus Communications, Waltham, MA, USA).

Hamel, G., & Heene, A. (eds) (1993). *Competence-based Competition*. Chichester: John Wiley & Sons.

Heene, A., & Sanchez, R. (eds) (1996). *Competence-based Strategic Management*. Chichester: John Wiley & Sons Ltd.

McKelvey, B. (1998). Can strategy be better than acupuncture? A realist/semantic conception of competence-based research. Fourth International Conference on Competence Based Management, Oslo, Norway, June 1998.

Prahalad, C. K., & Hamel, G. (1993). Strategy as stretch and leverage. *Harvard Business Review* March–April, 75–84.

Richardson, G. (1991). *Feedback Thought in Social Science and Systems Theory*. Philadelphia: University of Pennsylvania Press.

Sanchez, R. (1997). Strategic management at the point of inflection: systems, complexity, and competence theory. *Long Range Planning, 30(6)*, 939–946.

Sanchez, R. (ed.) (2001a). *Knowledge Management and Organizational Competence*. Oxford: Oxford University Press.

Sanchez, R. (2001b). Building blocks for strategy theory: Resources, dynamic capabilities, and competences. In H. W. Volberda & T. Elfring (eds) *Rethinking Strategy*. London: Sage Publications.

Sanchez, R., & Heene, A. (eds) (1997a). *Strategic Learning and Knowledge Management*. Chichester: John Wiley & Sons Ltd.

Sanchez, R., & Heene, A. (1997b). Reinventing strategic management: New theory and practice for competence-based competition. *European Management Journal, 15(3)*, 303–317.

Sanchez, R., Heene, A., & Thomas, H. (eds) (1996). *Dynamics of Competence-based Competition: Theory and Practice in the New Strategic Management.* Oxford: Elsevier Science Ltd.

Senge, P. (1990). *The Fifth Discipline: The Art and Practice of the Learning Organization.* New York: Doubleday Currency.

Sterman, J. (2000). *Business Dynamics: Systems Thinking and Modeling for a Complex World.* Boston: Irwin McGraw-Hill.

Teece, D., Pisano, G., & Shuen, A. (1997). Dynamic capabilities and strategic management. *Strategic Management Journal, 18(7)*, 509–533.

Wernerfelt, B. (1984). A resource-based view of the firm. *Strategic Management Journal, 5(2)*, 171–180.

PART I

Systems Concepts, Modeling Techniques, and the Analysis of Organizations as Dynamic Resource Systems

Chapter 2

Resource Management Under Dynamic Complexity

John Morecroft

Introduction

This paper examines resource management policies in dynamically complex systems as a basis for explaining differences in firm performance.[1] A firm is viewed as embedded in a network of interdependent resources linked through feedback loops (Sanchez & Heene, 1996). Resource management is represented in terms of operating policies, goals, and feedback loops used to control the build-up and retention of strategically important resources. A model is developed to represent managerial policies for a single tangible resource — staff. Even in this simplified model, considerable dynamic complexity arises through time delays inherent in building staff skills, through misperceptions of productivity, and through goal conflict. The analysis suggests how different firms may handle dynamic complexity by adopting distinctive policies for resource management that reflect the dominant strategic logic of influential policymakers.[2] Simulations show that differences in firm performance then arise from firm-specific patterns of resource accumulation determined by each firm's dominant logic and resulting feedback structure.

The systems approach is applied to an analysis of the rise and fall of People Express airlines. People Express was a fascinating example of the challenges in managing the complexities of resource building and leveraging. The company grew from obscurity to industry prominence in a period of only five years — in spite of facing powerful entrenched rivals. But dramatic growth was followed by an even more dramatic demise. The paper outlines a dynamic analysis of the People Express resource system and its management processes governing resource accumulation. The first step in the analysis identifies the tangible and intangible resources of the fledgling airline, such as planes and service reputa-

---

[1]An earlier version of this paper was presented at the Fourth International Conference on Competence-Based Management. Norwegian School of Management, Oslo, June 18–20, 1998 in a panel session on "Resource Dynamics, Competence and Firm Performance."

[2]The term *dominant logic* in this paper corresponds to the term *strategic logic* in the Sanchez and Heene (1996) model of the firm as an open system, and the term *policy* corresponds to *management processes* in the Sanchez and Heene model. For further discussion of parallels in terminology, see Chapter 1 of this volume.

Systems Perspectives on Resources, Capabilities, and Management Processes, pages 19–39.

tion. The second step examines the dominant logic of the management policies that controlled the evolution of these resources. A combination of partial and whole model simulations then unfolds the dynamic complexity of the resource system and reveals why the firm's resource accumulation policies eventually caused the firm to lose its competitive advantage. The paper concludes with comments on the potential contributions of feedback concepts and system dynamics modelling to resource-based and competence theory.

Dynamic Resource Systems

The traditional resource-based literature seeks to explain superior firm performance and competitive advantage in terms of unique configurations of firm resources that rivals find difficult to acquire or imitate (Barney, 1991; Foss *et al.,* 1995). Firms are viewed as complex bundles of resource endowments. However, a widely recognized limitation of the resource-based literature (Mosakowski & McKelvey, 1997) is the lack of a clear or agreed basis for *selecting* which of a firm's resources are in fact those that contribute most critically to performance. Part of the difficulty arises from the fact that "pure" resource-based thinking seeks to identify idiosyncratic resources solely from a static analysis of resource endowments. As Conner (1991) has observed "at some level, everything in the firm becomes a resource and hence resources lose explanatory power."

This paper proposes that competitive advantage and ultimately superior performance stem not only from the uniqueness and variety of the firm's current resources, but also from the ways resource endowments change over time as a result of management policies. This view shifts attention from static comparisons of resource endowments to dynamic analyses of resource accumulation and the dominant logic of policies and feedback processes that control accumulation processes and drive the evolution of resource stocks over time. Such an approach allows for the discovery of firm idiosyncrasies in approaches to managing the dynamic complexity[3] of a *resource system* rather than in the composition of a firm's resource stocks at a single point in time. This dynamic view of resource accumulation processes offers a way to overcome the implicit tautology in the ex post resource-based reasoning often cited by critics.[4]

Resource accumulation is a fundamental part of any dynamic resource system (Warren, 1997). The idea of resource accumulation was explained by Dierickx and Cool (1989) using the bathtub metaphor shown in Figure 1. Dierickx and Cool propose that competitive advantage may persist for some period of time because of the inertia of resource accumulation, processes which they call *asset stock accumulation*: "While flows can be adjusted instantaneously, stocks cannot. It takes a consistent pattern of resource flows to accumulate a desired change in strategic asset stocks."

---

[3]Senge (1990) suggests that dynamic complexity is present in business or social systems whenever cause and effect are subtle or where the effects over time of interventions are not obvious. For example, when an action has dramatically different effects in the short run and the long run, or when the local consequences of an action differ from consequences elsewhere in the system, then there is dynamic complexity.

[4]See for example Heene and Sanchez (1997), pp. 26–28, for a discussion of the apparent circularity in resource-based arguments about successful firms and resources as their sources of competitive advantage.

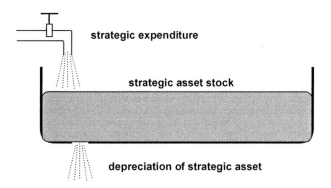

Figure 1: The Bathtub Metaphor: Visualizing the Accumulation of Resources.

Dierickx and Cool's thesis redirects attention from static endowments of resources to the dynamics of resource accumulation, but has little to say about what determines a firm's pattern of resource flows or how one might gauge whether such a pattern is internally consistent or superior to rivals. They thus suggest why performance differences between firms may persist, but not why or how these differences come into existence. Their model of resource stocks and flows is framed in terms of generalised strategic expenditures and does not deal directly with specific managerial policies and feedback processes that control resource flows by directing those expenditures.

More recently Sanchez and Heene (1996) have proposed a systems view of the firm as the basis for developing a theory of competence-based management. Their approach characterises the firm as a system of tangible and intangible assets organised under a *strategic logic* for achieving the firm's goals. Building on Dierickx and Cool, Sanchez and Heene introduce management processes organised under a strategic logic that control resource accumulations in competence building (developing entirely new assets and capabilities in response to a changing environment) and use of resource stocks in competence leveraging (applying existing assets and capabilities to market opportunities). Their conceptual model includes a hierarchy of system elements for managing firms' assets and capabilities, ranging from higher-order cognitive elements to lower-order operating elements. The conceptual model provides a framework for new avenues of research in competence-based management focusing on coordination, governance, and managerial cognition.

System dynamics, a special branch of systems theory,[5] can be used to study the coordination of dynamic resource systems through modelling and simulation. Figure 2 is an information feedback view of resource management using standard system dynamics notation (Forrester, 1961; Morecroft, 1994; Sterman, 1989). The rectangles in the top half of the diagram represent resource accumulations or stocks (corresponding to the level of

[5]Strictly speaking, system dynamics belongs within a tradition of thought focusing on feedback mechanisms (e.g. servomechanisms). By contrast, general systems theory, as developed by von Bertalanffy and others, belongs within a second tradition of feedback thought called cybernetics. The distinctions and ancestry of these two traditions are described with scholarly precision in Chapter 3 of Richardson's (1991) book *Feedback Thought in Social Science and Systems Theory*.

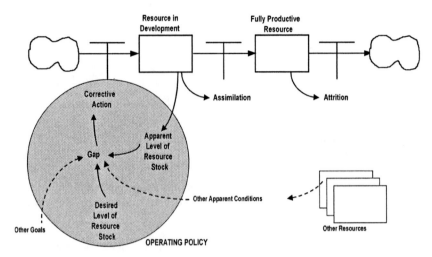

Figure 2: Operating Policy for Resource Management — Goals and Information
Feedback.

water in the bathtub in Figure 1). The solid arrows represent resource flows which either
increase or decrease the level of a resource (like water flowing in or out of the bathtub).
The valves represent the processes that regulate resource flows. The irregular cloud-like
shapes represent either the source or final destination of the resource flows. Typically, the
accumulation of a resource happens in two stages. The resource must first be developed (or
acquired) and then it must be assimilated into the resource system in order to become fully
productive. The two rectangular boxes in Figure 2 distinguish these two stages in the stock
and flow network. Corrective action (to close a perceived gap in the resource level)
controls the inflow of a new resource into the resource development stage. Assimilation
processes control the rate at which resources in the development stage are converted into
fully productive resources. Processes of attrition control the rate at which fully productive
resources leave the organization through obsolescence, retirement, or turnover.

    Some practical examples will illustrate the use and versatility of this representation.
Consider a resource such as staff. In this case, corrective action to increase staff means
hiring. Assimilation corresponds to training and gaining work experience, and attrition is
the loss of staff through voluntary departures or firing. Both the source and the final destination of the staff flows is the external labor market. Fully productive resource
corresponds to the number of experienced staff, while resource in development is the
number of newly arrived or "rookie" staff.

    In the case of capital equipment, to take another example, corrective action means
ordering new equipment. Assimilation corresponds to the arrival and commissioning of
new equipment, and attrition is the withdrawal of equipment through obsolescence or sale.
The source of capital equipment is the equipment supplier and the final destination of old
and used equipment is the scrap heap or the second-hand market. Fully productive
resource corresponds to the capacity of equipment currently available for operations, while
resource in development is equipment being built to fill the firm's order.

The large grey circular region of Figure 2 circumscribes the operating policy for resource management. Corrective action takes place whenever there is a gap between the apparent level of the resource stock and the level desired by management. For example, the apparent level of staff as a resource could be a simple measure of headcount (the sum of experienced staff and rookies) or it could be a more sophisticated measure that makes a distinction (e.g., a difference in productivity differential) between new recruits and fully assimilated members of staff. The desired level may be a fixed target over some time period, but in practice is much more likely to vary with the level and apparent condition of the resource in question, as well as with the level and the condition of resources elsewhere in the firm.

For example, an aggressive capital investment policy for a fast growing mobile phone producer might set an evolving goal for capacity which is always 25 percent higher than current capacity. Such a policy continually stretches the organization to expand capacity regardless of potential constraints to growth. On the other hand, a more cautious producer in the same industry may set an evolving goal for capacity that depends on the current size of the sales force or on expected cash flow.

At the heart of a managed resource system is a process of *balancing feedback*.[6] A *perceived* shortage of a given resource generates corrective action by management to eliminate the gap between perceived and desired resource levels. New resource then flows into the organization, leading first to an increase in resources under development and subsequently to an increase in fully productive resources available for use. Management monitors changes in a resource stock to arrive at a new view of the level and apparent condition of the resource, and that view may form the basis for further corrective action, thereby closing the balancing feedback loop. (As noted, Figure 2 contains a balancing feedback loop for regulating resource flows.)

Feedback loops thus provide a basis for understanding the coordination of a dynamic resource system. An important question, however, is whether or not explicit strategic logic and management processes exist for resource management within a firm. If so, we can expect the evolution of a given resource to be purposive and goal-directed. If not, then it may be the case that resource accumulation just drifts, responding to unmanaged pressures arising from imbalances of resources elsewhere in the system. The components of a firm's operating policy determine the likely degree of intent behind the evolution of a given resource. A prerequisite for proactive resource management is the existence of a clear and communicable goal for resource accumulation. Without a goal, there can be no corrective action. It is easy to imagine a goal for staff arising from output objectives or an annual

---

[6]Simple balancing feedback devices have fascinated engineers, social scientists, and philosophers since they were first invented. Such devices embody purpose and primitive intelligence because they relentlessly strive to achieve their desired condition or goal regardless of changing conditions in their immediate environment. Consider, for example, the automatic speed control in a car. The desired condition or goal is the set-speed — let's say 70 miles per hour for motorway driving. The speed controller monitors the current speed of the car. If current speed is below desired then the speed controller initiates corrective action by advancing the accelerator linkage, leading to a burst of acceleration (or "speed accumulation") which causes speed to rise. Anyone who has driven a car with automatic speed control has experienced the uncanny intelligence of balancing feedback as the accelerator moves up and down depending on the road terrain. The car begins to climb a steep hill and the accelerator advances automatically, just as you the driver would depress the accelerator pedal in the same circumstances.

budget. But formulating goals for an intangible resource which lacks an accepted metric, such as employee motivation, may be more difficult.

Another prerequisite for proactive resource management is the ability to accurately monitor the current level and condition of a given resource. Without knowledge of what resources are currently available, it is impossible to take effective corrective action to adjust the resource level toward the goal. This statement may seem obvious, but there can be practical situations where the condition of a resource is difficult to gauge with confidence, even when the level of the resource stock is quantifiable. A classic example (which is developed below in more depth) is the condition of skilled staff. Which is a more appropriate measure of staff resource — pure headcount, experienced staff, or some combination thereof? Different people may legitimately have different views. The monitoring problem can be especially difficult for intangibles. How can one reliably measure employee motivation or customer perceptions of quality? At best, only indirect measures can be used and may be subject to bias and distortion. For example, the current quality of a consumer durable rolling off a production line may be a poor indicator of perceived quality in the minds of consumers whose perceptions of a product's quality take shape over the course of a product's normal lifetime.

Exploring Dynamic Complexity in a Professional Service Organization

In many service organizations such as hospitals, schools, and professional practices (lawyers, doctors, consultants, software developers), staff are the key strategic resource and effective management of staff recruitment, retention, and development is vital to high performance. Common features of such organizations include high staff costs (often more than 90 percent of total operating costs); the need for assimilation, careful screening, indoctrination, coaching, and prolonged on-the-job training; and the difficulty of objectively measuring productivity.

To explore the dynamic complexity of resource flows in such situations, we examine the simplified case of an imaginary software organization employing specialist software staff. A resource map of the software firm as a system is shown in Figure 3.[7] The stock and flow network shows two resource accumulations — new software staff and experienced software staff— together with flows for hiring, assimilation, and departures. The output of the organization is measured in lines of software code written, and its success is judged in terms of its ability to meet an output target arbitrarily set at 6000 lines of code per week. If there is a current shortfall in output, then additional staff are hired. We assume that it takes one month to recruit new staff, and a further three months before they become fully

---

[7]The resource map and subsequent simulations of the imaginary software organization are created with the graphical modelling package "ithink" developed by High Performance Systems (1997). The design philosophy of the modelling package builds on a graphical user interface that supports both expert and less skilled practitioners of the modelling process. The user interface uses standard system dynamics icons for stocks, flows, converters and connectors to represent resources and feedback loops in business and social systems. Within each stock, flow and converter symbol is a repository for storing equation logic and documenting assumptions. More details of the design philosophy behind ithink are provided in Peterson (1994).

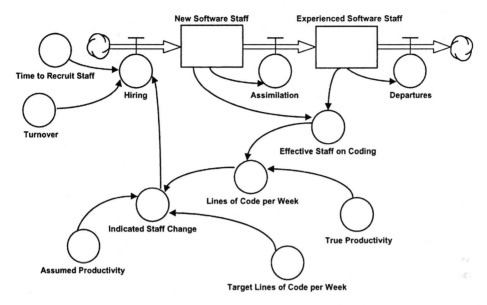

Figure 3: Resource System Map for Software Staff.

experienced. New staff are assumed to be half as productive as experienced staff. Moreover, new staff generate a workload for experienced staff, because each new recruit requires on-the-job coaching which (on average) absorbs 50 percent of the time of an experienced member of staff.

Initially there are 50 experienced staff, on average they write 100 lines of code per person per week, and initially there are no new staff. So the total initial output of the organization is 50*100 = 5000 lines of code per week — a gap of 1000 lines of code below the firm's target. A simulation model of the resource system traces how the organization adjusts output to meet its target through staff expansion. Dynamic complexity arises from the time delay involved in training new staff, from the relatively low productivity of new staff, and from the coaching workload that new recruits impose on experienced staff. (In this simplified example, the coaching workload is set to exactly cancel the higher productivity of new staff, so the effective number of staff working on coding is always equal to the number of experienced software staff, no matter how many recruits are in training.)[8] Essentially, new staff make no net contribution to output until they are fully experienced (after three months of coaching), making the contribution of the current hiring process to increased output capacity more difficult to gauge.

The top half of Figure 4 shows a simulation of the performance of the software organization over a period of twelve months, given these initial conditions and policies. Target

---

[8]Effective Staff on Coding is made up of new staff and experienced staff. New staff are half as productive as experienced staff and absorb half an expert in staff training. So the formula is: Effective Staff on Coding = (Experienced Staff − .5 * New Staff) + .5 * New Staff = Experienced Staff.

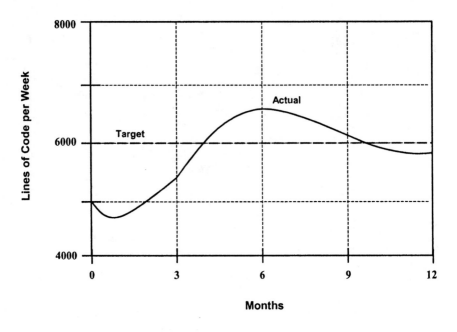

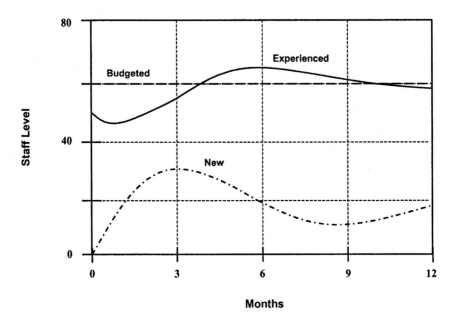

Figure 4: Time Charts of Output and Staff Levels for Software Organization.

output is steady at 6000 lines of code per week. Actual output starts below target at 5000 lines of code per week, falls briefly, then overexpands to about 6,500 lines of code per week by month seven. After peaking, output gradually falls to just less than target by the end of the simulation. Performance is inversely related to the area between the two lines (i.e., the cumulated absolute difference between target output and actual output, whether shortfall or overshoot), so there is room for improvement if we can define resource management policies that accelerate the expansion of output and reduce the amount of shortfall and overshoot.

Why is it difficult to achieve exactly the output target? The answer lies in the behavior of staff resource stock shown in the bottom half of Figure 4. The initial gap in output leads to a rapid increase in new software staff which grows from zero to a peak of around 30 by month three. As new staff complete their training, the number of experienced staff begins to rise. By month four, experienced staff equal budget staff, which represents the number of staff needed to meet target output at full productivity. However, in month four there are still more than 20 new staff in training. As they complete their assimilation and become fully productive, the number of experienced staff grows, leading to surplus staff and output levels rising above target (i.e., overshoot). Gradually, surplus staff are reduced through attrition.

Impact of Operating Policy on Performance: Time Compression Diseconomies

Imagine a competing software organization that begins with the same endowment of staff resources as in the above example: 50 experienced software staff and zero new staff. The competitor is also aiming for a target output of 6000 lines of code per week. In an effort to be more responsive, the competitor accelerates hiring by cutting the time to recruit new staff from one month to two weeks. How will this change of hiring policy affect performance?

The top half of Figure 5 shows that although the new hiring policy helps to reduce short-fall more quickly, it leads to much greater overshoot. Thus, the quicker hiring policy surprisingly causes *performance to worsen,* in the sense that the cumulative gap between target and actual output becomes greater. By comparison with Figure 4, actual lines of code reaches the target more quickly — which is a direct and beneficial consequence of accelerated hiring. However, the overshoot of output is much bigger than before. Output reaches a peak of almost 7000 lines of code per week in month five, and then declines to equal the target once more in month nine. Thereafter there is a noticeable undershoot as output falls below the target.

The bottom half of Figure 5 shows the staff resource dynamics that drive overshoot and undershoot in output. The more responsive hiring policy leads to a faster build-up of new software staff, which peaks at almost 40 people just before month three. But these new recruits still take three months to train and continue to absorb the time and attention of more experienced colleagues. The excessive build-up of new staff eventually translates into a large increase of experienced staff which reaches a peak in month five at a value

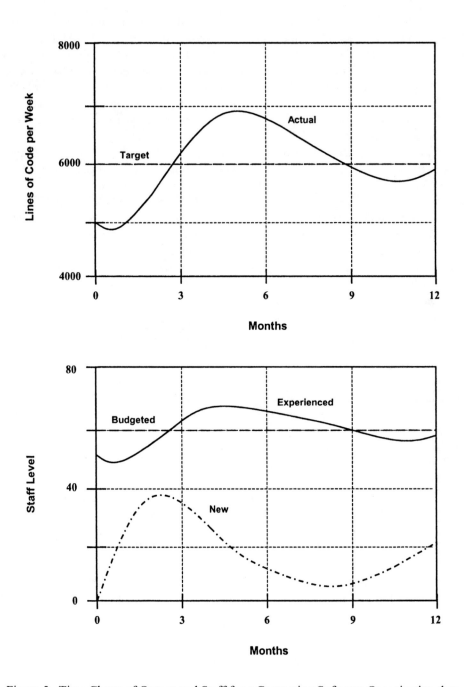

Figure 5: Time Charts of Output and Staff for a Competing Software Organization that Adopts a more Responsive Hiring Policy.

much greater than the budget staff, leading to excess output. In this case, a seemingly simple and well intentioned change in hiring policy causes a deterioration of performance, even though the new hiring policy seeks the same equilibrium staff resource as the original, less responsive policy. The resource dynamics in Figure 5 illustrate a dynamic form of Dierickx and Cool's "time compression diseconomies". Faster hiring may be a means to make up a shortfall in output more quickly, but may lead to higher costs resulting from overhiring. Also, simply forcing more recruits into the system is not necessarily the most *effective* means to make up a shortfall in output, because a corresponding number of experienced staff must spend time on on-the-job training.

Strategic Logic for Operating Policies

Competing firms with identical starting resources often adopt quite distinctive approaches to building and retaining strategic resources. These distinctive approaches reflect different operating policies that can be the basis of a divergence of resource stocks over time and sustained differences in performance. Capital investment policies vary, for example, because some firms invest only when there is a convincing financial case for doing so (as indicated by criteria such as net present value or rate of return), while other firms take a more visionary approach and invest primarily on the basis of market growth potential. Honda's investment in the post-war Japanese motorcycle industry is an example of visionary investment to support future growth. During an early stage of industry growth the company approved an expansion of capacity equal to ten times current Japanese industry capacity! Honda's strategic logic guiding capital investment was rooted in the founder's confidence in the future of the motorcycle, rather than in specific financial analysis.

The term *dominant logic* was introduced by Prahalad and Bettis (1986) to describe a distinctive style of managing resources and investments in a multi-business enterprise, reflecting mindsets and attitudes of business leaders shaped by their experience of the firm and industry. Extending this concept, Sanchez and Heene (1996) use the term *strategic logic* to denote the "operative rationale [of a firm] for achieving its goals," expressed for example in a firm's resource management policies. Rival firms can therefore be distinguished by the distinctive logics that shape their policies for investment, resource accumulation, and retention (Morecroft, 1985).

Strategic Logic for a Hiring Policy in a Software Organization

Hiring in the example in Figure 3 is driven by the need to achieve an output target. When output falls below target, hiring tries to correct the gap by increasing staff to (eventually) increase output. However, the firm's resource accumulation behavior would be quite different if the organization's hiring policies were constrained by a staff budget. Figure 6 shows the logic underlying a staff resource management policy based on budgetary control. Budget allocation for staff is determined by the target lines of code per week, divided by the assumed productivity per staff member. The greater the

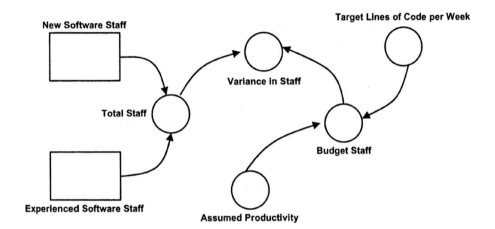

Figure 6: Hiring Policy Dominated by Variance Based on Budgeted Staff.

output target, the more staff are authorised by the budget; however, the higher the average productivity per staff member, the fewer the number of staff authorised by the budget. Average productivity of staff is difficult to gauge, of course, especially when the mix of new and experienced staff is changing over time. Assumed productivity may just be an estimate based on surveys of experienced staff. In the model the estimate is set equal to the true productivity of experienced staff at 100 lines of code per person per week. Budgeted staff is compared with current staff to arrive at the perceived variance in staff.

Recall that the original hiring policy in the example (see Figure 3) is the "indicated staff change" determined by the gap between current output relative to target output. The new policy determines staff needed based on variance from budgeted staff. Either of these policies could be perceived as a legitimate basis for hiring. Each choice of hiring policy a manager makes reflects a different underlying logic for achieving the output goal. If a budgetary logic dominates, then hiring responds to variance in budgeted staff. If the focus is on output levels, hiring responds to shortfall in output.

Figure 7 is a simulation of a software organization in which a budgetary logic determines hiring policy. The dynamics of the resource system are radically altered compared with the dynamics shown in Figure 4. In the top half of Figure 7, actual output settles at a value that remains lower than target output. In other words, the organization *never* achieves its output target. The lower half of the figure shows why. Budget staff imposes a rigid ceiling of 60 on the total number of staff that can be employed. In principle this ceiling should be adequate because 60 staff working at full productivity (100 lines of code per person per week) can generate 6000 lines of code per week—exactly equal to the output target. But the budget overestimates productivity by failing to take account of productivity dilution that results from the need for experienced staff to spend time training new recruits. The result is that the organization reaches its budget headcount of 60 staff, yet fewer than 50 are experienced. The rest are new staff who (because of their training demands on experienced staff) make no net contribution to output. Output therefore settles

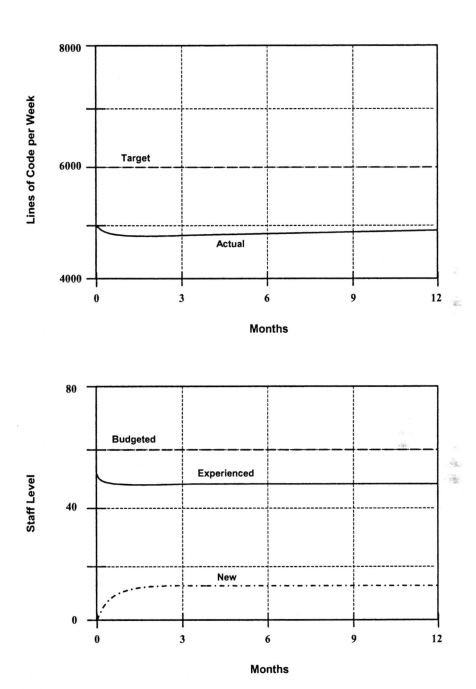

Figure 7: Time Charts of Output and Staff for a Software Organization with a Dominant Budgetary Logic for Hiring.

at a value lower than target. Note that the organization, by following a budgetary logic for hiring policy, now experiences *goal conflict*. The budgetary goal can only be met at the expense of the output goal!

Now, imagine the possible explanations of the relative shortage of experienced staff shown in Figure 7 an outside observer might make if looking only at static resource endowments. One might suspect imperfections in the labor market, and perhaps infer that staff are a scarce, difficult-to-replicate resource. By contrast, a dynamic resource system analysis is capable of revealing that the reason for staff shortage is the use of a budget-driven policy controlling staff hiring.

In fact, severe distortions in resource accumulation processes can arise from the use of policies based on inaccurate static measures of resource productivity, and the budgetary logic for hiring in Figure 7 is flawed only because it is based on an overestimate of average productivity.

To illustrate this point, Figure 8 shows a simulation of a more dynamic budgetary logic that takes into account the impact that initial training for recruits on average productivity which in this example is reduced by 20 percent, from 100 lines of code per person per week to 80. Using an accurate productivity figure leads to the staff budget needed to achieve the output target in the near future. In the top half of the figure, actual output approaches the output goal with no tendency for overshoot. In this example, budgetary discipline still keeps tight control over new staff hiring, but prevents overhiring *without* compromising the output goal. This effect shows up in the lower half of Figure 8. New software staff grow quickly to a peak of 20 people in month two. The budget then puts a limit on further hiring. As new staff become fully productive after completing training, experienced staff rise gradually to reach 60 people, which is the staff level required to achieve the output goal. If such improvement in hiring can be introduced, then a budgetary logic for hiring policy allows the firm to achieve the output goal.

Clearly the new budgetary logic for controlling hiring improves the firm's resource accumulation. It eliminates goal conflict and allows the organization to achieve both its output goal and its budget goal. However, note that this improved policy requires deriving an appropriate estimate of average productivity — i.e., one that takes into account the dilution of productivity that results from asking experienced staff to train new recruits. Too small an estimate of this effect would restrict output, and too high an estimate would lead to excess output or idle staff.

Applying the Dynamic Resource System Framework to a Multi-Resource System: The People Express Case

The analysis of the foregoing simplified example of a software organization suggests that firm performance depends greatly on the policies and feedback processes organizations use for managing key resources. Now we demonstrate this relationship with an example of a multi-resource system, drawing on analyses of the well-known case of People Express airlines (Whitestone, 1983; Sterman, 1989). People Express was a 1970s start-up airline that grew from obscurity to industry prominence in a period of only five years while

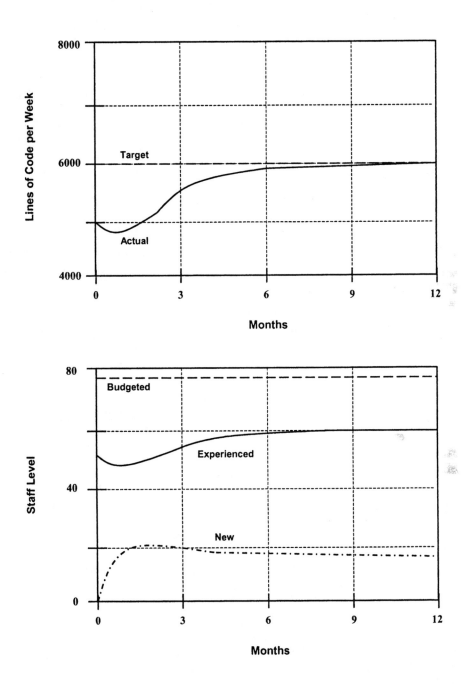

Figure 8: Time Charts of Output and Staff for a Software Organization with Flexible
Budgetary Logic for Hiring.

competing against powerful rivals. However, its dramatic growth was followed by an equally dramatic demise.[9]

In our dynamic resource system analysis, the first step is to classify resources into tangible or intangible and managed or unmanaged. For People Express, obvious tangibles are planes, staff, and passengers. Intangibles include, for example, service reputation and staff morale. The classification into managed and unmanaged resources is subtle but vital, because unmanaged resources (which are intangible and thus usually invisible at the operating level) often tend to be ignored and prove to be the undoing of a strategy that requires resource accumulation.

Recall Figure 2, which provides clues of what to look for in assigning strategic resources to the managed or unmanaged classification. For a typical tangible managed resource, there is usually a fairly clear desired condition or goal, and the condition of the resource is often measurable. As a result, the gap that drives corrective action to acquire some resources can be regarded as objective and beyond dispute, and a managerial feedback and control process can be established that is purposive and goal-directed. However, for key intangible resources, the desired condition or goal may itself not be clear or easy to define. As a result, the accumulation process for such resources may be neglected as managers focus their attention on processes for accumulative, more readily measurable resources.[10] In the case of People Express, unmanaged resources include potential passengers, (the condition of) newly-hired staff, service reputation, and staff motivation.

A classification of resources into managed *versus* unmanaged leads to the second step of inferring the logic underlying a firm's resource accumulation policies. This phase of analysis is demanding but important because it reveals the managerial rationale for the firm's resource accumulation strategy. Let's start with the tangible resources at People Express. What was the logic guiding fleet expansion? Such capital investment decisions could have been governed by funding constraints, market share goals, near-term financing return criteria, demand forecasts, or staffing constraints. The dominant logic at People Express, however, appears to have been CEO Don Burr's ambitious personal growth target, stemming from his vision of precipitating an industry revolution (Whitestone, 1983). Clearly such a logic could be both powerful and persistent, and the logic leads to a reinforcing feedback process that works to rapidly increase the resource stock of aeroplanes.

The dominant logic for staff expansion, however, was quite different. From the published sources, one gathers the impression of a Human Resources VP who was insistent on hiring only high-quality recruits, carefully screened (with input from the top

---

[9]The analysis of People Express in this paper is based on a synopsis of a fully developed dynamic resource system analysis used in the London Business School course "Dynamics of Strategy." For details, readers are referred to Morecroft (1999), which is an educational document comprising software and slidepack, designed around the People Express case.

[10]The classification of firm resources into managed and unmanaged reflects the notions of *lower order* and *higher order* control loops in the Sanchez and Heene (1996) systems model. Lower order loops represent managers' bottom-up adaptation of system elements for which hard, quantified data are available. Higher order loops represent managers' efforts at top down adaptation which requires "significant processing of ambiguous qualitative data... to discover plausible interpretations about the states of the firm's higher system elements."

management team) and then intensively trained on the job by experienced staff. Following this logic leads to reinforcing feedback in which the resource stock of experienced staff is a primary determinant of the rate of hiring the firm undertakes.

The logic for managing passenger growth is also noteworthy at People Express. Customers are a fundamental resource stock for all companies. Some companies explicitly try to manage their stocks of customers by setting sales targets, tracking customers in huge databases, and implementing marketing programmes to close gaps in goals for market share. Other companies, however, may not actively manage the size of the customer base at all, but instead allow the numbers of customers they have to vary with advertising, word-of-mouth endorsements, and "churn". People Express seems to have adopted an ambitious — but essentially unmanaged — approach to the growth of customers as a resource. Deep price discounts and targeted advertising unleashed a powerful word-of-mouth effect that caused a very rapid build-up of potential passengers (those fliers willing to try People Express should the opportunity arise). Very low prices (as little as one-third of competitors' fares) attracted media attention and became a topic of conversation among the flying public. The more people who heard the news, the more people passed it along. Pricing policy was thus designed to drive a reinforcing feedback that rapidly increased the resource stock of potential passengers.

The model of People Express' resource accumulation processes therefore includes a tangible resource system that contains three reinforcing feedback loops, each a compelling engine of growth in its own right, but each operating independently of one another to produce an essentially *uncoordinated* expansion of planes, staff, and passengers. Simulations reveal the power of these three growth engines to accumulate resources needed to drive the kind of spectacular growth actually achieved by People Express.[11]

Intangible Resources in Complex Growth Dynamics

The third step in our dynamic resource-based analysis looks to the behavior of two intangible resources — service reputation and motivation — to explain the company's mounting resource problems and, ultimately, the demise of People Express. From the case, it appears that neither stocks of service reputation nor stocks of staff motivation is managed. The basic requirements for proactive resource management are absent: operating goals for maintaining resource stocks are not clearly defined, and the condition of the resource stocks is unknown. Of course, it is not easy to get inside the minds of customers to measure service reputation, or to capture the emotions of staff to discern staff motivation. In People Express, reputation and motivation were apparently allowed simply to be driven by operating conditions. Reputation responds (with a time lag) to the balance struck between numbers of flying passengers and service capacity, and service capacity itself represents a complex dynamic mix of the number of experienced and

[11]The simulations of these resource accumulation subsystems in People Express show exponential growth of planes, staff and passengers over a five-year period, but all at different annual growth rates. These simulations are not shown in this paper, but are included in the educational document (Morecroft, 1999) that accompanies the People Express case in the "Dynamics of Strategy" course.

newly-hired staff and their joint productivity. Employee motivation responds to a range of dynamic factors, such as company growth rate and profitability, and in turn greatly influences staff productivity.

The three engines of tangible resource growth are not well coordinated because the underlying policies governing resource accumulation are so different. As fleet expansion and passenger growth begin to outstrip staff expansion, problems become evident in the intangibles of perceived service level, customer satisfaction, and employee motivation. No management action is taken to fix these problems, however, because: (1) the unmanaged intangible resources initially provide relatively weak signals to the rest of the organization of latent growth stresses; and (2) the powerful logics underlying the policies governing tangible resource accumulation are insensitive to such weak signals. This seeming lack of alignment of resource accumulation policies, leading to a virtual paralysis in the face of growing problems and, eventually, an impending doom, is symptomatic of a loss of management coordination under conditions of dynamic complexity.

As Figure 9 shows, a simulation of People Express that includes these dynamics shows that service reputation declines steadily for the first six years in an eight-year simulation of People's growth strategy. (Note: The apparent recovery of service reputation in the last two years results from an unintended surplus of service staff as disillusioned passengers switch to competing airlines.)

In Figure 10 staff motivation (an intangible resource that People Express did not directly manage) remains both steady and high for the first six years, contributing to People's competitive advantage. But as the growth in customer base overwhelms growth

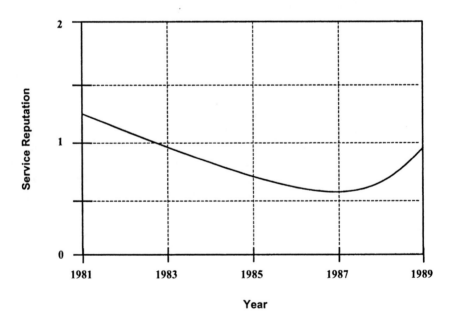

Figure 9: Service Reputation at People Express.

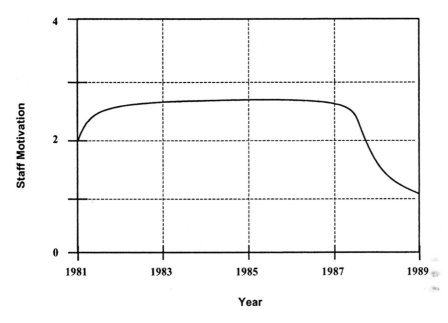

Figure 10: Staff Motivation at People Express.

in trained staff, leading to a collapse of the customer base, the excitement and profit-lure of the fast-growth enterprise evaporates. Employees become demoralised as planes begin to fly half-empty. The company begins a downward spiral with a configuration of resources (both tangible and intangible) that is markedly inferior to its major competitors. People Express was unable to find a commercially viable route of recovery from this resource trap.

Implications of a Dynamic Resource System View of the Firm

A dynamic resource system view of firm performance leads to insights into the rise and fall of People Express airlines. At the heart of this view is a synthesis of two powerful and influential sets of ideas from the strategy field: (1) processes of *resource accumulation* as a way of understanding firms' distinctive resource endowments and enduring differences in firms' strategy and performance; and (2) the dominant logic or strategic logic under-lying resource accumulation policies as a key to understanding firm-specific approaches to resource management and their effects on firm performance.

System dynamics models offer tools for investigating these ideas. Stocks and flows capture the dynamics of resource accumulation, while policies and associated information feedback embody the essence of the logic that initiates resource flows. The stock/flow and policy framework provides a versatile approach to articulating and visualizing firms' resource systems and for formulating equations to represent those systems. Simulation of the resulting dynamic model is a reliable way to understand how the dynamics of strategic resource accumulation arise from underlying resource management policies and feedback structures.[12]

The system dynamics framework also incorporates vocabulary and concepts now well established in the competence-based management literature. Firms, for example, are viewed as dynamic resource systems. Resources can be classified into tangible or intangible and managed or unmanaged. Distinctive patterns of resource accumulation (both effective and ineffective) result from a firm's policy logic for managing resources. Strategies that lead to failure after dramatic success can often be analysed and explained in terms of flawed logics for managing resource accumulations. These flaws may stem from operating goals and information feedback loops that are inadvertently at odds with each other — and perhaps even with overall strategy — as well as from unintended accumulations of intangible or unmanaged resources that interact with managed resources in unexpected (and sometimes detrimental) ways.

Competence and resource processes are at the heart of competitive strategy, diversification, corporate portfolio management (joint ventures and acquisitions), and international strategy (geographical diversification). As the People Express case illustrates, dynamic resource system models provide a means to understand and manage the dynamically complex resource flows in single businesses, the multi-business firm, and multi-firm industries. Dynamic resource system models thus offer new possibilities for model-based theory building that can explain and help to manage the dynamics of competition, diversification, organizational transformation, and internationalization.

References

Barney, J. (1991). Firm resources and sustained competitive advantage. *Journal of Management, 17(1)*, 99–120.

Conner, K. R. (1991). A historical comparison of resource-based theory and five schools of thought within industrial organization economics. *Journal of Management, 17(1)*, 121–154.

Coyle, R. G., & Morecroft, J. D. W. (eds) (1999). System dynamics for policy, strategy and management education. *Journal of the Operational Research Society, 50(4)*, special issue.

Dierickx, I., & Cool, K. (1989). Asset stock accumulation and sustainability of competitive advantage. *Management Science, 35(12)*, 1504–1510.

Forrester, J. W. (1961). *Industrial Dynamics*. Waltham, MA: Pegasus Communications.

Foss, N. J., Knudsen, C., & Montgomery, C. A. (1995). An exploration of common ground: Integrating evolutionary and strategic theories of the firm, *1*, 1–17. In C. A. Montgomery (ed.) *Resource-Based and Evolutionary Theories of the Firm*. Boston MA: Kluwer.

---

[12]More information on system dynamics modelling, including conceptualization, mapping, equation formulation and simulation analysis is available in Sterman's comprehensive textbook "Business Dynamics: Systems Thinking and Modeling for a Complex World" (Sterman, 2000). The book also includes a host of practical examples taken from business and public policy; a thorough guide to contemporary and historical literature in system dynamics; and a description of the most widely used software tools including ithink, Powersim and Vensim. The application of the approach to business policy, competitive strategy and management education is described in Coyle and Morecroft (editors, 1999), Larsen and Lomi (editors, 1999) and Warren (2000).

Heene, A., & Sanchez, R. (eds) (1997). *Competence-Based Strategic Management*. Chichester: John Wiley and Sons.

High Performance Systems, (1997). *ithink Strategy* (software and documentation). Hanover, NH: High Performance Systems Inc.

Larsen, E. R., & Lomi, A. (eds) (1999). System dynamics. Management Focus section of the *European Management Journal, 17(2)*, 117–163.

Mosakowski, E., & B. McKelvey (1997). Predicting rent generation in competence-based competition, Chapter 3, 65–85. In A. Heene and R. Sanchez (eds), *Competence-Based Strategic Management*. John Wiley and Sons: Chichester.

Morecroft, J. D. W. (1999). *Managing a Dynamic Resource System: The Curious Case of People Express Airlines* (software and slidepack), System Dynamics Group educational document ED-0002-A, Decision Technology Centre, London: London Business School.

Morecroft, J. D. W. (1994). Executive knowledge, models and learning, 1, 3–28. In J. D. W. Morecroft & J. D. Sterman (eds), *Modeling for Learning Organizations*. Portland, OR: Productivity Press.

Morecroft, J. D. W. (1985). The feedback view of business policy and strategy. *System Dynamics Review, 1(1)*, 4–19.

Peterson, S. (1994). Software for model building and simulation: An illustration of design philosophy. In J. D. W. Morecroft & J. D. Sterman (eds), *Modeling for Learning Organizations*. Portland, OR: Productivity Press.

Prahalad, C. K., & Bettis, R. A. (1986). The dominant logic: A new linkage between diversity and performance. *Strategic Management Journal, 7*, 485–501.

Richardson, G. P. (1991). *Feedback Thought in Social Science and Systems Theory*. Philadelphia: University of Pennsylvania Press.

Sanchez, R., & Heene, A. (1996). A systems view of the firm in competence-based competition. In R. Sanchez, A. Heene & H. Thomas (eds), *Dynamics of Competence-Based Competition*. Oxford: Pergamon.

Sanchez, R., Heene, A., & Thomas, H. (eds) (1996). *Dynamics of Competence-Based Competition*. Oxford: Pergamon.

Senge, P. M. (1990). *The Fifth Discipline: The Art and Practice of the Learning Organization*. New York: Doubleday.

Sterman, J. D. *Business Dynamics: Systems Thinking and Modeling for a Complex World*. Irwin/McGraw-Hill. (forthcoming).

Sterman, J. D. (1989). Modeling managerial behavior: Misperceptions of feedback in dynamic decisionmaking. *Management Science, 35(3)*, 321–339.

Sterman, J. D. (1988). *People Express management flight simulator* (software and documentation), available from author, Cambridge, MA 02142: Sloan School of Management, MIT.

Warren, K. D. *Competitive Strategy Dynamics*. Chichester: John Wiley & Sons. (forthcoming).

Warren, K. D. (1997). Building resources for competitive advantage. *Mastering Management* 591–598. London: FT Pitman Publishing.

Whitestone, D. (1983). People Express (A). Case No. 483–103. Boston: HBS Case Services.

Chapter 3

Operationalizing the Impact of Competence-Building on the Performance of Firms' Resource Systems

Kim Warren

Introduction

The practice of strategic management requires tools to help firms diagnose, anticipate and influence the evolution of their competitive performance through time. Whilst analyzing resources at a point in time may provide some indication of an organization's competitiveness, static comparisons of current resources may not be good predictors of long-run competitive performance. Resource-poor firms can emerge and grow by rapid accumulation of new resources, through a process of leveraging resources they already hold. Conversely, dominant firms can find that the strategic value of their resource-holdings are eroded or bypassed by rivals and new entrants who discover and pursue new means of building both traditional and novel resources.

To understand and improve an organization's effectiveness at building a powerful and coordinated portfolio of resources, a rigorous, comprehensive set of tools for operationalizing the accumulation and depletion of strategic "asset-stocks" (Dierickx & Cool, 1989) is required. System dynamics provides ideal tools for this purpose, including a rigorous means of formulating the mathematical integration underlying these accumulation and depletion processes. Furthermore, system dynamics frameworks can capture the dynamic interdependencies between resources, leading to powerful models of a firm's performance as a "dynamic resource-system".

A key determinant of a firm's effectiveness as a resource-building system is its relative capability in each resource-building task. Given equal resource-building capabilities, firms with comparable resource-attributes are unlikely to diverge in competitive performance. However, since the long-run development of a resource system is highly sensitive to small differences in growth rates for individual resources, even modest capability differences between competing firms may result in substantially divergent paths of performance over time. If a firm is able to learn from its success and failure in building and retaining resources, its capabilities will accumulate over time, a process that can be modelled in just the same manner as is applied to resources. The sum total of these increasing capabilities

Systems Perspectives on Resources, Capabilities, and Management Processes, pages 41–55.

across the entire system is a good indicator of a firm's organizational learning effectiveness.

The dynamic behavior of resource-systems is difficult to grasp intuitively. Accumulation and depletion of resources, combined with feedback and delay, often result in counter-intuitive behaviors and outcomes. Capability differences between rivals, their impact on the behavior of firms' resource systems, and the resulting time-paths of performance, can therefore be understood only through dynamic simulation. This paper describes the dynamic resource-system of a consumer products firm attempting to develop a new brand, and demonstrates through a system dynamic model how the firm's capabilities may enable — and limit — its ability to build performance over time.

A Dynamic Tool for Strategy Analysis

Over the last 15 years, research and debate regarding strategic management has divided broadly into concern with the "content" of strategy (*what* the firm should do to pursue sustainable competitive advantage) and the "process" of strategy (*how* strategic managers can stimulate and embed strategic initiatives in the firm). The strategy process agenda is extremely broad, spanning the formulation of strategy by management groups and participants from the wider organization, the strategic manager's role as designer and leader, and organizational issues such as structure, culture, power, and politics (Mintzberg & Quinn, 1992).

The strategy content agenda has struggled to make progress over the last decade. The analytical approach of Porter's (1981, 1985) micro-economics-based frameworks provided a rigorous method for strategy analysis throughout the 1980s, and still dominates the methodological approaches of major consulting firms. This framework took analysis of *external* history structural conditions (market shares, buyer power, threat of entry, etc.) as its starting point, and encouraged managers to search for opportunities to manage the external forces that constrain a firm's ability to achieve above-average profitability. The *internal* issues facing the firm were dealt with largely by analyzing the activities and associated costs within its "value chain".

Whilst this focus on analyzing industry and firm economics can be useful, its contribution to strategy development is limited by three principal shortcomings. First, such analysis has little to say about intangible issues — such as staff morale, customer-perceived quality or investor support — that are increasingly recognized by managers and scholars as crucial to creating a competitive advantage. Second, although recognizing that a firm consists of many separate activities and entities, industry and firm-level "structural analysis" usually neglects to operationalize the interdependencies between the structural elements it identifies. Third, such analytical approaches are essentially static. At best the evolution of strategic competition is represented by comparing industry conditions at different points in time, whilst trends in market conditions, costs and prices are generally represented by linear models.

Managers and scholars share a need for frameworks that can capture the *time-path* of a firm's evolving strategy, and its interactions with rivals (Sanchez, Heene & Thomas, 1996), in a rigorous, yet accessible manner, to help them understand history, anticipate emerging changes and influence the future time-path of their firm's strategic performance.

Understanding historical developments may be important for understanding how a firm now works, and for identifying forces that may already be driving it towards certain future outcomes.

Figure 1 shows dynamic representations of strategically important challenges facing two firms, as developed in recent case work. Note that both cases include three specific features: a (vertical) *scale* for measuring the indicator of concern, a (horizontal) *time-scale* over which the indicator is expected to change, and a curve representing the *time-path* of the indicator's evolution. Note also that case A relates to an exogenously imposed challenge (competitive entry following deregulation), whilst case B concerns a largely internal, though no less "strategic" issue.

Building an analytical tool-set to capture, interpret and test such performance dynamics can be tackled by building on two important components of recent strategic management theory, namely the concepts of *strategic resources* (Wernerfelt, 1984; Barney, 1991; Mahoney & Pandian, 1992; Amit & Schoemaker, 1993; Peteraf, 1993) and *organizational capabilities* and *competences* (Prahalad & Hamel, 1990; Hamel, 1994, Hamel & Heene, 1994; Sanchez *et al.*, 1996). The tool-set must also integrate the processes of managerial goal-setting and policy-making, reflecting a stream of work on behavioral decision-making (Cyert & March, 1963; Allison, 1971; Simon, 1976; Hall, 1981; Kahneman & Tversky, 1982; Morecroft, 1983, 1985, 1997).

Strategic Resources and Competences[1]

Whilst the terms "resources" and "capabilities" have been the subject of much semantic debate, the following definitions by Amit and Schoemaker (1993) provide a starting-point for the discussion that follows.

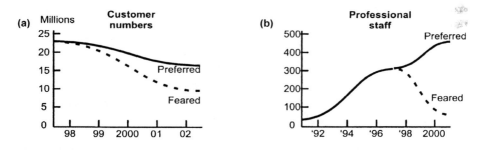

Figure 1: Time-charts of Dynamic Challenges Facing Two Illustrative Firms.
(a) Possible competitive intrusion against an incumbent telecommunications firm facing deregulation of its market.
(b) Possible staff-losses by a professional services firm.

---

[1]This even applies to new business start-ups, where the entrepreneur appears to start with nothing, but nonetheless depends upon some vital intangible resources, such as credibility with investors.

Strategic resources — "stocks of available factors that are owned or controlled by the firm... converted into final products or services by using a wide range of other firm assets and bonding mechanisms..."

Organisational capabilities — "a firm's capacity to deploy resources, usually in combination, using organizational processes... that are firm-specific and are developed over time..."

Such resources and capabilities are examples of "strategic assets" — "anything tangible or intangible the firm can use in its processes for creating, producing and/or offering its products to a market" (Sanchez *et al.*, 1996). This source also defines resources as "assets that are available and useful" in achieving the goals of a firm, and takes resources to include capabilities. For the present discussion, however, the term resources does *not* include capabilities.

Sanchez *et al.* (1996) go on to define "capabilities" as "repeatable patterns of action in the use of assets" and "competence" as *"an ability to sustain the coordinated deployment of assets in a way that helps a firm achieve its goals"*. Distinctions between resources and capabilities are made in the following discussion. Both will be treated in a manner consistent with the Amit & Schoemaker and Sanchez *et al.* definitions. Subsequent discussion will propose that the term "competence" requires a further conceptual distinction if it is to be made operational for strategy dynamic analysis.

Although strategy writers have recognized the importance to competitive advantage of strategic resources and capabilities, progress has been slow in making these concepts usable for analysis of the scale and rate of change in a firm's competitive advantage. Managers generally understand the importance of building and conserving the resources of their business. These resources may be "hard" or *tangible* items, including cash, plant, customers, products and staff, or soft, *intangible* factors, such as product quality, staff morale, and service standards. Having identified the relevant resources, further work must then be done to identify the *sustainability* of any advantage that might exist (Barney, 1991; Amit & Schoemaker, 1993).

The criteria for resources to provide sustainable advantage are well-established (Wernerfelt, 1984; Barney, 1991; Mahoney & Pandian, 1992; Peteraf, 1993). They must be *durable,* should not be *mobile* or *tradeable,* should not be easy to *replicate* and should also be difficult for others to *substitute* with alternatives. Finally, they should be *complementary,* i.e., capable of working well together. The last is a particularly challenging criterion to fulfil, or even to specify, since analytical techniques for capturing interdependence between resources are not yet well developed.

These criteria, whilst appearing to be reasonable tests of the likelihood that any strategic resource may be a sustainable source of advantage, suffer two problems. First, each of the criteria above generally applies not absolutely, but *to some greater or lesser degree.* Few resources are totally durable, absolutely non-tradeable, never replicable or impossible to substitute. Second, the durability, mobility, replicability and substitutability of resources are fundamentally *dynamic* issues, and firms always face the problem of the *rate* at which they, or rivals, may be able to change resource-levels. Some means of measuring and representing rates-of-change in resource-levels is thus vital to understanding the scale and rate of change in competitive advantage.

Static criteria for sustainability limit the usefulness of resources per se as "barriers to entry" — i.e., as factors that firms must possess in order to participate in an industry. Characterizing resource-ownership as a barrier to entry is a poor description of reality, since a firm may be able to participate in an industry to some extent with *a little* of each strategic resource, may compete more strongly with *more* of each resource, and may build competitive advantage if it can *grow* additional resources. Strategic resources are therefore not so much barriers to entry as "hills" of varying height and steepness, which firms must climb and from which they can compete to a greater or lesser degree, depending on how high they have managed to climb.

Operationalizing the Dynamics of Strategic Resources

Strategic management writers have recognized the importance of building and maintaining the *level* or *stock* of each resource (Dierickx & Cool, 1989). Resources are built by boosting the flow of additional resource into a stock, or by working to prevent resources being lost from the stock. Note that this description is as applicable to intangible resources, such as staff morale or market reputation, as it is to tangible factors, and as we shall see, it is also suited to describing the changing levels of capabilities.

The stock-and-flow framework can be operationalized as a simple integration device to represent resource accumulation and depletion. This simple structure alone in Figure 2 captures important aspects of the dynamic complexity of real business systems. Although the in-flows and out-flows to the resource-stock of staff are both following simple time-paths, their interaction creates a resource dynamic that is not intuitively obvious. Add some further stocks and flows — for instance, junior managers, managers and directors in a staff hierarchy — and it becomes increasingly difficult to estimate the time-path of growth for the stock of "managers", especially if the rates of resignation, promotion *to* and *from* the manager grade are all changing.

This simple graphical representation of strategic asset-stocks and their corresponding flows illustrates some important principles for modelling how resource-levels change over time:

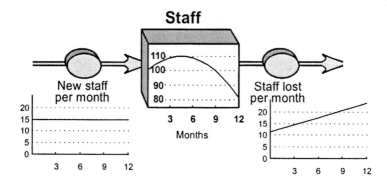

Figure 2: The Dynamics of an Isolated Strategic Resource.

- If a resource consists of certain units (people, customers, products etc.) then its accumulation and depletion *must be* a rate of change, expressed in units per time period (people per month, customers per quarter, new products per year);
- Resources can *only* be altered by changing the in-flows or out-flows i.e., the firm must do something about *getting* the resource at a faster rate, or *losing* it less rapidly;
- Both stocks and flows — and their trajectory over time — are vital to resource-dynamics, but firms are often poorly informed about their values;
- Although managers often worry about in-flows (recruitment, marketing etc.) they typically give less attention to out-flows (staff losses or customer lapse-rates); where different forces are known to be influencing in-flows and out-flows, analysis *must* split these two items.

Having identified these dynamic drivers of asset-stocks, some means is needed to formulate them in a rigorous manner. Stock accumulation and depletion lie at the heart of the system dynamics method (Forrester, 1961), making it ideally suited to capturing resources as "stocks" of strategic assets together with the "flows" that drive changes to the levels of such assets.

Resource Interdependence

The second contribution of system dynamics to understanding time-paths in strategy is its ability to capture *interdependence* between strategic resources. This is achieved by recognizing that *managers use resources they already have in order to develop other resources they need.* Marketing staff need a credible product or service to build a customer base, sales people cannot sell a product unless manufacturing has cost-effective production capacity, a firm needs a good reputation in the recruitment market to hire the people it wants, and so on. Such interdependence is illustrated in the larger graphic in Figure 3. Here, the more of resource A the firm has, the faster it can build resource B, and *vice versa.*

In this case, neither resource A nor B is consumed in this process. Whilst this is a common feature of interdependence, some resources can be used only by being consumed, common examples including cash and raw materials (see smaller graphic in Figure 3).

Note: the "R" inside the feedback loop indicates that this system "reinforces" its own growth i.e., an increase (decrease) in one resource-stock leads to an increase (decrease) in the other resources, the consequences of which is exponential growth (decline) in the entire system.

Although Figure 3 indicates a direct link *from* each resource to the accumulation of the other, in practice these connections tend to operate through intermediate factors. In brand management, for example, an increase in aware consumers is driven by advertising expenditure. Although not a resource-stock itself, advertising spending depends on revenues, which in turn arise from the stock of outlets offering the product. The *direct* connection, whereby outlet availability of the product directly boosts consumer awareness, is present, but is typically weaker than advertising-driven growth in consumer awareness.

Widening the perspective to a more comprehensive view of the firm, the framework introduced in Figure 3 can be generalized to a statement that:

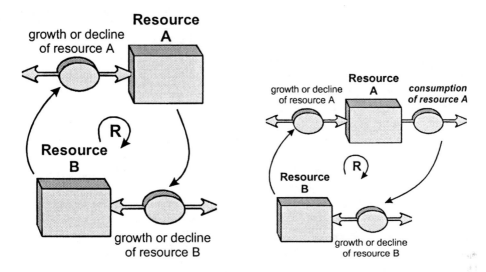

Figure 3: Interdependence Between Resources.

> *the current rate of change of a resource is a function of the current levels of all resources in the system, including that resource itself.*

Driving a firm's resource-system growth requires the management of intangible resources, which are crucial to competitive performance, yet difficult to acquire and maintain. It may be possible quickly to raise cash from investors, to buy or build production facilities, or to hire staff, for example, but it is more difficult, and generally takes more time, to build and sustain the morale of a workforce, the support of investors, a reputation in the market-place, or a cost-efficiency advantage over rivals. Moreover, such resources can rarely be bought (Itami, 1987). Not only are intangibles hard to build, they can be easily destroyed (e.g., by a high-profile failure), and may have powerful and immediate effects on critical tangible resources (e.g., catastrophic loss of customers when a reputation for quality is destroyed).

Further, many intangible resources are not independent, but are closely tied to some tangible resource. Staff experience, for example, flows through the firm with the staff members (i.e. human resources) who carry that experience, so loss of key staff does not just damage the quantity of tangible resource (people), but also diminishes the intangible resource of average staff experience (years). Recruiting may replace the people, but cannot so easily replace their experience. A parallel argument applies to other tangible/ intangible resource pairs, such as customer-quality (average profit contribution per customer), or the cost-efficiency of a portfolio of production plants (average cost per unit produced).

Whilst some intangibles may be closely tied to tangible resources, the firm may still be able to act to change their level directly. Staff skills can be increased directly by training (without increasing numbers of staff), as well as indirectly by recruitment and retention of skilled staff. Similarly, unit cost can be enhanced by improving plant performance, as well as by closing inefficient sites.

Finally, certain intangible resources tend to respond with a significant time delay to changes in other resources (Sanchez & Heene, 1996) — staff morale may deteriorate with continuing work-pressure and customer-reputation may build or deplete in response to historic service-quality. Such intangibles may be labeled *indirect,* to indicate that they depend on the reaction of other parties to conditions, and thus are not solely in the hands of management to alter.

The Role of Capabilities in the Firm's Resource System[2]

One of the continuing puzzles in strategic management is to explain how resource-poor firms are able to emerge and challenge dominant, resource-rich rivals. Whilst differences in resource-system design may partly explain such phenomena, there remains the question of how one firm may be able to grow a single key resource more quickly than rivals when it appears to have no more (or perhaps even less) of the other resources needed for the task. A plausible explanation for such superior performance is that the firm may be more *capable* than its rivals at building the resource in question.

This observation exposes an important issue concerning the definitions of "capability" discussed earlier. Whilst the importance of capabilities is widely accepted, better insights are needed into the mechanisms by which capabilities actually contribute to the accumulation of resources, and hence to competitive advantage. Since firms cannot operate at all without strategic *resources,* (i.e. asset-stocks other than capabilities), capabilities must somehow contribute to resource-accumulation and maintenance. Indeed, it can be argued that *capabilities have no strategic value in isolation from the resources of the firm.*

The following thought experiment illustrates this key relationship. Imagine that the entire staff of a firm is taken to a deserted island. Although the staff presumably carry with them at least some of their capabilities, they have no resources, no prospect of accumulating them, and thus no opportunity whatever to build a firm. If the same staff were put in a location rich in *potential* resources, they could feasibly begin to accumulate new resources, in effect creating a system that can build a firm. Thus, the notion of "capability" must be redefined as *"the rate at which the firm is able to build a strategic resource, for any given availability of the other resources needed for that task".*

It is now possible to represent the contribution of capabilities to the resource system framework. Figure 4 represents graphically the notion that the firm's rate of net

---

[2]Mathematically, this is represented by equation 1, and the current level of each resource is captured as the integral over time of its historic net accumulations (equation 2).

$$v_i(T) = \frac{dR_i(T)}{dT} = f_1[R_1(T), ..., R_n(T)] \tag{1}$$

$$R_i(T) = \int_0^T v_i(t)dt + R_i(0) \tag{2}$$

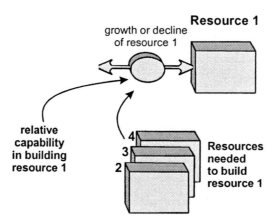

Figure 4: Representing "Capability" in the Building of a Resource.

accumulation for resource one is a function, not just of the other resources it holds, but also of its capability at that task.

Learning — or "capability-building" — arises from a firm's accumulated experience in applying its capabilities to managing the resource.[3] Figure 5 illustrates this relationship for the ease of site-acquisition by a multiple-retail operation. As a new entrant, this retailer is unlikely to be very skilled at site-acquisition — it will choose poor sites, be slow to find them, and pay too high a price. As it acquires more sites, however, the collective skill of its site-finding team may grow, provided that they learn from both successes and mistakes. The site-finding capability grows as a function of the flow of the strategic resource that it accumulates. Such learning may be possible from both positive and negative flows, i.e. site disposals as well as acquisitions. Note also that the capability is more than the aggregate of the skills of individual team members — loss of a single individual may cause little damage to the accumulated capability of the team as a whole.

---

[3]The mathematics of the resource system can be extended to incorporate capability building. Equation (3) says that capability i builds at a rate reflecting the current rate of change in its corresponding resource, and (4) says that the current level of capability i is the integral of all changes since time 0 plus its initial level. Equation (5) adapts equation (1) to indicate that the accumulation of resource i depends on its corresponding capability as well as the state of any or all of the system's resources.

$$c_i(T) = \frac{dC_i(T)}{dT} = f_2[r_i(T)] \qquad (3)$$

$$C_i(T) = \int_0^T c_i(t)dt + C_i(0) \qquad (4)$$

$$r_i(T) = f_3[R_1(T),...,R_n(T),C_i(T)] \qquad (5)$$

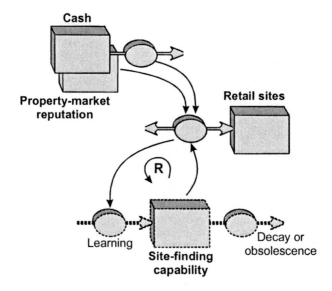

Figure 5: Representing Capability-building in Acquiring Retail Sites.

Capability-building can now be extended to the resource-system as a whole. Recognizing that the effectiveness of the firm as a *learning* resource-system reflects the contribution of all these individual capabilities, organizational competence appears as an interdependent composite of all those individual capabilities (Figure 6). This formulation of capability, organizational competence and learning is essentially consistent with treatments of these terms by Sanchez *et al.* (1996) and Sanchez & Heene (1997).

Illustrating the Dynamic Impact of Capabilities and Learning on Firm Performance

System dynamics is able to represent important aspects of interdependence and feedback between strategic resources. The same representation can readily be extended to incorporate the role of capabilities, learning and competences, as depicted in Figures 4 to 6. This can be demonstrated with a small research model, simplified from empirical evidence, of a consumer products company's efforts to build a brand in the spirits sector.

The strategic resources required to build a brand are *aware consumers* (of which there are potentially 5m in the sector), *retail stores* to stock the brand (potentially 50,000) and a *sales force* (typically about *50* people, though this number can be changed quickly). Consumers are made aware of the brand through advertising, but lose interest without constant reinforcement. Stores can be persuaded by the sales force to stock the brand, and keep stocking it, but only if the product offers a good retail profit contribution, which in turn depends on strong consumer demand and a healthy margin. Retail availability also helps to support consumer awareness, though more weakly than advertising spending. The resource-system diagram for the model is shown in Figure 7.

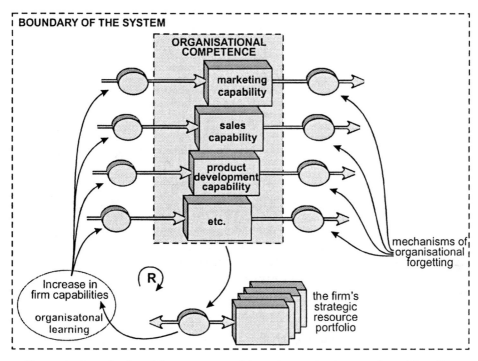

Figure 6: Organisational Competence and Learning as the Aggregation of Specific Capabilities.

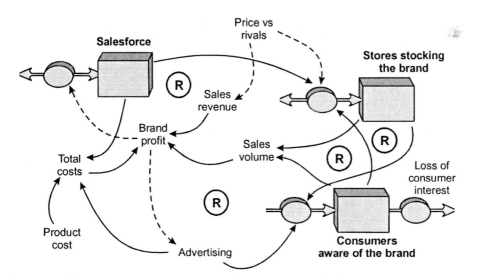

Figure 7: Resource-system Diagram of the Brand-building Model.

Note — "R" inside the feedback loop again indicates "reinforcing feedback". This structure will also be subject to "balancing" effects that will constrain growth, notably limits to the number of potential consumers and stores, limits to the reach that advertising can achieve, and declining performance of additional sales staff.

This business relies on two key capabilities. It must have a *marketing* capability to ensure that its advertising expenditure creates a strong base of consumers, and it must have a selling capability to ensure that high consumer awareness generates high levels of brand-stocking by stores. "Capability" here is measured on an index basis, where the index value of 1.0 is defined as "the highest capability management can imagine for this resource-building task", which can be estimated by reference to the capability of most-admired rivals.

Capability Differences — with no Learning

The model is first simulated to compare different, but static levels of the two capabilities. Figure 8 illustrates the impact of both isolated and combined capability-differences on sales and marketing, under fixed policies for advertising expenditure, pricing and sales force size.

- The firm's capability in both sales and marketing is initially (run 1) believed to be about 60 percent of the best imaginable for each capability. Modest marketing capability builds awareness over twelve months to a modest level, which the limited sales capability struggles to turn into retail distribution. Eventually, distribution rises to the point where brand availability helps support the modest marketing achievements, and the brand eventually takes off, becoming profitable by about month 30;
- Run 2 shows the impact of improving sales capability alone to 80 percent of peak performance. The brand's take-up by retail stores rises faster, in spite of little initial improvement in consumer awareness. From about month nine, though, consumer awareness also improves, due to the brand's increased visibility in stores;
- Run 3 shows the impact of improving marketing capability alone to 80 percent of optimum. Consumer awareness rises considerably faster than in Run one. Strong

Figure 8: Performance Dynamics Arising from Capability Differences in Brand-building.

awareness also creates rapid store take-up for the brand, in spite of the modest sales capability;

- Run 4 shows the effect of stronger performance by *both* sales and marketing. Both consumer awareness and store distribution rise strongly, with the brand becoming profitable much earlier and growing to higher long term levels of profitability than in Run one, two or three.

These outcomes lead to two observations. First, the relationships observed call into question the concept of "core competence"[4] (Prahalad & Hamel, 1990) — a question raised previously by Sanchez *et al.* (1996) and Heene & Sanchez (1997). Whilst originally specified for the multi-business firm, managers and consultants often seek to identify the core competence of individual business units. Yet the resource-system framework suggests that *no* capability (equivalent to "competence" as used by Prahalad and Hamel) can be expected to be "core". No matter how well a firm performs in any one resource-building task, it will fail if the rest of the system is ineffective. The same might be expected to apply to capabilities that are "core" to the multi-business corporation — if the firm applies a single capability to competing in an activity in which it does not have access to the other capabilities required by the rest of the system, it will fail.

Second, the described relationships call into question the widespread focus on customer-facing capabilities alone. The firm must be capable of building *all* strategic resources in its system. A common example concerns a firm's capability in operational control, which ensures continuing high rates of cash-flow into its financial resource. This cannot be described as "customer-facing", but a firm that retains 20 cents of cash-flow from every dollar of revenue has considerable advantages over a rival that only retains 15 cents, since it can deploy those stronger cash-flows to build other resources in its system.

Conclusions and Implications

This paper has explained that firm performance is a function of the resources the firm possesses, and that these resources have the characteristic that they *accumulate and deplete* over time. Furthermore, the rate at which a firm can build each of its resources depends critically upon the levels of resources that it *already* holds. "Capability" is best understood as a powerful determinant of a firm's *relative* ability, compared with rivals, to build a specific resource. This capability is built over time by continued experience in the corresponding resource-building task. Looking at the firm as a whole, *competence* may be viewed as the aggregate of a firm's capabilities at all strategically important resource-building tasks. *Organizational learning* then becomes an expression of a firm's effectiveness at building this overall competence.

The analytical perspective offered in this paper for understanding resources and capabilities has further implications for the dynamics of rivalry and industry change. Having

[4]Note that Prahalad and Hamel's use of the term "competence" corresponds to the term "capability" used throughout this article.

applied system dynamics to the dynamics of strategic resource building for a single firm, the framework can be extended to reflect the dynamics of rivalry, both between individual firms and between "strategic groups" of firms with similar resource-attributes and policy-sets (Porter, 1985; McGee & Thomas, 1986) and different competence-leveraging and building activities (Gorman, Thomas & Sanchez, 1996). This in turn may make it possible to explain and communicate otherwise intractable issues of industry dynamics, such as cyclicality and industry rationalization.

References

Allison, G. L. (1971). *The Essence of Decision.* Boston: Little, Brown.

Amit, R., & Schoemaker, P. (1993). Strategic assets and organisational rent. *Strategic Management Journal, 14,* 38.

Barney, J. B. (1991). Firm resources and sustained competitive advantage. *Journal of Management, 17,* 99.

Cyert, R. M., & March, J. G. (1963). *A Behavioral Theory of the Firm.* Englewood Cliffs: Prentice-Hall.

Dierickx, I., & Cool, K. (1989). Asset stock accumulation and sustainability of competitive advantage. *Management Science, 35,* 1504.

Forester, J. W. (1961). *Industrial Dynamics.* Cambridge, MA: Productivity Press.

Gorman, P., Thomas, H., & Sanchez, R. (1996). A competence perspective on industry dynamics. In R. Sanchez, A. Heene & H. Thomas (eds) *Dynamics of Competence-Based Competition.* Oxford: Elsevier Pergamon.

Hall, R. I. (1981). Decision making in a complex organisation. In G. W. England *et al. The Functioning of Complex Organisations.* Cambridge, NLA: Oelgeschlager. 111.

Hamel, G., & Heene, A. (eds) (1994). *Competence-based Competition.* New York: John Wiley.

Hamel, G. (1994). The Concept of Core Competence. In G. Hamel & A. Heene (eds) *Competence-based Competition.* New York: John Wiley. 11.

Itami, H. (1987). *Mobilising Invisible Assets.* Cambridge, MA: Harvard University Press.

Kahneman, D., & Tversky, A. (1982). The psychology of preferences. *Scientific American, 246,* 160.

Mahoney, I., & Pandian, J. R. (1992). The resource-based view within the conversation of strategic management. *Strategic Management Journal, 13,* 363.

McGee, J., & Thomas, H. (1986). Strategic groups: theory, research and taxonomy. *Strategic Management Journal, 7,* 141.

Mintzberg, H., & Quinn, J. B. (eds) (1992). *The Strategy Process.* Englewood Cliffs: Prentice Hall.

Morecroft, J. D. W. (1983). System dynamics: portraying bounded rationality. *Omega, 11,* 131.

Morecroft, J. D. W. (1985). The feedback view of business policy and strategy. *System Dynamics Review, 2,* 4.

Morecroft, J. D. W. (1997). The rise and fall of People Express: A dynamic resource-based view. *Proceedings of the 1997 System Dynamics Society Conference,* Istanbul, Turkey.

Peteraf, M. A. (1993). The cornerstones of competitive advantage: A resource-based view. *Strategic Management Journal, 14,* 19.

Porter, M. E. (1981). *Competitive Strategy.* New York: Free Press.

Porter, M. E. (1985). *Competitive Advantage.* New York: Free Press.

Prahalad, C. K., & Hamel, U. (1990). The core competence of the organisation. *Harvard Business Review* Mar/Apr, 75.

Sanchez, R., & Heene, A. (1996). A systems view of the firm. In R. Sanchez, A. Heene & H. Thomas (eds) *Dynamics of Competence-Based Competition*. Oxford: Elsevier.

Sanchez, R., & Heene, A. (eds) (1997). Preface and Introduction to *Strategic Learning and Knowledge Management*. Chichester: John Wiley.

Sanchez, R., Heene, A., & Thomas, H. (eds) (1996). *Dynamics of Competence-based Competition: Theory and Practice in the New Strategic Management*. Oxford: Elsevier.

Simon, H. A. (1976). *Administrative Behavior* (3rd edition). New York: Free Press.

Wernerfelt, B. (1984). A resource-based view of the firm. *Strategic Management Journal, 5*, 171.

Chapter 4

Innovation Management Under Uncertainty: A System Dynamics Model of R&D Investments in Biotechnology

L. Martin Cloutier and Michael D. Boehlje

Introduction

Whether in agriculture, pharmaceutical, or manufacturing industries, biotechnology-related firms are engaged in a wide range of research, development, regulatory approval, manufacturing, and commercialization activities in support of new product innovation. Maier (1998) has described the diffusion of an innovation as a complex system of reinforcing and balancing feedback loops with significant time delays and timing decisions. The sequence of activities from research and development (R&D) to commercialization also involves technology choices subject to substantial uncertainty. For example, one of the decision problems for a genetics company developing new kinds of seeds is R&D investment allocation between (1) a biotechnology-based event research program, and (2) the natural breeding research program. With the advent of other new technologies, more complex decision situations will arise involving investment trade-offs over time between and within platforms.

The essential problem for any firm investing in R&D and new technology is whether streams of expected profits earned through innovation will create sufficient economic value to justify investments that must be made not just in R&D, but also throughout the value chain during commercialization. The specific objectives of this chapter are to present a conceptual framework illustrating the decisions that must be made in innovating — in this case developing new corn genetics from R&D investment to commercialization. A system dynamics model is used to explore decision trade-offs associated with alternative investment decisions and their patterns of value capture, taking into account time delays.

Relevant Literature and Concepts

Economic research into innovation in the agricultural sector has resulted in explanations of the aggregate rates of return on investment (Huffman, 1998), highlighted the economic incentives for various types of technological change (Biswanger, 1974; Hayami & Ruttan,

Systems Perspectives on Resources, Capabilities, and Management Processes, pages 57–68.
Copyright © 2002 by Elsevier Science Ltd.
All rights of reproduction in any form reserved.
ISBN: 0-08-043778-8

1985), and clarified the structural implications of various types of technology transfer and R&D investments (Sunding & Zilberman, 2000). Other researchers (particularly sociologists) have looked at the innovation adoption process and the characteristics of various adopters of new innovations (Rogers, 1957). Thus far, however, studies have not focused on the management issues and decision problems involved in choosing a technology or technology platform and the commercialization of the results of the R&D activity.

Barney and Lee (1998) have argued that economic uncertainty breeds tensions between the transactions cost concepts of minimizing opportunism and the strategic options concepts of maximizing flexibility. These tensions are further exacerbated by the need for firms to establish coordination mechanisms that secure property rights from endogenous learning activities. It has been posited by Sanchez (1995) that "the concept of strategic flexibility (that is, strategic options) in product competition represents a fundamental approach to the management of uncertainty." The term *strategic options* refers to a firm's ability to alter decisions about resource access as well as interfirm relationships over time to achieve economic returns in dynamic product competition.

At the foundation of the systems approach are positive feedback (represented by a rein-forcing loop) and negative feedback (represented by a balancing loop). Positive feedback creates reinforcing behavior and negative feedback moderates a system towards an equilib-rium position. The identification of positive and negative feedback structures in economic and management systems are key to modeling and gaining insight into accelerating the speed of development of an innovation (Sterman, 2000). From a management of technology perspective, Sanchez has suggested that the dynamic product competition problem can be conceptualized using the reinforcing loop among technologies, product strategies, interfirm coordination mechanisms, and the business environment (see Figure 1). In biotechnology, the reinforcing loop could be substituted by a balancing loop if any of the changes identified in the reinforcing loop of Figure 1 were to oppose one of the changes at a given point in time. For example, changes in conducts and competitive environments could act to oppose changes in technology. We have represented this possibility by adding a minus sign to the top left feedback loop in Figure 1. The impact of a negative feedback loop would be to slow down or impair the potential adoption of a biotechnology innovation. However, the long time delays between the many strategic decisions that drive the positive feedback loops of Figure 1 forward require empirical inquiry and modeling to better understand how both economic uncertainty and time delays may affect the outcomes of strategic decisions. In this discussion, we provide a systems model for such an exploration.

A Decision Model

The R&D choice between natural breeding programs or biotechnology as a technology platform for bringing new crops to market (or some optimal combination of these two plat-forms) can be best framed as a dynamic multi-stage decision problem. We represent this problem as an investment decision in which the economic payoff of investing in a tech-nology platform is the result of (1) the market penetration as measured by acres of a particular variety of crop grown from the new seed to be developed, and (2) the margin on sales after all production costs (that is, the net revenue that can be allocated as a return to

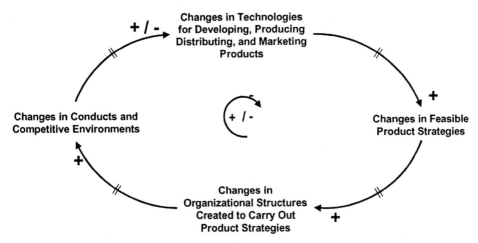

Figure 1: Systemic Relationships and Positive Feedback among Technologies, Product
Strategies, Organization Structures, and Competitive Environments. (Adapted from
Sanchez, 1995).

the R&D investment). Both market penetration and margins follow time paths that depend
on market acceptance and competition, as we detail later. The decision criteria used in
making the technology platform choice is to choose the most valuable real option — the
natural breeding technology platform or the gene-splicing biotech platform (or some
combination or mixed strategy) — expected to result from sequential R&D investments.

Figure 2 provides an overview of the key components/stages and drivers of our decision
problem. This conceptualization identifies three key stages in the decision problem: R&D,
multiplication (technology transfer) and ramp-up, and market introduction and commercialization. R&D involves the identification and development of seeds with a particular
desired trait or attribute such as yield, drought resistance, pest resistance, protein content,
etc. This stage also involves obtaining whatever regulatory approvals are necessary to
proceed to the next stage of multiplication and ramp-up.

In the multiplication and ramp-up stage, the volume of product obtained from the R&D
stage is expanded and multiplied to obtain sufficient volume for commercial sales. In
natural breeding programs, the biological growth process imposes on the ramp-up stage
both time delays and uncertainties resulting from the natural laws of biology. With genetic
modification technology, opportunities for gene-splicing may alter these time delays and
reduce the uncertainty of growth processes. Once ramp-up provides adequate volumes for
commercial sales, the new product is released to the third stage of market introduction and
commercialization.

In the commercialization stage, the new variety is made available to the marketing/sales
force, and it is adopted by producers depending upon a number of factors, including availability of competitive products and producers' expectations of the net benefits of the new
seed's attributes or variety.

Each stage in this process can be impacted by various drivers or influences that affect
the rate of development, as well as the cost and effectiveness of performing other functions

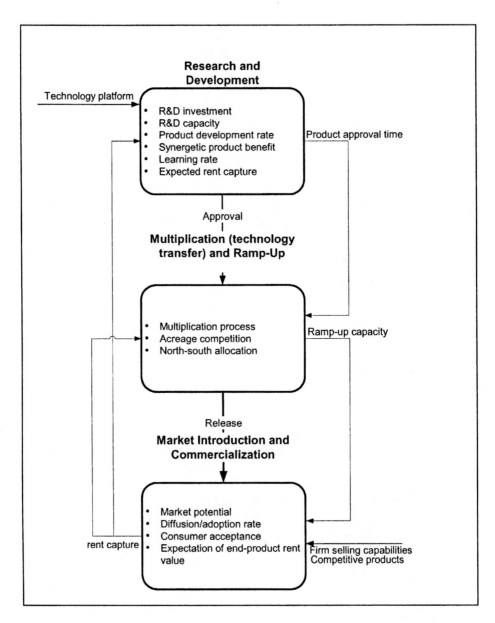

Figure 2: The Process of Transforming Technology from R&D to Commercialization.

or activities at each stage. In the R&D stage, a major determinant of performance will be the technology platform selected for development. Natural breeding programs have fairly well understood cost, efficiency, and effectiveness parameters, as well as typical rates of improvement in identifying and isolating specific traits or attributes. Biotechnology platforms accelerate this rate of advancement, but frequently do so only at a higher cost. R&D

in biotechnology tries to generate a genetic characteristic or "event" (for example, insect or herbicide resistance, or some nutritional characteristic) and to insert this characteristic into a plant species. Expected benefit streams combined with the availability of R&D funding will also impact the rate of investment in R&D activities. Finally, any regulatory requirements and the speed with which any regulatory approvals can be obtained are usually major determinants of R&D activity. In general, regulatory processes will be much more significant in driving R&D when using a biotechnology platform compared to a natural breeding program.

Although the multiplication and ramp-up stage can be much more complicated than that depicted in Figure 2, the two major drivers of the speed, effectiveness, and efficiency of this stage are the multiplication process and the capacity to multiply. The multiplication process is the biological and/or biotechnology determined procedure for taking germplasm from the R&D stage and increasing the volume to a level adequate for market introduction. This process is driven by the biological growth process of plants in the case of natural breeding programs, but with the biotechnology platform, it is accelerated through gene splicing and other technologies. The second determinant, capacity to multiply, depends on two major decisions: (1) how much acreage is available for seed stock production, given development of competitive products that also are demanding multiplication and ramp-up acreage, and (2) whether the seed stock production activity will take place only in the northern hemisphere, only in the southern hemisphere, or in both hemispheres (which could double or even triple annual multiplication and ramp-up capacity).

Once a product is released to the marketing and sales organization for introduction and commercialization, its acceptance by producers will depend significantly on their understanding of end-users' net benefit expectations. Technology adoption is typically represented by an adoption/diffusion pattern summarized by a cumulative logistics (or S-shaped) growth curve (see, for example, Day & Schoemaker, 2000; Sterman, 2000). But the shape and characteristics of this adoption curve will also depend on the performance of competitive products; if an effective competitor has been introduced into the market, the level and rate of adoption can be substantially reduced. Furthermore, the capability and capacity of the marketing program and the sales force will impact the purchasing behavior of producers and their level and rate of adoption of the new product. Adoption levels and rates and commercialization may also be a function of end-user acceptance of the biotechnological platform and its transgenic products. And equally important is the concept of value decay for products that have enhanced attributes, such as increased protein content. If producers think that this enhanced value will be retained over a number of years, then more producers may be willing to adopt seeds based on a new technology. If the value is expected to decay rapidly for some reason, then the adoption level and rate will be lower.

A Dynamic Model Representation

We now examine dynamic product competition in the agricultural biotechnology market using a dynamic systems simulation model. System dynamics modeling and simulation can be used in scenario analysis to understand the influence of uncertainty and time delays in the sequential decisions of firms developing new seed products or new technology in general (Coyle, 1998; Morecroft & Sterman, 1994). The simulation results explore and contrast the consequences of adopting seeds developed using natural breeding methods versus biotechnology-based methods. The simulation explores the impacts of time delays, and differences in adoption, diffusion, and producer acceptance related to both technologies. The natural breeding technology has a longer time-to-market than the biotechnology method. Producer acceptance, however, is represented as having a higher degree of uncertainty for biotechnology-based products. By simulating alternative illustrative scenarios, the model helps to develop a deeper understanding of the underlying economic dynamics and the impacts of timing of decisions on economic value creation and decay.

The influence diagram of Figure 3 elaborates the innovation process summarized in Figure 1 and captures the dynamics of the three innovation process stages depicted in Figure 2. The influence diagram is a means to represent the process "microstructure" underlying the dynamic and nonlinear "macrobehavior" of the system of interacting processes that may be carried out by a single firm or through governance structures that include joint ventures, strategic alliances, etc. The three stages of Figure 2 are depicted within the dotted-line boxes in Figure 3 and include the main reinforcing and balancing feedback loops within the innovation process.

The R&D stage includes two reinforcing loops (R1a,b) and one balancing loop (B1). The reinforcing loops (R1a) and (R1b) illustrate the R&D capacity expansion trade-offs between natural breeding and biotechnology platforms. The development of the biotechnology platform emphasizes investment in R&D to generate a particular genetic "event". The biotechnology event could eventually be commercialized in the seed of any compatible naturally bred crop species. Investments in the biotechnology R&D platform may be commercialized across many crops, while a natural breeding program involves the incremental selection of traits within a crop species. Thus, the outputs of these R&D investments programs are complementary, even though they compete for budget and land inputs over time. Thus, genetics companies while pursuing biotechnology research programs must also maintain natural breeding technology platforms across a number of crops.

Note that there is a key time delay between the expected capture of profits and any increase in R&D capacity through making investments in R&D capacity.[1] Overall R&D capacity is also constrained by the trade-offs between the technology platforms. The R&D capacity in the natural breeding and biotechnology programs influences their respective discovery/invention rates and ultimately influences expected R&D rents. Added R&D capacity may translate into increased discovery/invention rates for both platforms. The balancing loop (B1) shows the effect of approval time delays on the synergetic benefits of the natural breeding and biotechnology platforms and moderates the potential for rapidly expanding profits through R&D exploitation.

The choice of technology platform in the R&D stage influences the dynamics within the multiplication and ramp-up stage. Depending upon the choice of a natural or a biotechnology-based breeding process, the time delay between the multiplication process and the

---

[1] In a fully developed system dynamics model, time delays would be quantified explicitly.

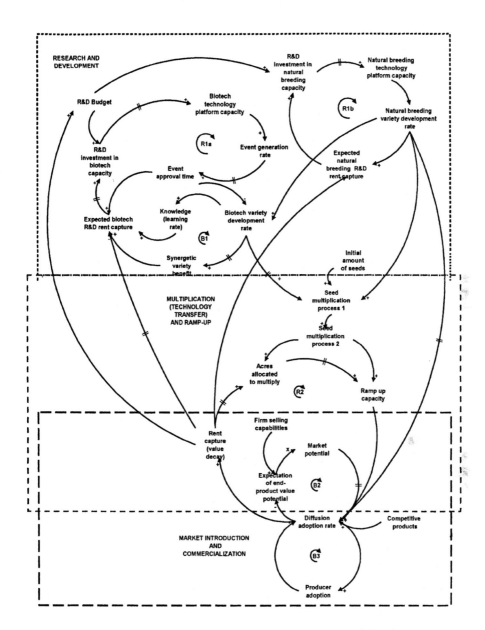

Figure 3: Influence Diagram: From R&D to Commercialization.

acres planted for seed production will be accordingly greater or smaller. This depends on the initial quantity of seeds available. The genetics company must then, in a second stage, combine acreage allocation decisions with the number of seeds available. An acreage allocation decision must be made between growing seeds that contain the biotechnology event and the ones that are identical in all respects but for the event. The reinforcing loop (R2) shows the acres allocated to planting with the seed that may contain the biotechnology event which influences the ramp-up capacity, which in turn then influences the adoption/diffusion rate. Finally, the adoption/diffusion rate influences profits captured and acres allocated.

The market introduction and commercialization stage is premised on a cumulative logistics (or S-shaped) growth curve (see Figure 4). This stage contains two balancing feedback loops (B2 and B3) and one reinforcing loop (R3) within its internal microstructure, which also influences the behavior of the multiplication and ramp-up and the R&D stages. The balancing feedback loop (B2) shows the microstructure of the diffusion/adoption process. Expectations of end-product value, influenced by sales force capabilities and the new product adoption rate by producers, influences the size of the potential market. The market potential influences the diffusion/adoption rate, with a time delay. As the diffusion/adoption rate increases, the adoption process eventually slows down because the market potential is being fully addressed. The diffusion/adoption rate is reflected in the growing number of product users, hence in market acceptance (also with a time delay), as seen in the balancing loop (B3). The diagram also includes the influence of exogenous competitive products that limit the rate of diffusion/adoption. Finally, the rate of adoption influences the profits captured, and profit capture increases R&D investments (with a time delay). The profits obtained are part of the feedback loop that influences R&D budget, the future allocation of that budget, and further allocations between the biotechnology and the natural breeding programs (R3).

Illustrative Results

We next present the results of simulations of a numerical simplification of the influence diagram presented in Figure 3. The results illustrate the market introduction and commercialization stage of the technology transformation process introduced in Figures 2 and 3, as well as the most critical influences from the R&D and multiplication and ramp-up stages. These results suggest the importance of the dynamic and non-linear behavior of the underlying microstructure of the model.

Three simulations presented below illustrate some of the adoption tradeoffs between a natural breeding program and a biotechnology-based breeding program. The first results are presented in Figure 4 and are based on the assumption that the rate of adoption of products based on natural breeding or biotechnology platforms will be identical. The evident difference between the two technology platform choices is the greater profit gained from the biotechnology-based platform and its resulting larger number of producers and higher rate of adoption.

The next results, shown in Figure 5, show what would happen if the expected profits were the same for both natural breeding and biotechnology products, but adding the condition that the adoption time delay is greater for the biotechnology-based product. In that case, the model shows that the product based on natural breeding achieves a higher adoption level.

The third simulation results, shown in Figure 6, show what happens when products of natural breeding methods are assumed to have a speedier time of adoption than

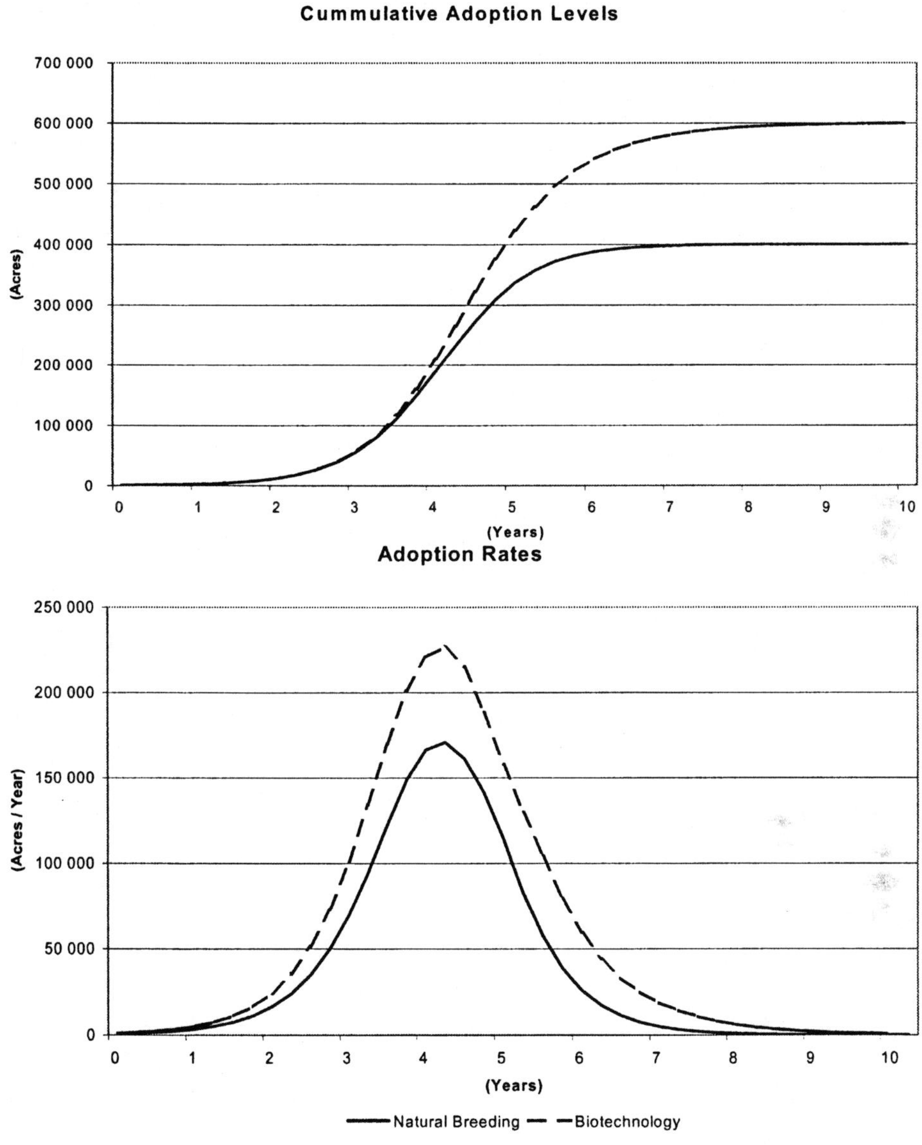

Cummulative Adoption Levels

Adoption Rates

Natural Breeding ▬ ▬Biotechnology

Figure 4: Assumes Same Adoption Time Delay but Longer Value Decay for
Biotechnology than for Natural Breeding.

biotechnology-based products, and when the products of the biotechnology platform are
assumed to have a greater profit potential because the platform can support further
improvements over a longer period or can be distributed over a large number of plant
species. These results show that the path of adoption is actually slower at first for the
biotechnology-derived seed, but eventually the biotechnology-based product creates a
larger market in spite of its initial slower adoption rate.

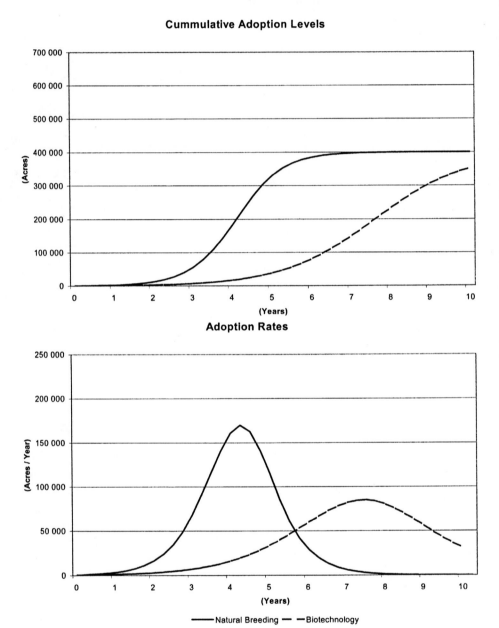

Figure 5: Assumes Faster Adoption for Natural Breeding than Biotechnology, and Same Time Delay for Value Decay.

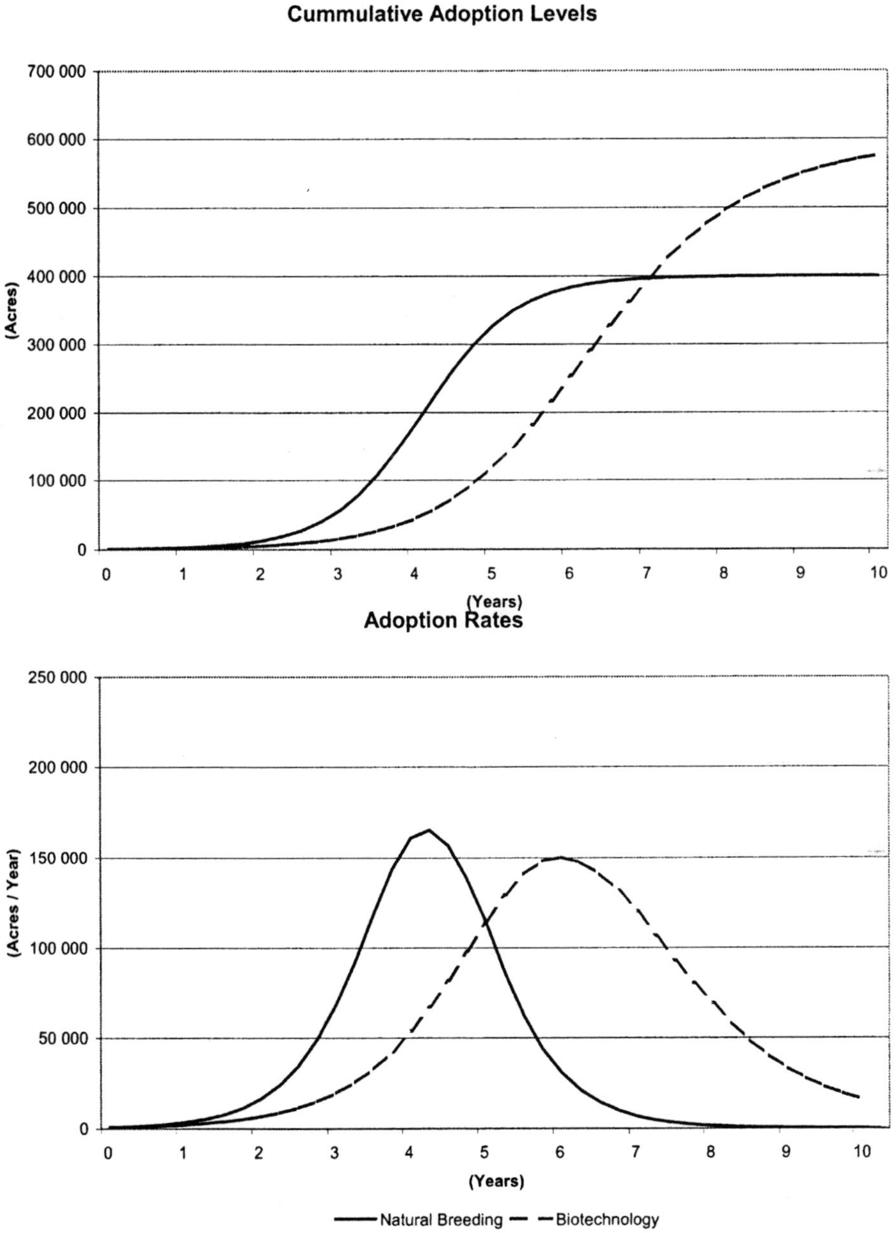

Cummulative Adoption Levels

Adoption Rates

Figure 6: Assumes Faster Adoption and Value Decay for Natural Breeding than for Biotechnology Breeding.

Conclusions

We have illustrated the application of system dynamics modeling in the investigation of technology adoption and diffusion processes for a genetic improvement developed through biotechnology and natural breeding platforms. The results presented here establish the importance of time delays and feedback loop interactions (reinforcing and balancing) in building up R&D capacity, market acceptance, and profit streams. Developing insights into the impacts of various time delays is essential to improving our understanding of the dynamic and non-linear behavior of such systems. Systems modeling also facilitates analysis of the synergetic components of natural breeding and biotechnology platforms. The results presented in this discussion suggest how systems modeling can be employed by decision-makers to achieve greater understanding of such issues before committing large amounts of resources.

References

Barney, J. B., & Lee, W. (1998). *Governance under uncertainty: Transactions costs, real options, learning, and property rights*. Reference No. 124140. Ohio: Fisher College of Business, Ohio State University.

Binswanger, H. P. (1974). A microeconomic approach to induced innovation. *Economic Journal, 84*, 940–958.

Coyle, G. (1998). The practice of system dynamics: milestones, lessons and ideas from 30 years of experience. *System Dynamics Review, 14*, 343–365.

Day, G. S., & Schoemaker, P. J. H. (2000). A different game. In P. J. H. Schoemaker, G. S. Day & R. E. Gunther (eds), *Wharton on Managing Emerging Technologies*. New York: Wiley & Sons. 1–23.

Hayami, Y., & Ruttan, V. M. (1985). *Agricultural Development: An International Perspective*. Baltimore, MD: Johns Hopkins University Press.

Huffman, W. E. (1998). Finance, organization and impacts of U.S. agricultural research: Future prospects, paper prepared for conference. *Knowledge Generation and Transfer: Implications for Agriculture in the 21st Century*. Berkeley: University of California.

Maier, F. H. (1998). New product diffusion models in innovation management – a system dynamics perspective. *System Dynamics Review, 14*, 285–308.

Morecroft, J. D. W., & Sterman, J. D. (eds) (1994). *Modeling for Learning Organizations*. Portland, OR: Productivity Press.

Rogers, E. (1957). *Diffusion of Innovations, Iowa State Agricultural Experiment Station*, Special Report No. 18. Ames, IA: Iowa State University.

Sanchez, R. (1995). Strategic flexibility in product competition. *Strategic Management Journal, 16*, 135–159.

Sterman, J. D. (2000). *Business Dynamics: Systems Thinking and Modeling for a Complex World*. Boston, MA: Irwin McGraw–Hill.

Sunding, D., & Zilberman, D. (2000). The agricultural innovation process: Research and technology adoption in a changing agricultural sector. *Handbook of Agricultural Economics*.

PART II

Systems Approaches to Building and Leveraging Organizational Competences

Chapter 5

Managing Strategic Change: A Systems View of Strategic Organizational Change and Strategic Flexibility

Ron Sanchez and Aimé Heene

Introduction

As the environments of many organizations become increasingly dynamic,[1] managers face a growing challenge to continuously improve the systemic ability of their organizations to identify and respond to strategic changes. In the following discussion, we use the term *strategic flexibility* to refer to the systemic ability of an organization to change in strategically important ways, and we explain a systems model of organizations that helps to develop insights into five interrelated forms of organizational flexibility on which the achievement of overall strategic flexibility depends.

Our model represents organizations as *open systems* that depend for their survival and success on assuring inward flows of a changing array of useful resources, on effective coordination of the resources currently within or accessible to an organization, and on setting appropriate goals for the deployment of an organization's resources in strategic processes of value creation and value distribution. We then use this open systems model to identify and clarify some key dynamics that must be managed well to create a strategically flexible organization.

The systems properties that affect an organization's ability to sustain adaptive change have been studied for some time by systems researchers as well as by strategists. In formulating his "law of requisite variety," for example, Ashby (1956) observed that to survive in a complex environment while maintaining internal stability, a system must be able to generate a requisite variety of responses to a changing environment. Forrester's (1961, 1968) industrial dynamics modeling helped to clarify the important impacts on the

---

[1] *Dynamic environments* are characterized by rapid technological changes, the frequent emergence of multiple (and often conflicting) market opportunities and threats, and resulting high levels of irreducible uncertainty about the long-term direction and extent of strategic change in the environment. These uncertainties may apply not just to future scenarios, but to present circumstances as well. Even current market needs and customer preferences may be unclear, often forcing an organization to pursue rapidly shifting market demands and opportunities.

Systems Perspectives on Resources, Capabilities, and Management Processes, pages 71–91.

dynamics of industries and economies of information feedback loops and time delays in adjusting stocks of resources. Researchers in the systems dynamics field have extended the industrial dynamics framework to the analysis of organization processes and dynamics (e.g., Morecroft, 1988, 2001 in this volume; Warren, 2001 in this volume; Sterman, 2000). Herbert Simon (1981) also identified a number of basic properties shared by systems of all types, whether purely physical systems, natural systems, or human systems.

In the strategic management field, Beer (1994) and Ansoff (1988) have investigated designs of organizations as systems that can improve their responsiveness to changing competitive conditions. Dierickx and Cool (1989) further characterized organizations as systems composed of stocks of interrelated, strategically useful resources. They argued that organizations with current stocks of strategically useful resources may be able to sustain their resulting competitive advantages for some time, because competing organizations that try to change their stocks of resources quickly will be disadvantaged by time-compression diseconomies, the lack of asset mass efficiencies, inadequate asset interconnectedness, and causal ambiguity about the most appropriate ways to deploy and coordinate available resources. These effects result from the systemic interrelatedness of resources in an organization and impose higher costs and longer time requirements on competitors trying to duplicate a successful organization's current stocks of resources. In a closely related argument, Teece, Pisano, and Shuen (1997) proposed that an organization's capabilities are dynamic — i.e., they take time to develop — and therefore organizations that currently have certain capabilities may have competitive advantages during the time it takes competing organizations to develop comparable capabilities.

Strategists in the competence perspective have proposed a model of organizations as goal-seeking open systems composed of various tangible and intangible resources (Sanchez, Heene, & Thomas, 1996; Heene & Sanchez, 1997; Sanchez & Heene, 1997). This open-system view of organizations extends Dierickx and Cool's (1989) model of an organization as a collection of resource stocks and flows by explicitly recognizing that an organization's ability to strategically reconfigure its resources also depends on:

(i)   the *cognitive processes* through which managers try to determine what kinds of resource stocks and flows an organization should try to develop and what uses an organization's available resources may best be applied to;

(ii) managers' ability to *coordinate* both intraorganizational and interorganizational flows of resources and capabilities in processes of organizational change;

(iii) managers' ability to maintain processes of *organizational learning* that continuously renew an organization's base of knowledge as a critical strategic resource (Sanchez, 2001a).

By incorporating these three key aspects of organizational change, the competence-based open system model we explain below provides a conceptual framework for understanding some of the fundamental uncertainties managers face in managing strategic change and identifies the kinds of flexibilities managers must develop in their organizations to deal with those uncertainties.

The Open System Model of Organizations

Figure 1 presents our model of an organization as an open system. In this model, an organization's tangible and intangible resources are deployed and coordinated in a manner determined by the organization's *strategic logic,* which represents the organization's "operative rationale for achieving its goals" (Sanchez & Heene, 1996). An organization's strategic logic does not just represent the strategic thinking of top managers, but includes all the ideas that influence all decision makers who determine the composition of an organization's resource stocks and flows, the uses to which available resources will be applied, and the ways in which resources will be coordinated. Thus, an organization's strategic logic may include a spectrum of strategic ideas held by many organizational actors and generated through a variety of organizational processes.

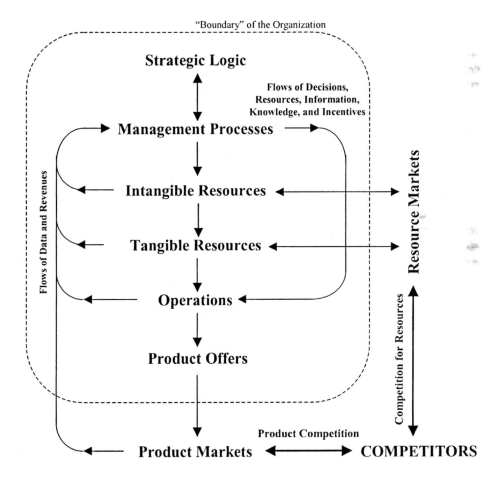

Figure 1: View of an Organization as an "Open System". (Adapted from Sanchez and Heene 1996).

Some organizations' strategic logics may be the result of "top-down" strategy making processes that are undertaken within a strong authority hierarchy and that lead to a detailed strategic plan for implementation through strict controls for allocating and monitoring resource flows. Other organizations' strategic logics, however, may both emerge from and be implemented through a "flat" organization design and an organizational culture of empowerment in which teams of employees have broad authority to make decisions about resource flows, uses, and methods of coordination. Many other processes for originating and implementing an organization's strategic logic are of course possible. In effect, the model in Figure 1 is intended to suggest that an organization's strategic logic is the aggregate set of ideas that motivates and guides the cognitive processes of *decision makers at all levels of an organization* in their acquisition, deployment, and coordination of an organization's resources. These ideas then find specific expression in the *management processes* an organization follows in interpreting its environment (i.e., its *sensemaking* activities) and in responding to environmental opportunities and threats through appropriate deployments of available resources.

Resource Flows.   As an open system, an organization must continuously replenish its stocks of both *tangible resources* (equipment, buildings, etc.) and *intangible resources* (including knowledge and capabilities necessary to use tangible resources effectively). An organization's *operations* are determined by the specific activities or organizational routines an organization can perform in using its resources (Nelson & Winter, 1982). The market's responses to the organization's *product offers* generate flows of revenues as well as data about its markets. Data about the organization's products, operations, and resource stocks also flow to decision makers within the organization's management processes. From an organization's management processes emanate the specific decisions, policies, procedures, budgets, and norms that direct the flows of the organization's financial and other resources to maintain or increase resource stocks in the organization's operations, tangible assets, intangible assets, or management processes.

Resource flows may also consist of firm-addressable resources, the use of which an organization can arrange through transactions in markets for resources or through strategic alliances of various types. In its processes for maintaining or increasing resource flows, organizations must compete against other organizations to obtain inputs of the best available resources. Competition to obtain both desirable resources as inputs and revenue flows from outputs creates important interactions and interdependencies that embed competing organizations in progressively larger open systems of market segments, product markets, and industries.

Perception of Strategic Gaps in Resource Stocks.   In the open-system model of organizations, strategic change consists of changes in the kinds of resources an organization uses, in the purposes to which an organization applies its resources, or in the processes an organization uses to coordinate its resources. Strategic changes are undertaken when decision-makers within an organization perceive that unacceptable *strategic gaps* exist between the organization's current stocks of resources, its processes for using resources, the purposes to which its resources are being applied in pursuit of the organization's goals, or the organization's overall goals, on the one hand, and the resource stocks, processes, purposes, and goals the organization's decision makers believe are desirable or necessary for the organization, on the other hand. Decision-makers' perceptions of the need to change an organization's resource stocks, processes, purposes, and goals are shaped by the *feedback* they receive about the current condition of the organization. In the competence framework, the term *control loops* is used to refer to the feedback flows through which decision makers gather and interpret flows of data about an organization's resource stocks, processes, purposes, and goals.

Data flowing to decision makers through control loops are subject to *increasing causal ambiguities* as the origin of the data flows moves from the bottom to the top of Figure 1. This means that it becomes progressively more difficult for managers to discover clear cause-and-effect relationships as they try to identify and interpret data originating from lower to higher levels in the open system model of Figure 1. For example, finding clear cause-and-effect relationships is more feasible in a organization's "operations" (e.g., the impact of alternative machine settings on yield rates) than at the level of an organization's strategic logic or management processes (e.g., the impact of a particular human resources policy on an organization's success or failure in a given product market).

Many forms of data typically have to be gathered and evaluated in an effort to assess the current effectiveness of an organization's intangible resources, management processes, or strategic logic, and the ambiguities in available data are unlikely to be definitively resolved no matter how much and how many kinds of data are gathered. Thus, the problem of increasing causal ambiguity means that initiating strategic change in an organization's "higher-order" stocks of intangible resources, management processes, and strategic logic cannot be made dependent on first obtaining "hard," quantitative, unequivocal evidence of a need for change. Rather, strategic change at this level must proceed on the basis of managers' judgmental perceptions of *implied* strategic gaps in an organization's higher-order resource stocks, processes, purposes, and goals.

Dynamic Response Times in Changing Resource Stocks. Processes of strategic change are also subject to increasing *dynamic response times* as an organization tries to change its resource stocks and processes at progressively higher levels in the open system model of Figure 1. In other words, an organization can change its mix of products more readily than it can change the way it operates, can change its operations more readily than its tangible assets, can change its tangible assets more readily than its intangible assets, and can change its intangible assets more readily than its management processes and strategic logic. In essence, the upward direction of increasing dynamic response times in Figure 1 means that it takes an organization longer to change the *ideas* it uses (i.e., its knowledge, concepts for coordinating resources, and goals) than the *things* it uses (i.e., its machines, buildings, etc.). The problem of managing changes in the essentially cognitive resources in an organization is accentuated when dynamic environments demand both fast and innovative changes in the ideas that motivate and direct an organization's strategies for value creation.

The Need for Strategic Flexibility. Researchers in the competence perspective (e.g., Sanchez & Heene, 1997) argue that the cognitive challenge of managing the increasing causal ambiguities and dynamic response times in organizations as open systems today cannot be overcome through a singular focus on trying to improve an organization's ability to predict future events. Rather, managers and theoreticians alike must recognize that today's complex competitive environments have substantial *irreducible uncertainties* that cannot be resolved adequately through heightened efforts to predict the future. In effect, the competence perspective argues that the most effective — and perhaps only feasible — approach to coping with irreducible uncertainties is creating *strategic flexibilities* in an organization to generate a range of timely responses to a range of potential future environmental conditions.

As we discuss further below, creating the strategic flexibility to generate the requisite variety of responses required from an organization as an open system requires developing both flexible resources and flexible capabilities to deploy and coordinate resources in alternative processes useful for a range of purposes (Sanchez, 1995, 1997). To respond flexibly to the changing opportunities and demands of dynamic environments, managers must help their organization develop several distinct "modes" of competence that will enable the organization to respond with appropriate levels and forms of flexibility as environmental conditions change (Sanchez, 2001b). We therefore summarize below five modes of competence (each of which represents an important form of flexibility), the contributions of each competence mode to the overall strategic flexibility of an organization, and some key dynamic interactions between competence modes that must be managed well. We also explain how developing the five competence modes needed to achieve strategic flexibility in turn requires management processes that use both "lower-order" and "higher-order" control loops effectively.

Building Strategic Flexibility from Flexible Resources and Coordination Capabilities

In the open system view, the strategic flexibility of an organization depends jointly on the *flexibilities of the resources* available to the organization and on the *coordination flexibilities* of managers in using the organization's available resources (Sanchez, 1995).

The flexibility of a resource can be represented in three dimensions. Resource flexibility increases as the range of alternative uses to which a resource can be applied increases, as the time required to switch a resource from one use to another decreases, and as the cost of switching from one use to another decreases. Thus, flexible resources are those that have more than one use and can be switched from one use to another quickly and inexpensively, while inflexible resources are those that cannot be switched to other uses or that may only be switched to alternative uses with significant cost, difficulty, and time.

Strategic management theory in the 1970s and 1980s typically emphasized the need to make significant commitments to specific-use resources in order to build future competitive advantage (e.g., Ghemawat, 1991). This prescription was essentially based on the two assumptions that specific-use resources (i.e., resources custom-designed to produce a specific product) enable lower unit costs of production than do flexible, general-purpose resources (Riordan & Williamson, 1985) and that low cost production of a specific product was the key to competitive success. In the increasingly dynamic product markets of the

1990s and beyond, however, this emphasis on *static economizing* in producing a given product has given way to recognition of the need for *dynamic economizing* in the form of efficiently generating a fast, flexible response to a changing array of market opportunities and threats (Sanchez, 2000).[2] The dynamic interdependencies of resources in an organization as a system mean that the inflexibility of the least flexible essential resource in an organization will act as a bottleneck that limits the overall flexibility of the organization to respond to change. Since the overall flexibility of a system cannot be greater than the flexibility of the least flexible essential resource to be used in the system, improving the flexibilities of *all* key resources is a prerequisite to building strategic flexibility in the organization as a system.

Of course, the overall flexibility of an organization as a system also depends on the cognitive flexibilities of its managers in changing the processes, purposes, and goals that motivate the organization's coordination and deployments of its resources in alternative uses. The concept of *coordination flexibility* represents the abilities of an organization's managers to coordinate new strategic uses for resources through reconfiguring and redeploying the resources available to the organization.

The building of strategic flexibility in an organization requires the development of resource flexibilities and coordination flexibilities that can be combined in various ways to achieve specific kinds of organizational flexibilities. We next consider how five forms of flexibility that are critical to achieving overall strategic flexibility in an organization are related to five forms or "modes" of competences that must be developed and maintained by a competent organization in a dynamic environment.

Five Modes of Organizational Competence

The open system model of organizations in Figure 1 can be used to identify five key forms or modes of organizational competence (Sanchez, 2001b), which are summarized in Table 1. The term *competence mode* refers to an important way in which the overall competence of an organization is expressed through specific kinds of activities and processes. Each competence mode depends on a specific kind of organizational *flexibility* to respond to changing or diverse environmental conditions, such as evolving market demands, technological change, and competitive developments in an industry. Each kind of flexibility can in turn be described by the specific kinds of *strategic options* that each flexibility brings to an organization (Sanchez, 1993, 1995).

Competence Modes I and II pertain to the ability of an organization's top managers to identify and embrace new strategic logics and new management processes. Competence Modes III, IV, and V relate to the abilities of middle managers, other employees, and other resources in an organization to actually enact new strategic logics and new management processes generated through Competence Modes I and II. The strategic changes that an organization can undertake are therefore determined jointly by the strategic boundaries top managers place on

---

[2]Moreover, technology advances in many resource markets have made available flexible resources with unit costs of production that now rival those of specialized, single-purpose equipment.

Table 1: The Five Competence Modes and the Strategic Options each Competence Mode Creates.

Competence mode	Strategic options created by competence mode
I. *Cognitive flexibility* of strategic managers to define alternative strategic logics	Portfolio of perceived market opportunities to create value
II. *Cognitive flexibility* of strategic managers to define alternative management processes	Portfolio of perceived ways of managing value creation processes
III. *Coordination flexibility* of managers to identify, configure, and deploy resource chains	Portfolio of resource chains managers can identify, configure, and deploy
IV. *Resource flexibilities* of resources to be used in alternative operations	Portfolio of alternative processes to which resource chains can be applied
V. *Operating flexibilities* of managers and other employees in applying skills and capabilities in alternative uses of available resources	Portfolio of feasible operations

the goals and purposes an organization may pursue (Competence Modes I and II) and the capabilities of the organization to adopt and sustain new resources and processes within the strategic boundaries set by top managers (Competence Modes III, IV, and V).

A summary of the "re-invention" of Chrysler Corporation in the late 1980s and early 1990s illustrates the five competence modes and the flexibilities derived from each mode.

Competence Mode I: Cognitive Flexibility to Imagine Alternative Strategic Logics

Competence Mode I derives from the *cognitive flexibility* of an organization to imagine alternative ways of creating value in markets. Competence Mode I therefore depends on an organization's ability to perceive market needs, to define products that can satisfy those needs, and to design supply chains and distribution channels for realizing new kinds of products. In the terminology of the competence perspective, Competence Mode I is the ability of an organization to define *alternative strategic logics* for using available resources in value-creation processes that help the organization achieve its goals (cf. Hamel's (2001) concept of "business system innovation").

Competence Mode I results largely from the cognitive flexibility of an organization's strategic managers, because they normally have the authority to launch or support important new strategic initiatives like creating new kinds of products. In this regard, strategic managers may lead their organization in launching new initiatives, or they may act as "bottlenecks" that limit strategic change by blocking new initiatives proposed by middle managers or others within an organization. The extent to which an organization's strategic managers are willing to bear the risks inherent in a change in strategic logic determines the extent to which Competence Mode I will be achieved in the organization.

The cognitive flexibility of an organization's strategic managers in Competence Mode I is expressed by the feasible strategic options managers believe the organization has to pursue new *market opportunities to create value.*

Competence Mode II: Cognitive Flexibility to Imagine Alternative Management Processes

Competence Mode II results from a second form of *cognitive flexibility* of managers — their ability to conceive of new management processes for implementing new strategic initiatives. This flexibility in turn derives from managers' abilities to identify and access the new kinds of resources needed to carry out a new strategic logic, to devise new organization designs (allocations of tasks, decision making, and information flows) for using new resources, and to define appropriate controls and incentives for monitoring and motivating new value-creating processes.

Like Competence Mode I, Competence Mode II depends primarily on an organization's strategic managers, who normally have ultimate responsibility for an organization's management processes, and who may be either willing to experiment with new forms of coordination or unwilling to depart from existing management structures and processes. Where an organization's managers lie on the continuum between openness to organizational innovation and reactionary organizational rigidity will determine the extent to which Competence Mode II is achieved in an organization.

An organization's Competence Mode II therefore results from its managers' flexibility to undergo strategic change in the organization's management processes and is expressed by the strategic options managers perceive are available to an organization to pursue alternative approaches to managing its value creation processes.

Competence Mode III: Coordination Flexibility to Configure and Deploy Resources

Competence Mode III pertains to the *coordination flexibility* of an organization to assemble alternative chains of resources that may be needed to carry out alternative strategic logics. Coordination flexibility generally depends on the ability of middle managers (or the top managers of smaller organizations) to identify, acquire or access, configure, and deploy alternative chains of appropriate tangible and intangible resources in effective ways. Appropriate resources may include both *firm-specific resources* that are internal to an organization and *firm-addressable resources* that an organization can access but that remain external to the firm (Sanchez & Heene, 1996). Effectively configuring a chain of resources requires devising appropriate designs for the specific ways the resources will interact in value-creating processes.[3] Deploying a resource chain requires focusing the

---

[3]The decomposition of product creation and realization processes into specific activities and the specification of the ways in which those activities interact defines a *process architecture.* See Sanchez & Mahoney (1996) and Sanchez (1999) for further discussion of the ways in which process architectures can affect an organization's coordination flexibility.

activities involved in using resources on clearly defined tasks in pursuit of a market opportunity.

The coordination flexibility of an organization creates a portfolio of strategic options to assemble the alternative resource chains required to create and realize a range of product offers, and those options increase in value as the time and cost an organization takes to assemble an effective new resource chain decreases.

Competence Mode IV: Flexibility of Resources to be Used in Alternative Operations

Competence Mode IV derives from the ability of the resources in an organization's resource chains to be used in alternative ways and is constrained by the intrinsic resource flexibility of the organization's available resources. The forms of resource flexibilities may include upgradeability to higher performance levels, scalability to increase capacity, and extendibility to add new functionalities, as well as the ability to switch a resource from one use to another. The intrinsic flexibilities of the resources an organization possesses or can access therefore determine its strategic options to use resources in alternative ways in value-creating processes.

Competence Mode V: Operating Flexibility in Applying Skills and Capabilities to Available Resources

Competence Mode V derives from the ability of an organization to use the flexibilities of its firm-specific and firm-addressable resources effectively and efficiently over a range of operating conditions. This *operating flexibility* essentially depends on the collective human skills and capabilities that an organization's front-line managers and employees can apply *at the working level* in using its available resources.

The operating flexibilities of an organization in using its available resources determine the reliability and efficiency with which a firm can sustain production and delivery of its products. In effect, Competence Mode V determines the *robustness* of a firm's operations over a range of operating conditions (cf. Leonard-Barton *et al.*, 1994). Thus, the operating flexibility of an organization determines its portfolio of operational strategic options — i.e., the operationally feasible ways an organization can bring its products to markets.

The Five Competence Modes in Action: The "Re-Invention" of Chrysler Corporation

An example may help to illustrate the nature of the five competence modes and the various flexibilities that result from them.

In the late 1980s Chrysler Corporation was on the verge of bankruptcy. Except for its minivans, Chrysler's automobile designs had fallen well behind the competition and could only be sold at deep discounts. As Chrysler's financial condition worsened, the company had to be rescued by a package of loans (guaranteed by the US government) that essentially gave Chrysler a grace period during which it had to fundamentally transform itself into a viable business. In one of the most dramatic turn-arounds in business history, Chrysler was able to re-invent itself and create a new set of competences at all levels of the organization.

Chrysler's new management team headed by Robert Eaton recognized that Chrysler's boxy and staid product designs no longer appealed to consumers. The management team launched several new product development initiatives that were intended to significantly reposition Chrysler in the American automobile market. These new product initiatives included an aggressively styled, limited production sports car called the Viper and the introduction of a sleek, revolutionary "cab-forward" vehicle design in its main line of LH platform family automobiles. Both vehicles received great public acclaim and established a new market position for Chrysler as the innovative design leader in the US market. The cognitive flexibility of Chrysler's management team to imagine a radically new set of market possibilities for Chrysler enabled a major increase in Competence Mode I of Chrysler as an organization.

Chrysler's management team also re-invented the way the company manages the development of new vehicles. Previously, development of new cars was subject to review by several layers of management, who often intervened to overrule new design approaches suggested by Chrysler's designers and development engineers. The heavily managed development process took five years or more and cost US$ 2–3 billion to develop a new vehicle, assuring that Chrysler's new product designs were out of date on introduction and likely to be unprofitable. Chrysler's new management team reorganized product development processes around a new "platform team" concept that gave broad decision making autonomy to product developers and allowed them to manage their own development processes within strategic guidelines for product market positioning outlined by Chrysler's management team. The new development management process at Chrysler reduced development time and costs by more than 50 percent and led to the development of innovative product designs with strong market acceptance. The flexibility of Chrysler's strategic managers to adopt a much more "empowered" approach to managing development processes gave Chrysler as an organization a new set of capabilities in Competence Mode II.

Chrysler's new management team also transformed Chrysler's relationships with its suppliers from an arm's-length, cost-focused, zero-sum game bargaining relationship to a more communicative, collaborative relationship with a mission to continuously improve quality and cost performance of components. Suppliers of key components were invited to join Chrysler's new platform teams and to share their ideas and expertise in creating Chrysler's new generations of vehicles. New contracts for sourcing components were also devised that established commitments to strict quality requirements and continuous cost reductions. Chrysler engineers began to work closely with suppliers to improve component designs and production processes, and as it recovered financially, Chrysler began to assist major suppliers in financing purchases of advanced production machinery. The flexibility of Chrysler's managers and engineers to conceive of and implement this new approach to coordinating supplier relationships significantly improved Competence Mode III within Chrysler.

Chrysler's new platform approach to developing new vehicles also enabled the carmaker to "leverage" a larger number of model variations from each development program. Production lines then had to be engineered to allow a greater mix of product variations to be assembled on Chrysler's vehicle assembly lines. The increased flexibility of Chrysler's new product designs and production systems represents an increase in Competence Mode IV.

By the early 1990s Chrysler Corporation also completed a materials and resources planning (MRP) system that created an elaborate "map" of the flow of all materials, parts, components, and subassemblies through every supplier's operations and through every transportation channel into each of Chrysler's auto assembly plants. Chrysler's production managers (assisted of course by computers) now use this MRP map to maintain an uninterrupted flow of materials, parts, components, and subassemblies into Chrysler's assembly plants. The MRP system can be used, for example, to reschedule or redirect shipments from alternate suppliers when a snow storm in the Midwest of the USA interrupts planned shipments from a given supplier. By having an accurate picture of the supply flexibilities that are "designed into" Chrysler's production system, production managers can make more effective and efficient use of those flexibilities in responding to a range of unexpected circumstances that otherwise could greatly impact its assembly operations. These capabilities have greatly improved Chrysler's operating flexibility in Competence Mode V, enabling it to achieve significant increases in plant utilization rates by avoiding interruptions in the flow of inputs to its assembly lines.

Systemic Interrelationships Among the Five Competence Modes

Achieving overall strategic flexibility in an organization requires developing a complementary balance among the five flexibilities in the organization's five competence modes. We now consider some key systemic interrelationships between the five competence modes that must be managed to achieve *coherence* among the dynamic complementarities between activities in the five competence modes (Christensen & Foss, 1997).

Since the ability of an organization to create value through its various processes depends on achieving adequate flexibility in each of the five complementary competence modes, each competence mode can act as a potential bottleneck that limits the overall competence and strategic flexibility of the organization. If an organization behaves like an adaptive system, in the long run the flexibility of any competence mode that is not put to full use is likely to diminish to a level that is simply adequate to function with the least flexible competence mode of the organization. In effect, we can expect the competence modes of the organization to equilibrate to the level of the least flexible competence mode, which acts as a *capability bottleneck* that limits the organization's overall competence leveraging processes.[4] Managers of organizations as competence leveraging systems must therefore understand which competence modes are or could become capability bottlenecks and take steps to develop and maintain an adequate level of complementary flexibility in each of the five competence modes.

As one moves upwards in Figure 1 from activities resulting from Competence Mode V to activities that lead to Competence Mode I, it generally takes longer for an organization

---

[4]For a discussion of how well defined product and process architectures can be used to discover an organization's capability bottlenecks, see Sanchez & Collins (2001).

to increase the flexibilities of its higher-level competence modes. Because each competence mode will tend to equilibrate with the least flexible competence mode of the organization, making long-term changes in lower-level competence modes will generally require making complementary changes in higher-level competence modes. Because higher-level competence modes take longer to change, however, the rate of change in an organization's lower-level competence modes will be constrained by the maximum rate of change in its higher-level competence modes. Thus, Sanchez and Heene (1996) have argued that to avoid becoming bottlenecks in the strategic change processes of an organization, strategic managers must meet "the never-ending challenge of continuously learning how to better manage their own cognitions," which is the source of the cognitive flexibilities that underlie Competence Modes I and II. The need for managers to find ways to manage their own cognitive processes is especially important — and challenging — in dynamic environments because of the high levels of causal ambiguity encountered at the levels of Competence Mode I and II.

Managing Through Control Loops: A Systems View of Strategic "Stretch"

Managers, through their collective impact on the five competence modes of an organization, can greatly influence the capabilities and behavior of an organization as an open system. In their sensemaking processes for identifying strategic gaps in an organization's five competence modes, managers generally rely heavily on the feedback flows of data and information established within the organization — which we refer to as the organization's *control loops*. Through an organization's control loops, managers try to monitor various aspects of its internal conditions and external environment, to identify the changing array of resources needed by and available to the organization, to direct and monitor the organization's processes for acquiring and using resources, to assess the success of the organization's value-creation processes, to "fine-tune" or radically transform the organization's value-creation processes, and thereby to adapt the organization to a changing environment.

From this perspective, an organization undertakes *strategic change* when its managers detect strategic gaps, and seek significant changes in the organization's current competence modes by pursuing qualitative changes in its stocks and flows of resources, capabilities, processes, or goals. Important differences in the strategic responses of organizations to a changing environment may therefore result from differences in the kinds of strategic gaps their managers perceive. We next consider how two kinds of control loops affect the sensemaking processes of managers and thus the actions they take to adapt their organizations to a changing environment (Sanchez & Heene, 1996).

Use of Lower-Order Control Loops to Drive Strategic Change

Lower-order control loops gather data on an organization's current product offers in its product markets, its operations and its tangible assets, as suggested in Figure 2(a).

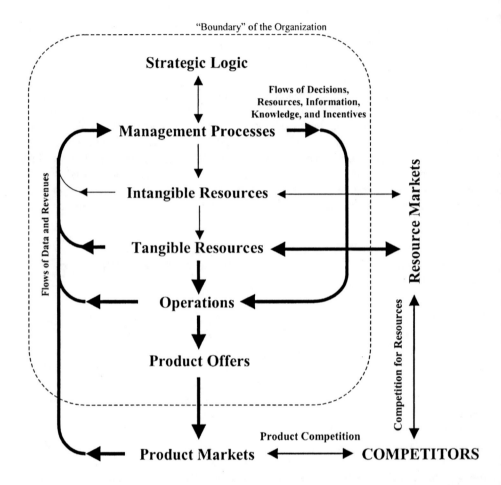

Figure 2(a): Lower-order Control Loops in an Organization as an "Open System".
(Adapted from Sanchez and Heene, 1996).

Lower-order control loops generally gather "hard" quantified data about current sales levels, market share, productivity, capacity utilization, inventory levels, and similar economic measures. Such data are essential inputs for managers assessing the adequacy of an organization's Competence Modes IV and V to carry out effectively the organization's existing processes within the current usual range of change and variation in its environment.

It has often been noted, however, that we tend to "manage what we measure." As a result, many managers may tend to focus on measuring and managing lower-level competence modes, whose resources, capabilities, and processes are easier to define, measure, and interrelate causally. The tendency to focus on issues that can be managed through lower-order control loops, however, may create cognitive "blind spots" (van der Vorst, 1997) about the current state of an organization's higher-level competence modes. The tendency to develop cognitive blind spots about higher-level competence modes may become acute when an organization's value-creation processes are currently successful and control loops bringing managers current operating data begin to act like positive or reinforcing feedback loops. Current market acceptance of an organization's products may lead to data on profitability, revenues, and market share that managers interpret positively, increasing their confidence in the adequacy of all the organization's current competence modes. Believing that the processes that have brought current success will also bring future success, confident managers may expand current operations quantitatively. If expanding operations leads to more sales and profits, managers may become even more strongly persuaded that the organization's current competences are adequate for meeting the future.

While the currently successful organization's managers are focused on carrying out and expanding current value-creation processes, the market environment may undergo a shift in consumer preferences, or competitors may undertake strategic change in higher-level competence modes that lead to introductions of more competitive products. Detection of such strategic shifts in the environment through lower-order control loops may be subject to considerable time delays before a long-term deterioration in an organization's market share and profitability becomes evident. Managers' first response to such data, moreover, is likely to be scrutiny of the processes that are directly monitored by the lower-order control loops (e.g., production, distribution, and sales) that are generating signs of deteriorating current performance. It may take considerable time for managers to suspect that the deterioration in current performance can only be reversed by development of new kinds of product offers, which may require new value-creation capabilities that can only be accomplished through changes in higher-level competence modes. Given the longer times required to change higher-order competence modes, however, managers who have been focused on managing changes in lower-order competence modes may not be able to identify and make needed changes in the organization's higher-order competence modes before the organization's condition has deteriorated beyond a point of no return.

Use of Higher-Order Control Loops to Drive Strategic Change

The inherent cognitive limitations of lower-order control loops as drivers of strategic change suggest that establishing control loops to monitor the adequacy of an organization's higher-level competence modes is essential for managing strategic change in a dynamic environment. This effort will rely on patterns of data gathering through higher-order control loops, as suggested in Figure 2(b).

To assess the adequacy of an organization's higher-level competence modes, however, managers must usually gather "soft" qualitative data whose interpretations are likely to be highly causally ambiguous. Thus, for managers the task of driving strategic change through higher-order control loops will necessarily be a cognitive exercise in "strategy as stretch" (Prahalad & Hamel, 1993). Leading an organization to stretch beyond its current higher-order competence modes requires a *stretch of managerial imagination* to identify potential strategic gaps in an organization's higher-order competence modes that may only be *implied* by the flows of "soft," causally ambiguous data through higher-order control

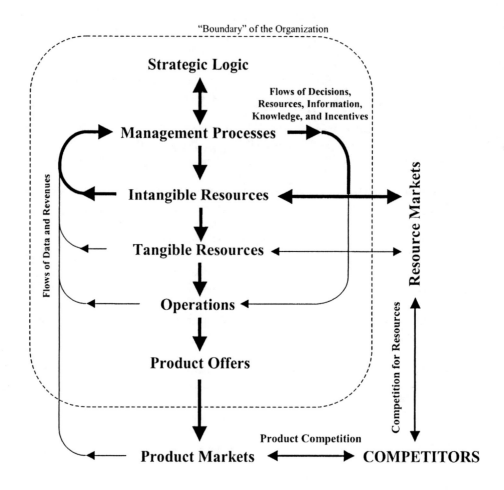

Figure 2(b): Higher-order Control Loops in an Organization as an "Open System".
(Adapted from Sanchez and Heene, 1996).

loops. Managers must also develop a collective corporate imagination that enables them to envision alternative strategic logics, management processes, and intangible resources unlike those currently constituting the organization's Competence Modes I, II, and III.

Like lower-order control loops, however, higher-order control loops can also behave like positive or reinforcing feedback loops. Current competitive success may increase managers' confidence in the adequacy of their organization's higher-level competence modes, and encourage them to focus on using lower-order control loops to fine-tune the organization's lower-level competence modes. Thus, even when current operating data indicate current profitability and a strong market position, strategic managers must initiate processes that continually question the adequacy of the organization's current Competence Modes I, II, and III to manage the uncertainty and change in its environment. Three approaches to challenging the adequacy of higher-level competence modes are summarized below.[5]

Benchmarking and Benchtrending. Benchmarking is a process for systematically comparing an organization's current strategic logic, management processes, intangible resources, tangible resources, operations, and/or products against their counterparts in organizations considered to be world-leading in their product markets (Karlof & Ostblom, 1993; Watson, 1993). To effectively challenge an organization's higher-level competence modes, however, benchmarking must look beyond comparisons of a firm's current operating data gathered through lower-order control loops. Benchmarking should include comparisons of processes for developing new technologies, creating new product and process designs, designing and changing organization structures, devising incentive plans, challenging and revising strategic logics, and identifying new sources of data that may be relevant to changing higher-level competence modes. To be most effective, comparisons should be dynamic and oriented towards the identification and understanding of trends and change trajectories being undertaken by world-leading organizations. Future-oriented process comparisons — often referred to as *benchtrending* — are critical in assessing Competence Modes I, II, and III, which must provide adequate flexibility to respond to a range of strategic contingencies in the future.

The ability to perceive implied strategic gaps in higher-level competence modes may be improved by benchtrending organizations that are best-in-world organizations in any industry for a given process or capability. When an automaker like Chrysler benchtrends a world-leading service company like Federal Express, for example, managers may acquire a new understanding of ways to define, create, and deliver highly appreciated services. This new understanding may then suggest new ways of providing new or improved service to customers in the automobile business. In some organizations, ongoing benchtrending has become an integral part of continuous learning processes that regularly and systematically challenge and improve higher-level competence modes.

Environmental Scanning. When cooperative benchtrending is not possible to arrange with world-leading firms within or outside an organization's industry, the assessment of higher-level competence modes may still benefit from environmental scanning for potentially significant changes in other organizations' technological, organizational, and marketing capabilities. Managers may scan for both technologies in current use and for apparent directions and rates in the evolutions of currently or potentially important technologies. Similar assessments may also be made for organizational innovations in use or being adopted by other organizations. New ways of discovering and serving emerging market preferences may also be monitored and assessed for their applicability to an organization's own value-creation processes.

---

[5]It is also possible that the causal ambiguity inherent in data gathered through higher-order control loops may prevent identification of better strategic logics and lead managers to make escalating commitments to failing strategic logics (Staw, 1981).

Managerial perceptions of emerging technological, organizational, and marketing possibilities could stimulate managers to ask how those possibilities might improve an organization's higher-level competence modes under a variety of future scenarios. When managers perceive implied gaps between an organization's current competence modes and the competences it will need or might advantageously use in the future, managers may begin to build new competences now that would significantly shorten the dynamic response times of its higher-level competence modes in responding to new competitive conditions in the future. Also, by beginning early to build new competences, managers may be able to resolve some of the causal ambiguities surrounding new technologies, new organizational forms, and new marketing approaches before competitors develop insights in these areas.

Challenging Cognitive Frameworks.   The thought processes of managers are limited by the bounded rationality that constrains the gathering and interpretation of data by all decision makers (Simon, 1954). Accepting the inevitability of bounded rationality may help managers to avoid falling into defensive routines (Argyris, 1986) that limit communication with others who might suggest new analytic frameworks and theories of value creation that could challenge managers' current interpretive frameworks for sensemaking. Managers may try to overcome the limits of their own bounded rationality by *hiring consultants* or other advisers or by *working with management researchers* investigating new models for competing in their industry or in other industries. Managers may also seek to *hire new executives* from other firms or other industries to bring new perspectives or new industry recipes (Spender, 1989) that would provide new perspectives for assessing and improving an organization's higher-level competence modes. In a growing number of cases in the USA, in particular, boards of directors are becoming active agents of strategic change by recruiting new managers with new cognitive frameworks when current managers are unable to let go of cognitive frameworks that are no longer capable of creating value.

Managers may also try to create a pool of different cognitive frameworks within an organization by seeking *diversity in its mix of managers*. Managers may also seek to build an organizational *culture of confrontation* with processes that promote "no-holds-barred" questioning of the basic assumptions underlying a current strategic logic. Managers may also seek to stimulate "*dissidence*" and constructive debate through the application of techniques such *Devil's advocate or dialectic inquiry* (Vennix, 1996).

Managers may also use *system dynamics models* to create microworlds that can serve as learning environments for testing managerial assumptions and designing higher-order control loops for assessing and managing higher-level competence modes (Senge, 1990). An organization may also choose to force continual redefinition of an organization's strategic logic and management processes through periodic "*zero-based strategy-making*" in which the appropriateness of current strategies, processes, and resources must be argued and affirmed in order to receive further resource allocations.

Conclusions

In organizations facing significant environmental change and uncertainties, a critical task of strategic managers is guiding the *strategic change processes* of their organization. We have used an open system model of an organization to describe this key managerial activity as an essentially cognitive process of perceiving possibilities for the creation of new strategic logics, new management processes, and new kinds of tangible and intangible resources for effective value-creation activities. We have also used the open system model to further characterize the task of managing strategic change as one of managing competence building in five distinct competence modes and managing key dynamic interrelationships between competence modes.

In managing the five competence modes, managers must use feedback loops or control loops that are appropriate for identifying and remedying strategic gaps in each competence mode. Important differences in the patterns of gap-closing actions undertaken by different organizations result from differences in the ways their managers detect strategic gaps in organizational competences. Relying on lower-order *versus* higher-order control loops in managing strategic change, for example, typically leads managers to focus on improving lower-level competence modes concerned with current products, operations, and tangible assets, as suggested in Figure 2(a). Use of lower-order control loops to drive strategic change may therefore deepen an organization's current capabilities and sustain incremental learning in lower-level competence modes, and may be the basis for competitive success in stable environments that reward progressive reductions in costs and steadily improving efficiency. Exclusive or excessive reliance on lower-order control loops, however, may transform an organization's current "core capabilities" into "core rigidities" (Leonard-Barton, 1992) if managers lose their ability to identify opportunities to improve or change higher-level competence modes that can generate new concepts and processes for value creation.

Managers that actively gather and interpret data through higher-order control loops ought to be more capable of identifying strategic gaps and pursuing gap-closing actions in an organization's strategic logic, management processes, and intangible assets — the objects of an organization's higher-level competence modes, and the primary locus of strategic change. Thus, *strategic learning* by managers who develop and use higher-order control loops to identify and pursue changes in an organization's higher-level competence modes plays a central role in the "perception-forming, direction-setting, decision-making, process-coordinating, and change-inducing activities of decision makers that result in a organization's distinctive patterns of competence building and leveraging over time" (Sanchez & Heene, 1996).

References

Ansoff, H. I. (1988). *The New Corporate Strategy.* Chichester: John Wiley & Sons.
Argyris, C. (1986). Reinforcing organizational defensive routines: An unintended human resources activity. *Human Resource Management, 25(4)*, 541–556.
Ashby, W. R. (1956). *An Introduction to Cybernetics.* London: Chapman and Hall.
Beer, S. (1994). *Diagnosing the System for Organizations.* Chichester: John Wiley & Sons.
Christensen, J. F., & Foss, N. J. (1997). Dynamic corporate coherence and competence-based competition: Theoretical foundations and strategic implications. In A. Heene & R. Sanchez (eds), *Competence-Based Strategic Management.* Chichester: John Wiley & Sons.

Dierickx, I., & Cool, K. (1989). Asset stock accumulation and sustainability of competitive advantage. *Management Science, 35*, 1504–1511.

Forrester, J. W. (1961). *Industrial Dynamics*. Cambridge, MA: MIT Press.

Forrester, J. W. (1968). *Principles of Systems*. Cambridge, MA: MIT Press.

Hamel, G. (2001). *Leading the Revolution*. Cambridge, MA: Harvard Business School Press.

Heene, A., & Sanchez, Ron (eds) (1997). *Competence-Based Strategic Management*. Chichester: John Wiley & Sons.

Ghemawat, P. (1991). *Commitment: The Dynamic of Strategy*. New York: Free Press.

Karlof, B., & Ostblom, S. (1993). *Benchmarking. A Signpost to Excellence in Quality and Productivity*. Chichester: John Wiley & Sons.

Leonard-Barton, D. (1992). Core capabilities and core rigidities: A paradox in managing new product development. *Strategic Management Journal 13* (summer), 111–125.

Leonard-Barton, D., Bowen, H. K., Clark, K. B., Holloway, C. A., & Wheelwright, S. C. (1994). How to integrate work and deepen expertise. *Harvard Business Review,* September–October.

Lippman, S. A., & Rumelt, R. P. (1982). Uncertain imitability: An analysis of interorganization differences in efficiency under competition. *Bell Journal of Economics, 13*, 418–438.

Morecroft, J. D. (1988). System dynamics and microworlds for policymakers. *European Journal of Operational Research, 35(3)*, 301–321.

Morecroft, J. D. (2001). Resource management under dynamic complexity. In R. Sanchez (ed.), *A Systems Perspective on Resources, Capabilities, and Management Processes*. Oxford: Elsevier.

Nelson, R. R., & Winter, S. G. (1982). *An Evolutionary Theory of Economic Change*. Cambridge, MA: Harvard University Press.

Prahalad, C. K., & Hamel, G. (1993). Strategy as stretch and leverage. *Harvard Business Review, 71(2)*, 75–85.

Riordan, M. H., & Williamson, O. E. (1985). Asset specificity and economic organization. *International Journal of Industrial Organization, 3(4)*, 365–379.

Sanchez, R. (1993). Strategic flexibility, firm organization, and managerial work in dynamic markets: A strategic options perspective. *Advances in Strategic Management, 9*, 251–291.

Sanchez, R. (1995). Strategic flexibility in product competition. *Strategic Management Journal 16* (summer special issue), 135–159.

Sanchez, R. (1997). Preparing for a uncertain future: Managing organizations for strategic flexibility. In *Preparing for the Future: Special Issue of the International Studies in Management and Organization, 27(2)*, 71–94.

Sanchez, R. (1999). Modular architectures in the marketing process. *Journal of Marketing 63* (special issue), 92–111.

Sanchez, R. (2000). Demand uncertainty and asset flexibility: Incorporating strategic options in the theory of the firm. In N. Foss & V. Mahnke (eds) *Competence, Governance, and Entrepreneurship*. Oxford: Oxford University Press.

Sanchez, R. (ed.) (2001a). *Knowledge Management and Organizational Competence*. Oxford: Oxford University Press.

Sanchez, R. (2001b). Understanding competence-based management: Identifying and managing five modes of competence. *Journal of Business Research* (forthcoming).

Sanchez, R., & Heene, A. (1996). A systems view of the firm in competence-based competition. In R. Sanchez, A. Heene, & H. Thomas (eds), *Dynamics of Competence-Based Competition*. Oxford: Elsevier.

Sanchez, R., & Heene, A. (1997). Competence-based strategic management: Concepts and issues for theory, research, and practice, 3–42. In A. Heene & R. Sanchez (eds), *Competence-Based Strategic Management*. Chichester: John Wiley & Sons.

Sanchez, R., Heene, A., & Thomas, H. (eds) (1996). *Dynamics of Competence-Based Competition.* Oxford: Elsevier.

Sanchez, R., & Mahoney, J. T. (1996). Modularity, flexibility, and knowledge management in product and organization design. *Strategic Management Journal, 17* (winter special issue), 63–76.

Sanchez, R., & Thomas, H. (1996). Strategic goals. In R. Sanchez, A. Heene, & H. Thomas (eds), *Dynamics of Competence-Based Competition.* Oxford: Elsevier.

Senge, P. M. (1990). *The Fifth Discipline.* New York: Doubleday.

Simon, H. (1981). *The Sciences of the Artificial.* Cambridge, MA: MIT Press.

Spender, J. C. (1989). *Industry Recipes: An Inquiry into the Nature and Sources of Managerial Judgement.* New York: Basil Blackwell.

Sterman, J. D. (2000). *Business Dynamics: Systems Thinking and Modeling for a Complex World.* Boston, MA: Irwin McGraw-Hill.

Teece, D., Pisano, G., & Shuen, A. (1990). *Firm Capabilities, Resources, and the Concept of Strategy*, CCC Working paper No. 90–8, University of California at Berkeley.

Teece, D., Pisano, G., & Shuen, A. (1997). Dynamic capabilities and strategic management. *Strategic Management Journal, 18(7),* 509–533.

Van der Vorst, R. (1997). The blind spots of competence identification: A system-theoretic perspective. In A. Heene & R. Sanchez (eds), *Competence-Based Strategic Management.* Chichester: John Wiley & Sons.

Vennix, J. A. M. (1996). *Group Model Building: Facilitating Team Learning Using System Dynamics.* Chichester: John Wiley & Sons.

Warren, K. (2001). Operationalizing the impact of competence-building on the performance of firms' resource systems. In R. Sanchez (ed.), *A Systems Perspective on Resources, Capabilities, and Management Processes.* Oxford: Elsevier.

Watson, G. H. (1993). *Strategic Benchmarking: How to Rate Your Company's Performance Against the World's Best.* Chichester: John Wiley & Sons.

Chapter 6

A Competence View of Firms as Resource Accumulation Systems: A Synthesis of Resource-Based and Evolutionary Models of Strategy-Making

Edoardo Mollona

Introduction

This paper tries to reconcile the dichotomy between content- and process-oriented studies in strategy.[1] It presents a model which integrates resource building decisions and an intra-organizational ecological process model of corporate strategy-making. The model describes critical feedback loops between resource accumulation processes and human and capital allocations. The model shows how firms can be investigated as complex dynamic systems, and how competences emerge as properties of the structure of feedback loops in complex self-organizing systems.

   The first section develops the conceptualization of firms as resource accumulation systems. The second section briefly illustrates some evolutionary theorizing on strategy-making. The third section merges the two approaches and develops a feedback model of corporate strategy-making and resource position evolution. A concluding section summarizes the findings of the model and suggests some implications of this model-based investigation for future research in strategy.

Resource-Based View of the Firm

Firms as Complex Systems of Resources and Capabilities

In strategic management a large body of literature, referred to as the resource-based view of the firm (RBV hereafter), focuses on the idiosyncratic characteristics of firms, stressing the role played by peculiar bundles of resources (Penrose, 1959; Barney, 1986, 1991),

[1] See, for example, Sanchez and Heene (1997a).

Systems Perspectives on Resources, Capabilities, and Management Processes, pages 93–125.
Copyright © 2002 by Elsevier Science Ltd.
All rights of reproduction in any form reserved.
ISBN: 0-08-043778-8

competences (Prahalad & Hamel, 1990), capabilities (Nelson & Winter, 1982; Amit & Schoemaker, 1993) and dynamic capabilities and competences (Teece *et al.*, 1990; Lei *et al.*, 1996; Helfat, 1997). Building on these concepts, firms can be represented as very complex social systems (Sanchez & Heene, 1996; Sanchez *et al.*, 1996), and competence building and adaptation may be analysed as self-organizing processes of such systems. Thus far, only a few scholars have focused on the system characteristics of such bundles of resources and the ways in which firms' differing behaviors and performance results from differences in the structure and resulting interactions of interconnected resources.

Dierickx and Cool (1989), in an innovative contribution, developed an interesting view of firms as complex and dynamic systems of resource accumulation whose behaviors are only partially directed and intended by decision-makers. Extending this view, Sanchez and Heene (1996) and Sanchez, Heene and Thomas (1996) developed a theoretical model of the firm as a system of resources linked by inter-chained, gap-closing feedback loops.

Throughout the strategic management literature, the very concept of capability has a systemic flavour. Amit and Schoemaker suggest, for example, that capabilities are grounded in organizational processes that are *developed over time through complex inter-actions among a firm's resources* (1993). In this sense, capabilities appear, using a chemical metaphor, as *compounded assets* (Schendel, 1994).

At a higher level of abstraction, firms are characterized as *architecture(s) of organizational competences* (Rumelt, 1995) or *hierarchies* of organizational capabilities (Nelson & Winter, 1982). In this hierarchical mode of analysis, a firm's "competences" can be seen as the "… ability to sustain the coordinated deployment of assets and capabilities in ways that promise to help a firm to achieve some desired results (goal) through specific actions." (Sanchez *et al.*, 1996). The existence of a capability in marketing, for example, relies on a prior "higher-order" capability in hiring, training, and coordinating marketing people. The long-term success of the firm, moreover, depends on the higher-order "strategic logic" for deciding what capability in marketing ought to be developed and what goals it should be applied to.[2] Therefore, a firm's competence is realized through its ability to integrate and connect together resources and capabilities.

The relationships among these different hierarchies of capabilities are complex. Not only do higher-order capabilities drive the creation of lower-level capabilities, but these latter influence and direct the evolution of the former. Strategic decision-making, if taken as an ex-post rationalization capability (Weick, 1979), is not an independent and illuminated act of creativity of a decision-maker, but rather an activity that is likely to be strongly influenced by accumulated resources to which management is committed (Ghemawat, 1991) and by lower-level decision-making routines (Noda, 1994; Noda & Bower, 1996; Burgelman, 1983a) — in other words, by the *structure* of the organization (Burgelman, 1983c).

In this light, firms are seen as complex systems in which different hierarchies of capabilities affect and depend on each other, so that different layers of management interpretations and decisions are inter-chained throughout the firm. An analytical perspective emerges from this view which, rather than focusing on how valuable resources generate advantageous competitive positions, emphasises how the heterogeneity of a firm is shaped by the holistic properties

---

[2]See Sanchez' levels of knowledge in Sanchez (1997b).

of its *system* of inter-linked resources and organizational processes. This perspective studies the whole system of a firm's resources,[3] rather than searching for a particular valuable resource or unique capability. A major interest in this approach is understanding how resource accumulation systems evolve, and to what extent this evolution is intendedly directed *versus* spontaneously emergent. In this respect, a number of authors (Montgomery, 1994) have pointed to the promise of a cross-fertilization between resource-based and capability-based views of the firm and evolutionary theories. Such a marriage would certainly go a long way towards explaining how systems of capabilities evolve, and why some systems of resources create *core competences*, while others lead to *core rigidities* (Leonard-Barton, 1993).

Decision-Maker Rationality and Shumpeterian Dynamics

Some scholars (Goshal & Moran, 1996) claim that under the RBV approach, competitive advantage is associated with the concept of *appropriation* and competition is reduced to a race for first-mover advantages in acquiring or building up resources. Such a theoretical framework would overlook, however, subsequent creative efforts of management to improve competitive positions. This "one period model" of competition derives from the fact that the "strong form",[4] content-oriented RBV emphasises Ricardian rents (obtained from control of scarce resources) rather than Schumpeterian rents (obtained from new combinations of resources applied to new opportunities). The RBV's lack of interest in Schumpeterian rents may be due to its strong inheritance from economics (Levinthal, 1995) directed at identifying only long-lived and durable rents in an equilibrium analysis.

Schumpeterian rents result from differences in competitive positions that are inherently dynamic. In a Schumpeterian framework, firms gain competitive advantages by finding new, more profitable, combinations of productive factors. Advantageous positions last until competitors begin to imitate the new combinations of productive factors. However, firms which introduce innovations can use their competitive advantage to conceive of further new combinations of inputs that might again place them ahead of the competition. On the other hand, competing firms might introduce a different, more advantageous combination of productive factors that destroy the competitive positions of incumbent firms. The Schumpeterian world situation is not one in which a favorable competitive position can be protected from imitation, but rather is one where competitive positions evolve dynamically.

The RBV's bias in focusing on Ricardian rents explains its implicit assumption that idiosyncratic resource positions can generate advantageous competitive positions that can persist in equilibrium (Peteraf, 1993). Thus, the RBV's major focus is on why firms differ in equilibrium, rather than on how they evolve differently to achieve those positions. At

---

[3]See Sanchez, Heene & Thomas (1996), and Heene & Sanchez (1997).
[4]By "strong form" I refer to that thread of RBV literature (Wernerfelt, 1984; Barney, 1986; Lippman & Rumelt, 1982) which inherited both a marked content-orientation and strong rationality assumptions on decision-making. For these reasons this line of contributions has been defined as the *High Church* in RBV (Levinthal, 1995) or the *formal* thread in RBV (Foss, 1995).

the heart of the RBV research agenda, therefore, are questions concerning the conditions for competitive advantage to be sustained, rather than the process by which the competitive positions may be created (Conner, 1991).[5] According to the RBV view, competitive advantage is obtained in discrete steps and is maintained as long as *ex-post* conditions hold.

In the RBV framework, managers that are lucky or far-sighted (or both) are able either to acquire valuable and scarce resources in the presence of imperfect factor markets and asymmetric information, or to enjoy valuable know-how stored within organizational capabilities. *Causal ambiguity* and *uncertain imitability* (Dierickx & Cool, 1989; Lippman & Rumelt, 1982) of organizational mechanisms for identifying and using resources prevent competitors from understanding and replicating a successful firm's capabilities. Successful organizations, in deploying their resources, are better at connecting actions to their consequences in order to achieve their objectives. However, the RBV does not tell us why unsuccessful firms failed in building similar capabilities, other than by assuming a difference in foresight and luck among decision makers. The possibility that unexpected and counterintuitive consequences may follow from intendedly rational actions is not recognized, nor are the boundedly rational decision-making processes of managers recognized in dealing with the issues that arise in firms as complex social systems.

In the RBV world, once they achieve a favorable competitive position, firms are portrayed being able to exploit such positions without error, i.e. *without leaving profits on the table* (Levinthal, 1995). However, if decision makers do not make errors in administrating their advantages, from where do differences and competitive advantage arise? If we are willing to relax the RBV's strong actor rationality assumptions, we can immediately see that one source of difference between firms is that even the best available routine might not be able to fully account for the complexity of a situation at hand, thereby allowing for errors by managers in connecting actions to their dynamic consequences. As Dierickx and Cool stressed (1989), integrating and accumulating resources is not an easy task, and the complexity of resource accumulation processes in organizations generates sufficient causal ambiguity to cognitively de-couple actions and decisions from their consequences to at least some extent.

In this vein, Lippman and Rumelt (1982) proposed that stable inter-firm differences in profitability may depend on the result of a draw from a probabilistic distribution. Lippman and Rumelt's model is a dynamic view of competitive positions evolution. However, in their model, decision makers may use sub-optimal routines, and they do not learn; rather,

---

[5] Some dynamic analyses, however, have been conducted in the RBV. In Rubin's (1972) exploration of the trade-off between using resources to generate products/services or to train new resources, he developed a programming model of the firm aimed at defining an optimal rate and direction of growth. Wernerfelt proposed a *resource-product matrix* (1984), a conceptual tool allowing the consideration of different growth paths when choosing between exploitation of existing resources and development of new ones. Some years later he suggested (1989) a methodology to analyse and define resources and leverage them when deciding in which market segment to compete. However, I argue that the significance of these efforts lies in their normative definition of a sequence of inter-temporal optimal decisions to be taken by completely rational decision makers, rather than in their capability to explore and describe effective resource accumulation processes of boundedly rational decision makers.

the consequences of their actions differ because of different luck in their original draw from the set of possible routines.[6]

On the other hand, Levinthal (1995) proposes that an evolutionary perspective may contribute to a richer repertoire of assumptions. In an evolutionary framework, actors are boundedly rational; they do not know which is the best routine. However, decision makers learn by searching for new, more efficient routines, thereby updating the content of their actions. In pursuing their search, decision makers are *procedurally* rational (Simon, 1955, 1964) — that is, they use heuristics to decrease the average number of searches (Nelson & Winter, 1982).

For example, a leading firm may be using a manufacturing routine to produce a certain product. Suppose that such a routine is the best among those used by competitors (in terms, for example, of the achieved quality-cost ratio); however, this manufacturing routine does not necessarily have to be the best achievable. In this case, another firm may take the lead by choosing an alternative routine that results in a better quality-cost ratio. Therefore, firms enjoying superior competitive positions may lose their lead at any moment, and competitive dynamics replace the RBV's notion of sustainable competitive advantage in a stable equilibrium. In an evolutionary framework, competitors are locally rational and may have different sets of choices because of their different histories (Nelson, 1995), so that at any time, firms are able to generate variations with the potential to revolutionize the competitive rules of the industry.

Modelling Firms as Resource Accumulation Systems

Resource-Stocks as System Rate Variables. Generally, in neo-classical economic termi-nology, *resources* refer to the productive factors of a firm, or inputs into the production function (Mansfield, 1975). Moreover, these productive factors are *items of property* of a firm (Winter, 1987). This definition of resources makes it awkward to consider assets like knowledge or competences as resources (Winter, 1987). Indeed, neo-classical economics generally considers competences as available without costs to all firms within a certain industry (Carlsson & Eliasson, 1994). Mansfield (1975), for example, states that techno-logical competences represent the patrimony of knowledge that a society has achieved. In the neo-classical framework, generally available know-how is assumed to shape the production function of all the firms within an industry. However, understanding the inner functioning of a firm requires recognition that firm-specific knowledge may be an impor-tant part of idiosyncratic capabilities.

In the RBV view of the firm, the term *resource* has a very broad meaning, comprising both assets (tangible and intangible) and capabilities (Hall, 1992, 1993). In this paper, however, I use the concept of resource-stock with a more restricted meaning, indicating

---

[6]Lippman and Rumelt clarify: *"One might, of course, choose to view uncertain imitability as the outcome of bounded rationality, but we prefer to distinguish between bounds on the quality of decisions and bounds on the quality of the best theory on which decisions may be based."*

the assets which are *tied semipermanently to the firm* (Wernerfelt, 1984) and therefore represent the *state* variables of the firm.

Resource-stocks in this analysis include only the assets that a firm can deploy, and in this respect are distinguished from other concepts such as *competences* or *capabilities.*[7] Capabilities and competences are broader concepts, including not only assets that a firm can deploy, but also what the firm is able to do with such assets. Consequently, competence and capability are terms that include both *state* and *control* variables (Winter, 1987) — in other words, both a firm's *Having* and its *Doing* (Hall, 1992, 1993).

Resource-stocks cannot be instantaneously modified. Rather, resource stocks must be accumulated over time. Thus, at each point in time current resource-stocks define the resource position (Wernerfelt, 1984) or the asset portfolio (Winter, 1987) of the firm. Resource stocks are the result of past actions and decisions. A firm's resource-stock collection is a snapshot of the state of its resources at any point in time; it is not dependent at that moment on what the firm is doing to modify its resource stocks. Resources represent what would remain observable if a firm's actions were frozen in time. In such a case, past resource accumulation actions would be embodied in the current state of the resource stocks.

Of course, the resource stock-variable includes intangible resources. In this respect, knowledge or reputation can be represented as resource-stocks, in that they incorporate, at each point in time, the results of past actions. Machlup (1983), for example, described knowledge as the product of the addition of information; in this scheme, information is a flow that accumulates into a stock called *knowledge*. Alternatively, knowledge might be thought of as a social construction emerging from the accumulation of *solved puzzles* (Kuhn, 1970; Sterman, 1985).

More generally, the conceptualization of resource stocks used here is strongly influenced by Forrester's extension of physical laws of conservation of matter, energy, and quantity of motion to the modelling of social systems (Forrester, 1968). All the stocks or "level" variables, whether they are tangible or intangible, share a common feature: they are *conserved quantities* that can be modified only by adding or subtracting an amount of the

---

[7]As for the relations between "competence" and "capability", the distinction between the two concepts seems to be blurred and strongly influenced by the intellectual and academic heritage of different scholars. Hamel (1994), for example, uses the terms "capability" and "competence" "interchangeably" (p. 12) and focuses instead on the difference between core and non-core competences. The term "capability" is often used by those scholars which have been influenced by the work of Nelson and Winter (1982) or by the concept of "organizational capability" originally used by Chandler (1962). More recently, the term "capability" has been used as a starting point to develop the concept of "dynamic capability" (Teece, Pisano, & Shuen, 1990). On the other hand, the term "competence", whose intellectual roots can be traced back to the concept of "distinctive competence" (Selznick, 1957), provided the base on which Prahalad and Hamel (1990) built the idea of "core competence". The concept of "competence" has recently received renewed attention in the work of a group of scholars who have focused upon competence-based management (Sanchez, Heene, & Thomas, 1996; Sanchez & Heene, 1996, 1997). Referring to this last thread of literature, in this work, the accepted meaning of *competence* is, as already mentioned, the "... ability to sustain the coordinated deployment of assets and capabilities in a way that promises to help a firm to achieve some desired results (goal) through specific actions" (Sanchez, Heene, & Thomas, 1996), and *capability* is a "... repeatable pattern of action in the use of assets." (p. 7).

same entity to or from the stock. The only way to change the quantity contained in resource-stocks is through resource flows to and from the stocks.

Routines and Capabilities as Control Variables. Capability is a recurrent concept in the RBV literature. A general definition is given by Amit and Schoemaker (1993), who referred to *capability* as the *firm's capacity to deploy resources*. Nelson and Winter (1982) stated that capabilities are *"... associated with the possession of particular collections of specialized plant and equipment, and the repertoires of organization members include the ability to operate that plant and equipment"*. From these definitions, a firm's capabilities are represented as resulting from the combination of its knowledge-stocks, its routines derived from such knowledge-stocks, and the assets to which routines are applied. No single element among these three provides an adequate description of a capability. Knowledge becomes effective when it informs how a firm operates — that is, when it is transformed into blueprints, manuals, or procedures and is applied in deploying other assets — such as raw materials and people.

Therefore, we can think of capabilities as incorporating both assets and the routines to deploy these assets; or, stated differently, capabilities result from systems that include a number of state variables, knowledge among them, and a number of mechanisms or routines used to deploy its state variables.[8] Thus, two fundamental elements are considered in modelling capabilities: routines and resource-stocks. A mathematical expression of these relationships is as follows:

In general, if $x_1, x_2, x_3, ... x_n$ are resource-stocks, a routine can be represented as a function

$$\frac{dx_1}{dt} = f(x_1, x_2, x_3, ..., x_n) \qquad (1.1)$$

where $\frac{dx_1}{dt}$ is the rate of change of the resource-stock x_1 at the time period dt.

In this representation, information concerning a firm's resource-stocks $x_1, x_2, x_3, ...,$ x_n is taken into account in deciding to modify the state of resource-stock x_1. For example, consider a simple decision making rule, called the means-ends rule (Simon, 1964; Forrester, 1968). According to this decision rule, decision makers modify the state of a variable in order to reduce the perceived discrepancy between the desired and the effective (or current) value of that variable. Therefore, a goal (G), with respect to the level of a resource-stock x_1, provides a comparator to control change in the state of x_1. The firm, in each time period, examines the difference ($G-x_1$) and tries to reduce the discrepancy between G and x_1 by creating a resource flow to x_1. In equation 1.2, G is

---

[8]Grant (1991) describes capabilities as routines, or a number of interacting routines, where routines are *regular and predictable patterns of activity which are made up of a sequence of co-ordinated actions by individuals*. Following this line of thought, it is assumed in this work that the mechanisms that transform information into actions can generally be understood not as creative and unpredictable acts but as routine processes, or *repeatable patterns of action* in the use of resources (Sanchez, Heene, & Thomas, 1996).

the desired state of x_1, and $\frac{dx_1}{dt}$ is the rate of change of the resource-stock x_1 during the time dt.[9]

$$\frac{dx_1}{dt} = (G - x_1) \qquad (1.2)$$

In this representation, information concerning resource-stock x_1, along with information concerning the desired state of the system, is used to determine the rate at which the firm tries to modify the state of resource-stock x_1. In this case, x_1 is the resource-stock, and $(G–x_1)$ represents the routine through which the resource-stock is modified.

To understand how resource-stocks and routines can be used to study capabilities, consider the following example. If we assume that x_1 is the resource-stock consisting of newly hired workforce, we can think of the capability of managing the workforce as encompassing the routines

$$\frac{dx_1}{dt} = (G - x_1) + a_2 x_2 + a_3 x_3 \qquad (1.3)$$

$$\frac{dx_1}{dt} \leq a_2 x_2 \qquad (1.4)$$

$$\frac{dx_1}{dt} \leq a_3 x_3 \qquad (1.5)$$

and the resource-stocks x_1, x_2, x_3.

If x_2 and x_3 for example, represent respectively experienced workforce and available financial resources, the routines explain how certain proportions in these resource-stocks may be combined with the desired level of workforce G to determine the process rate at which a firm will seek to modify the level of newly hired workforce.

Equations 1.3, 1.4 and 1.5 state that the firm hires new employees at a rate that is lower than a determined proportion a_2 of existing experienced workforce and lower than a proportion a_3 of available financial resources. Moreover, the firm hires workforce with the aim of achieving a particular state of the system that is defined by the optimal level for the variable x_1 (that is, G).

In equation 1.4, the use of parameter a_2 can be explained by considering that each new employee will need a certain period of training during which he works closely with an experienced employee. However, it is reasonable to conjecture that the productivity of an experienced employee will fall during the time he has to devote part of his time to transferring knowledge to the new employee. In this case, the firm may decide to hire new workforce only up to a certain ratio of experienced employees, to facilitate the process of knowledge transfer to new employees without lowering unacceptably the productivity of its existing workforce. Thus, equation 1.4 captures the routine that

[9]For the time being, how the desired state of a system is determined is not part of this investigation.

the firm utilises in deploying the resource-stock of its experienced workforce in building up the resource-stock of its new workforce. More generally, equation 1.4 explains how the firm leverages part of its current resource-stock to increase another resource-stock.

A firm's managers might, for example, use a wrong value for the parameter a_2, or completely ignore the fact that this parameter is important. In such a case, the firm's resource accumulation routine would not consider information flows from the current resource-stock of experienced employees. Equation 1.3 would then have a different form. Specifically, x_2 would not appear in equation 1.3, or may be substituted by another variable, say x_n, meaning that the firm considers information arising from another resource-stock when deciding its process for hiring new workforce. The use of a less effective routine for resource accumulation may either decrease workforce productivity dramatically or, conversely, jeopardize learning and experience transfer. Similarly, firms may differ in their choices of a sensible and appropriate desired state of the system (G), or in the proportion a_3 of financial resources they want to devote to hiring. Firms, therefore, differ in the ways they decide and design their routines for choosing which resource-stocks to consider, and for deciding how to weigh information flowing from the resource-stocks they consider. These differences lead to firms' having different abilities in building up resource positions and portfolios.

Firms as Dynamic Resource Accumulation Systems. The foregoing section has suggested how capabilities in building a certain resource — for example, the workforce — emerge from the ways a firm defines its routines and uses information about other resource-stocks. However, firms manage a number of different resource-stocks simultaneously, using interconnected routines. For example, in equations 1.3, 1.4 and 1.5 the firm accumulates x_1 at a rate determined by x_2 and x_3; however, at the same time the firm will use other routines to manage resource-stocks x_2 and x_3.

We might now ask how the resource-stock of experienced employees (x_2) is built up. First, the building up of experienced workforce resource-stock depends upon the number of newly hired employees. The larger the number of employees newly hired, the larger the number of employees that, during a time period dt, can become experienced. Such a process is essentially *physiological*[10] and stems from the fact that workers tend to learn by doing. Therefore, in principle, a natural flow should occur from the newly hired workforce resource-stock to the experienced workforce resource-stock. However, the question is whether a firm's decision making facilitates or impedes this process. Let us consider more closely how decision making routines and physiological processes are intertwined in firms' capabilities.

Suppose that a firm uses a certain proportion b_2 of its financial resources, x_3, to offer formal training to new employees, and that this training facilitates learning and amplifies the rate at which the experienced employee resource-stock grows. This resource accumulation routine can be represented as

---

[10] A *physiological dynamic* is a dynamic process that originates automatically or inexorably from the physical state of a system (see Forrester, 1961:102).

$$\frac{dx_2}{dt} = b_1 x_1 \bullet b_2 x_3, \tag{1.6}$$

where b_1 represents a physiological rate of learning, and $b_2 x_3$ is the effect of the expenditure devoted to training.

Thus, considering equations 1.3, 1.4, 1.5 and 1.6 together, the routines of the firm in building its resource stocks can be represented as

$$\begin{cases} \dfrac{dx_1}{dt} = (G - x_1) + a_2 x_2 + a_3 x_3 \\[2mm] \dfrac{dx_1}{dt} \le a_2 x_2 \\[2mm] \dfrac{dx_1}{dt} \le a_3 x_3 \\[2mm] \dfrac{dx_2}{dt} = b_1 x_1 \bullet b_2 x_3 \end{cases}$$

Extending this argument, this system of resource accumulation could be elaborated further by including the routine by which the firm accumulates financial resources, x_3. Assuming that financial resources derive from the activities of the current stock of experienced workforce, the amount of new financial resources earned during the period dt depends on the resource-stock of experienced workforce — for example, according to a linear relationship (given by parameter c_1). It could be further conjectured that the firm gains financial resources from a rate of return c_2 earned on previously invested resources x_3. The greater the level of x_3, the greater the amount of financial resources yielded.

The overall resource accumulation dynamics of the firm can then be modelled as follows:

$$\begin{cases} \dfrac{dx_1}{dt} = (G - x_1) + a_2 x_2 + a_3 x_3 \\[2mm] \dfrac{dx_1}{dt} \le a_2 x_2 \\[2mm] \dfrac{dx_1}{dt} \le a_3 x_3 \\[2mm] \dfrac{dx_2}{dt} = b_1 x_1 \bullet b_2 x_3 \\[2mm] \dfrac{dx_3}{dt} = c_1 x_2 \bullet c_2 x_3 \end{cases}$$

The above result is a system of differential equations that defines how a firm simultaneously manages a set of resource-stocks using a number of inter-connected *resource accumulation routines*. The equation therefore describes what, in this paper, is referred to as a *resource accumulation system* (RAS). In Figure 1, a graphical illustration is presented of the RAS described in the above set of differential equations. Boxes indicate state variables and double-line arrows with valves depict how *resource accumulation routines* are employed within the firm to control the levels of resource-stocks. Single-line arrows indicate information flows from resource-stocks to resource accumulation routines.

The presented resource accumulation system also includes dynamic processes that only loosely depend on the decision making activity of the firm. For example, the parameter c_2 defining the interest yielded during the period dt is likely to be, at least partially, exogenously given. Furthermore, although the experienced employee resource-stock increases physiologically as new employees learn, the experienced workforce also decreases over time as employees reach their retirement age and leave the firm. In the same vein, resource-stock representing productive capacity of the firm would decrease with the obsolescence of machinery. These outflows from resource stocks result from physiological dynamic processes inter-linked by the routines of the resource accumulation system, rather than from direct decisions of managers.

Dynamic Capabilities. Another important point of view for the study of capabilities is the concept of dynamic capabilities (Teece *et al.*, 1990). What makes capabilities dynamic is an organization's ability to change its existing decision rules. Reflecting the concept of learning used in the literature on behavioral decision theory (Cyert & March, 1963), dynamic capabilities are created when an organization can generate learning rules that modify lower-level routines and search rules.

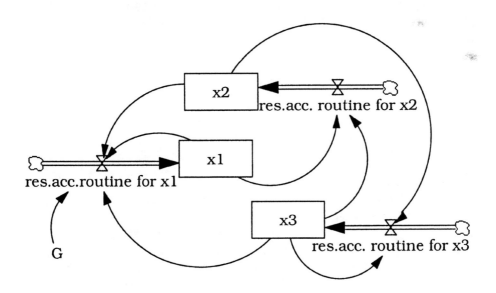

Figure 1: Stock and Flow Representation of a Resource Accumulation System.

The model of capabilities as derived from resources and routines, as presented above, can be extended to include dynamic capabilities, which are defined for this purpose as *dynamic accumulation routines*. Whereas resource accumulation routines act directly upon resources, the characteristic of dynamic resource accumulation routines is that they modify resource accumulation routines. In equation 1.3, for example, G represents the desired state of a system. This information was used to define a routine that modifies the actual state of the system. A dynamic routine would then be represented as a change in the goal of G:

$$\frac{dG}{dt} = f(\bullet) \tag{1.7}$$

This dynamic routine states how the routine in equation 1.3 will change. In this respect, G assumes the features of a resource-stock. In other words, we begin to think of an organization's goals as a resource stock that influences routines that drive other resource stocks. In equation 1.7, G can be considered as a resource, a part of the cognitive assets of the firm and its memory.

The intriguing feature of goals as a resource-stock is that they incorporate an idea or a projection about another resource-stock. In this case, for example, G signifies the desired state of another resource-stock, the workforce. Both the workforce and its desired state G are measured in numbers of employees, but while the workforce resource-stock refers to the tangible, concrete, existing workforce, the goal indicates an intangible idea or projection about the workforce. Resource-stocks that are projections, goals, or speculations about other resource-stocks are intangible resource-stocks which incorporate the knowledge and aspirations of an organization. Dynamic capabilities are driven by such higher-order, intangible, knowledge-like resource-stocks that seek to modify lower-order capabilities by changing their tangible or intangible resource stocks and/or co-ordination routines.

Synthesis of Content-Oriented and Process-Oriented Strategy Perspectives

Having conceptualized the firm as a complex system of interconnected capabilities and resource-stocks, and stated our objective of understanding how such a system actually behaves, we next need a set of assumptions about the process that sets the system in motion. We need to understand which actors and decision-making processes influence the aggregate behavior of the system, and how firms decide which resources to grow and what organizational processes they want to improve. Of particular interest is how a firm decides how to allocate capital in developing and managing a portfolio of different resources and capabilities.

The strategy-process literature investigates how firms decide to accumulate resources, to build capabilities, and ultimately, to manage their asset portfolios. In contrast, a large part of the resource-based view and core competence literature has focused on prescriptive, content-oriented explanations of how capabilities must be effectively grown and managed by firms. In order to create the foundations for a descriptive theory of the evolution of organizations as resource accumulation systems, we need to develop more process-oriented theoretical frameworks and generate a synthesis between process-oriented and content-oriented theoretical frameworks (Sanchez *et al.,* 1996).

The Bower-Burgelman Model of Strategy-Making

The Bower-Burgelman (BB) process model suggests how firms dynamically decide to allocate capital to different strategic initiatives for building business level resources and capabilities (Bower, 1970; Burgelman, 1983a,b,c). Within this framework, strategy-making is represented as *an iterated process of resource allocation* (Noda, 1994; Noda & Bower, 1996).

At the heart of this model is the analysis of corporate strategy-making as four sub-processes carried out by groups of actors at three hierarchical levels. The three groups of actors are top managers, middle managers, and front-line managers. The four sub-processes are the two bottom-up processes of *definition* and *impetus* and the two corporate-level processes of *structural context determination* and *strategic context determination*. Figure 2 explains the role played by each of the three groups of actors in the phases of these processes.[11]

In the definition phase, strategic initiatives emerge from front-line managers who are close to the market and possess specific information, knowledge, and skills. These initiatives may then be supported by middle-managers in the impetus phase. Top managers contribute to this process by defining the structural context, which includes creating the administrative mechanisms for framing bottom-up strategic initiatives in the definition phase and for selecting initiatives in the impetus phase. In defining the structural context, top management are influenced by the organization's current concept of its corporate strategy (Noda & Bower, 1996). Middle-managers play a key role in this process by negotiating with top managers the specific configurations of administrative and organizational mechanisms. Strategic context results from top managers' *rationalization* process (Burgelman, 1983a,b; 1991), which refers to managers' learning gained through development of prior strategic initiatives. Strategic context is also influenced by middle managers' role in *delineating new fields of business development* (Burgelman, 1983a, b, 1991; Noda, & Bower, 1996).

Intra-Organizational Strategy-Making

The Bower-Burgelman model has been further developed (Burgelman, 1991; Burgelman & Mittman, 1994) to include an *intra-organizational ecological perspective* intended to explain organizational change and renewal. In this perspective, an evolutionary variation-selection-retention framework underpins the process of corporate strategy-making. Variation is generated at the operational level by managers who pursue both *induced* and

---

[11]Figure 3 is adapted from Burgelman (1983a). The reported diagram highlights only some among the key activities pursued by managers at different levels of the organization.

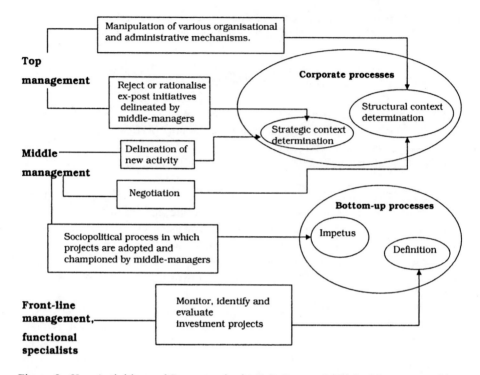

Figure 2: Key Activities and Processes in the B-B Process Model of Strategy-making.

autonomous strategic initiatives. Induced initiatives are those that "*... are intended to preserve the coupling ... with the organization's strategy*" (Burgelman, 1991), while autonomous initiatives are those that are *outside the scope of current strategy*. Strategic initiatives are then selected in the structural context, which includes an internal selection mechanism. The structural context is influenced by the values, beliefs, goals, and perceived action domains in top management's rationalized concept of strategy.

Rationality Assumptions in the Bower-Burgelman Model

The Bower-Burgelman and Burgelman models acknowledge certain biases and cognitive limits of actors in three behavioral aspects of decision making. First, the strategy process is conceived of as a *cognitive process* (Noda & Bower, 1996), as distinct from a perfectly rational decision making model. In the definition phase, for example, actors search for strategic initiatives motivated by problems (Cyert & March, 1963). In the impetus phase, the decision process is one of selection rather than optimization, relies on heuristics, and is biased by the firm's history. Selection often relies on the track records or credibility of middle managers supporting emergent strategic initiatives (Noda & Bower, 1996).

Second, strategic behavior also depends importantly on socio-political processes (Noda & Bower, 1996). In the selection phase, for example, in which different actors compete for scarce resources, selection rules are informed by the need to mediate requests from different middle-managers. In this light, allocation routines may reflect *truces* that prevent conflict from being *expressed in highly disruptive forms* (Nelson & Winter, 1982). Decision making is influenced by *quasi solution of conflicts* (Cyert & March, 1963) — a characterization that suggests the intellectual proximity of this model with behavioral decision theory.

Third, the decision-making framework is highly dynamic. The strategic context and the structural context (through its administrative mechanisms) define which strategic initiatives will be pursued. As time goes by, the consequences of strategic initiatives that have been implemented alter the corporate context: corporate context changes as the result of experience. In this way, firms learn. The accumulated learning of firms then expresses itself in a critical way: in setting company objectives, top managers develop aspiration levels that are the result of the past history of strategy implementation (Cyert & March, 1963).

This behavioral framework helps to look inside the black-box of the firm, explaining how external stimuli are internally amplified or distorted. Initial events — for example, the perception of a new market opportunity — alter the state of the system, but the evolution of the firm ultimately depends on the way decision-makers in the organization react to such perceptions and transform them into strategic initiatives. The history of the firm thus forges corporate context by its influence on aspiration levels, goals, and expectations, and the corporate context provides the environment in which locally boundedly rational actors take decisions.

Noda (1994) and Noda and Bower (1996) have studied how decision-making structures define the path of resource allocation. In their interpretation, initial events are amplified by iterative and path-dependent processes of resource allocation, with the result that firms may become locked into sub-optimal, undesirable processes of resource accumulation.

By showing how a sequence of managerial activities at multiple levels of the organization generates trajectories of resource allocation, Noda and Bower demonstrate how corporate context creates a structure that orients and integrates local decision making processes, and how this effect leads to aggregate strategic behavior. In their model, strategic behavior emerges from processes carried out by locally rational decision makers and may often be sub-optimal.

The model of the strategy-making process as *an iterated process of resource allocation* provides the fundamental conceptual link between the *content* of strategic decision making and the *process* of resource accumulation — a key objective of the competence-based management agenda for theory development (Sanchez *et al.*, 1996).

A Synthesis of the Resource-Based View and the Intra-Organizational Model of Strategy-Making

The model presented in Figure 3 combines key elements of the resource-based perspective and the evolutionary perspective on organizations. From the evolutionary perspective, internal and external selection mechanisms are seen as drivers of organizational change.

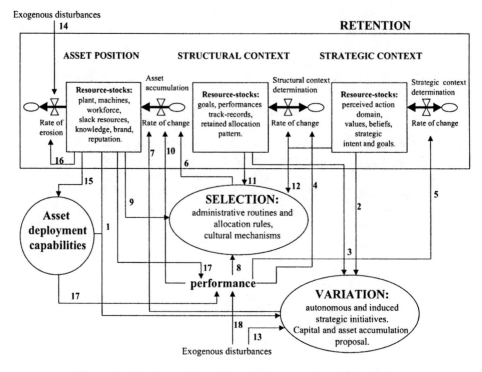

Figure 3: The Dynamics of the *Resource Accumulation System.*

The influence of history on the present, which is expressed through an organization's decision-based retention mechanisms, is represented in the model through resource-stocks that both represent the cumulative result of past decisions and function as powerful retention mechanisms that affect future behavior. The model also incorporates an evolutionary perspective in representing emerging firm capabilities as flowing from the self-organizing processes of a system composed of many locally boundedly rational decision-makers who are embedded in and act upon an inter-connected network of resource-stocks. Capabilities emerge systemically and holistically from the co-evolution of inter-connected resource-stocks and resource-stock accumulation routines.

Variation and Search Behavior

The variation process presented in Figure 3 is strongly influenced by the strategic initiative generation described by Burgelman. In the figure, the variation process occurs through asset accumulation routines as they respond to different proposals for changes in capital allocation and resource-stock accumulation. Through this variation process, firms originate new ideas about which resource-stocks and assets they should accumulate.

Search is sometimes represented in evolutionary models as random. In an ecological model, for example, random variations of genotypes create the opportunities for species to adapt and survive (Monod, 1970). Random variation in organizations, on the other hand, may result from unexpected outcomes of institutional experiments with a new problem solution (Miner, 1994) or errors and mistakes in imitating competitors' successful routines (Levinthal, 1991; Levitt & March, 1988; Lant & Metzias, 1990; Baum & Singh, 1994; Fombrum, 1994).

In the intra-organizational ecological model developed here, the variation process is not completely random.[12] New strategic initiatives arise from front-line managers who are close to opportunities arising at the business level.[13] Managers act to close gaps between existing opportunities and perceived current performances (Sanchez & Heene, 1996). The gap closing behavior in this model may include not only motivated or problemistic searches by front-line managers, but also their *innovative* search (Cyert & March, 1963; Lant & Metzias, 1992).[14]

In the model in Figure 3, variation is influenced by managers' knowledge about the historical path of selection retained in the structural context (Link 3), by their knowledge of the prior results of applying decision routines (the retention mechanism) in the strategic context (Link 2), by the content of opening business opportunities (Link 13), and by constraints imposed by current assets and operative capabilities (Link 1) (Burgelman, 1991).

In Link 1, variation is influenced by current operative capabilities in the sense that current ways to deploy resources define the frame of reference within which decisions are made to generate new deployment routines. Decision-makers normally search in the neighbourhood of existing routines (Cyert & March, 1963; Hannan & Freeman, 1989; McKelvey, 1982; Miller & Friesen, 1980a, b) and retain elements of old problem solutions (Levinthal, 1991; Holland, 1975; Hannan & Freeman, 1984, 1989). Variation is also influenced by current assets because the content of new strategic initiatives may pertain to changes in deployment routines for exiting assets.

In Links 2 and 3 the retained selection pattern of the structural context and the values and beliefs crystallized in the strategic context also constrain variation, because the initiatives that front-line managers conceive of are likely to be inspired by their beliefs about "… which types of initiatives are likely to be supported by the organization" (Burgelman, 1991).

The influence of retention on search and variation is the basis for the distinction in Burgelman's framework between autonomous and induced strategic initiatives. Autonomous strategic initiatives concern "… initiatives that emerge outside (the scope of

---

[12] *"While* [autonomous strategic initiatives] *often emerge fortuitously and are difficult to predict, they are usually not random because they are rooted in and are constrained by the evolving competence set of the organization"* (Burgelman, 1991:246).

[13]*"… [initiatives] are most likely to emerge at a level where managers are directly in contact with new technological developments and changes in market conditions, …"* (Burgelman, 1991).

[14]The difference between *motivated*, or *problemistic*, and *innovative* search refers to the kind of stimulus leading to search behaviors. *Motivated* or *problemistic* search is the consequence of the emergence of a problem such as a decline in a firm's performances. On the other hand, *innovative* search is not necessarily stimulated by the emergence of a problem. Rather, it might be inspired by managerial creativity and attitude to experiment. In both cases, it is possible to envision gap-closing mechanisms at work. In the first case, the gap to be closed is the one between the historical, or expected, performances and the actual ones. In the second case, the gap is the one between desired as possibly obtainable performances and actual performances.

organizational strategy) and provide potential for new organizational learning" (Burgelman, 1991). On the other hand, induced strategic initiatives concern the exploitation of "...growth opportunities remaining in the current domain". Such initiatives may include "... core technology advances, new product development for existing product families, new approaches to marketing and manufacturing ..." (Burgelman, 1991).

Selection Mechanisms in the Corporate Context

Perhaps the central premise of our model is that organizations produce a certain amount of variation by conceiving strategic initiatives that involve adjustments to their existing resource accumulation routines. In modifying existing routines, firms nevertheless follow internal selection mechanisms that "maintain order" by rejecting possible strategic initiatives that seem too far from the entrenched idea of the firm's action domain or that are unlikely to generate results consistent with accepted performance criteria. In Figure 3, Link 6 represents the influence of a firm's strategic selection processes on its resource accumulation routines. Link 7, on the other hand, indicates that some new variations in initiatives will survive the selection process and subsequently will influence future resource allocations and accumulation.

Generally, Link 12 from the strategic context to the selection routines signifies that rigidities in the way a firm selects its strategic initiatives depend on the extent to which top managers are or are not willing to tolerate[15] deviant initiatives.

The model in Figure 3 also introduces into the intra-organizational model some behavioral assumptions about organizational decision-making. The model assumes, for example, that the thoroughness with which initiatives are explored and selected in the structural context is influenced by the search behavior of the firm. In this regard, Link 9 in the model suggests that accumulated slack resources increase the organization's willingness to search and to experiment with deviant strategic initiatives (March, 1981).

Further, performance below aspiration level motivates search for new strategies, and firms are more likely to consider initiatives which imply changes in the existing allocation routines. Therefore, Link 8 in the model indicates that tolerance of deviant initiatives in the selection mechanism increases as current performance falls below expectations. Links 11 and 12 connect the selection mechanism with the organization's aspiration levels, which are resource-stocks in both the structural and the strategic context. In the structural context, aspiration may be expressed as expected returns on assets from strategic initiatives; in the strategic context, aspiration may take the form of longer-term, higher-order goals such as growth in market share.

---

[15]This hypothesis represents a simplification of the original framework proposed by Burgelman who, more precisely, stresses that autonomous and induced strategic initiatives follow two separate selection procedures. The induced initiatives are selected in the structural context selection mechanism, whereas autonomous initiatives are selected outside the structural context by acting directly on the strategic context determination and therefore by modifying incrementally top managers' concept of strategy. Figure 3 was a simplified representation focusing on the scope or neighbourhood of search as influenced by three factors: past performances, unabsorbed slack resources, and top managers' tolerance of deviant initiatives.

The idea that decision-makers generally tend to repeat actions that have produced good results and abandon actions that have generated bad results is found in the early studies of micro-sociology (Homans, 1974), in behavioral decision theory (March & Simon, 1958; Cyert & March, 1963; Winter, 1994; Ginsberg & Baum, 1994), and in prospect theory's notion that receptivity to risk and experiment increases in loss domains (Tversky & Kahneman, 1986). Current behavior in selection is thus influenced by the results of past selection behavior. Routine decision-making and strategic initiative selection strongly depend on the relative performance track-records of alternative selection criteria crystallized in the structural context (Link 11).

Retention, Accumulation and Inertia

The view of firms as resource accumulation systems suggests a number of possible characteristics of retention processes. First, given the stock-representation of resources, firm evolution is determined by the way in which flows to and from stocks are governed in organizations (Dierickx & Cool, 1989). Organizations are represented as complex feedback systems where rates of change of stocks depend on information concerning the state of the system as perceived by managers as they monitor resource stocks. The representation of resources as stocks is thus consistent with the concept of *accumulation*. As Levinthal points out (1994), the notion of accumulation is germane to the understanding of inertia in organizations both at a structural and at a cognitive level. Indeed, the distinction in systems models between resource-stocks in general and knowledge-like resource-stocks in particular reflects the essential difference between structural and cognitive inertia.

Resource systems of the structural type cannot be changed instantaneously, because some resource-stocks need to be depleted and others must be accumulated, and the processes of depletion and accumulation take time. When designing a particular strategy — a product differentiation strategy, for example — a particular bundle of resources will have to be accumulated to pursue that strategy. If environmental conditions change, so that customers are more sensitive to prices and less sensitive to product differentiation, a firm will face two sources of structural inertia in reacting to such change. First, the firm will need time to deplete the accumulated current resource-stocks like specialized plants, inventory, and workforce. Second, a firm needs time to build new kinds of resource-stocks. For example, the firm might need to acquire new product or process technologies to differentiate its products, and this requires selling large volumes by accumulating a new brand awareness and customer base. Building up such new resources cannot be accomplished instantaneously.

Knowledge resource stocks represent the cognitive context of the firm and are the sources of cognitive inertia. One form of cognitive inertia occurs when firms take time to recognize the need for change. For example, the objective of becoming a "memory company" in the early days of Intel Corporation (Burgelman, 1991) or the objective of entering the wireless telephone business at South Bell (Noda, 1994; Noda & Bower, 1996) developed over some time. Because goals and objectives emerge and evolve over time, goals and objectives in fact behave like stocks (Levinthal, 1994) that adjust through incremental accumulation over time.

The pace at which knowledge and other intangible resource stocks will adapt and evolve depends on the effectiveness of the learning processes embedded in a firm's dynamic routines (Teece *et al.,* 1990) and on the nature of the resource. For example, Sanchez and Heene (1996, 1997) suggest that stocks embodying higher-order knowledge and information such as a firm's *strategic logic* will be characterized by longer adjustment times.

Drawing on both resource-based literature and the intra-organizational evolutionary model, the model in Figure 3 illustrates three categories of stocks that represent retention processes at three different levels of an organization.

The lowest order refers to stocks of tangible resources like plants, machines, capital, and workforce. Intangible resources (reputation, knowledge) of the firm refer to retained information regarding routines for deploying tangible assets, such as routines for producing or selling. Stocks of knowledge inform the resource deployment routines (Link 15), but are subject to rates of erosion as knowledge is "retired" or lost in an organization (Link 16). Current resource stocks and resource-stock deployment routines determine a firm's near-term competitive performance (Link 17). The erosion rate (Dierickx & Cool, 1989) represents the fact most resource-stocks erode over time: machines and plants age, knowledge and technology become obsolete or forgotten, and brands decay in their market power.

Asset accumulation routines in Figure 3 determine the rate of change in accumulation of resource-stocks. Asset accumulation routines, however, are influenced by the selection mechanism in the structural context (Link 6). The selection of a strategic initiative usually implies the allocation of capital or labor, and this allocation decision often leads to the accumulation of a resource-stock. For example, a new product development initiative might imply the building of a new team of designers and engineers — that is, the accumulation of stocks of human resources. The rate at which resource-stocks are accumulated by resource accumulation routines is also influenced by competitive performances (Link 10), because the capital available to a firm to allocate to resource accumulation depends on how well it performs in competing in the market place. A firm's ability to create value can be represented in terms of Figure 3 as the ability to sustain a net inflow of resources in the firm's resources accumulation processes.

The structural context in Figure 3 is the locus of administrative and cultural mechanisms. At this level resource-stocks are intangible and consist of retained information about strategic planning and control systems, approaches to measuring and rewarding managers, rules governing resource allocation (administrative mechanisms), and socialization rules and behavioral norms (cultural mechanisms) (Burgelman, 1991:244). The resource-stocks at this level are accumulated through the rate of change called *structural context determination* in Figure 3. This rate of change is influenced by the strategic context in that it strongly depends on top management's concept of strategy. In other words, the administrative and cultural mechanisms which constitute the selection environment in the structural context represent the crystallization of top management's ideas, objectives and beliefs (Link 12), and their embedding in the firm's control systems and sensemaking processes (Sanchez, 2001).

The model elaborated in Figure 3 acknowledges the fact that the rates of change of the stocks in the structural context are also governed by a firm's current competitive performance (Link 4). This occurs because these resource-stocks often incorporate such accumulated expectations as past budget targets and performance track records (Cyert & March, 1963). These expectations are an important part of the cognitive background of the organization and form the basis for the scanning and selection of strategic initiatives (Noda, 1994; Noda & Bower, 1996).

The strategic context is the highest layer at which retention takes place in the organization's evolution. At this level the resource-stocks incorporate top management's concept of strategy (Burgelman, 1991) and represent the essential features of the firm's strategic logic (Sanchez *et al.,* 1996). The strategic context thus refers to the firm's perceived strategic domain, its ideas about the company's mission and about the relative importance of its accumulated resources and capabilities. This "… represents the more or less explicit articulation of the firm's theory about the basis of its past and current successes and failures. It provides a more or less shared frame of reference for the strategic actors in the organization, and provides the basis for corporate objective setting in terms of its business portfolio and resource allocation" (Burgelman, 1983b).

The top management concept of strategy is the state variable which embodies what is retained in top management's ex-post cognitive processes of learning about the bases of past/current successes and failures, the forging of perceived goals for resource allocations, the perceived action domain, and desired organizational character. In the model this process of ex-post rationalization from past action and performances regulates the functioning of the rate of change named strategic context determination. Link 5 therefore represents the effect of learning on the strategic context from experience and from enacted strategic initiatives. For example, as the result of a successful new initiative such as investment in a completely new business, the idea of corporate strategy might evolve by modifying its perceived action domain to incorporate the new business (Burgelman, 1991).

Exogenous Disturbances

Finally, the effect of exogenous disturbances must be considered. Environmental change such as the evolution of a technological standard, for example, might depreciate and erode the usefulness of a resource-stock such as existing technical know-how (Link 14). Other environmental changes like the opening of new business opportunities or the extinguishing of old ones could also stimulate adjustments in and orient the search behavior of the firm at the front-line level (Link 13). Changes in the overall economic context of an industry may also have an immediate effect on a firm's performance (Link 18).

The possibility for a system to *communicate* with its environment creates the conditions for the emergence of new behavior and evolution. As Burgelman (1983b) pointed out, a firm may react to environmental change by absorbing or mirroring exogenous disturbances, or by amplifying them. In the first case, a *homeostatic* tendency often brings a firm's behavior back to its original trajectory. In the second case, a firm undertakes an increasing divergence from its original trajectory. This latter case might generate difficulty in governing the system, but might also give rise to *homeoresis* — that is, a condition that brings out the capacity of a system not merely to return to its state prior to the occurrence of disturbances, but to seek out new development pathways through successive instabilities (Burgelman 1983b).

A Feedback Approach to the Synthesis of Teleonomic and Evolutionary Behavior

As presented in the model in Figure 3, the structure of intra-organizational ecology is an interconnected web of locally and boundedly rational actors who interact through decision-making routines. The ecology is therefore a dynamic and complex system, and both the strategic decision-making and resource evolution of a firm are emergent behaviors of such a system.

The system behavior of a firm (Sanchez & Heene, 1996) can be studied by looking at its inner structure and in particular at the web of inter-linked feedback loops in which decision-makers are embedded. Emergent dynamic properties of the firm as a system can be investigated by analyzing the structure, direction, and relative strengths of such feedback loops.

We can now add that there are two kinds of feedback loops, negative and positive. Negative feedback loops have the property that if a variable embedded in such a loop moves away from its desired value, the influence of the negative feedback loop on the overall system leads to interactions that tend to bring the variable back to its original level. On the other hand, in a positive feedback loop, if a variable moves in one direction, the effect on the overall system will be to precipitate interactions that amplify that movement and push the variable even further away from its original value.[16] Looking at the system in Figure 3 it is possible to identify a number of negative and positive feedbacks.

At front-line level, managers undertake strategic initiatives by trying to close gaps between desired performances or perceived attainable performances and actual performances (Sanchez & Heene, 1996). Figure 4 explains how front-line manager behaviour typically embodies a negative feedback. As new opportunity leads to new goals, managers "close the gap" between the new goals and current performance levels until performance matches the goal.

We can think of selection mechanisms in a firm's evolution as negative feedback loops that work to maintain coherence in the firm's current strategic initiatives. A firm's activities are maintained close to its original strategic trajectory by its selection mechanisms that suppress strategic initiatives deviating from the firm's action domain. Figure 5 shows how firms regulate the strength of such negative feedback loops through the degree to which they tolerate deviant strategic initiatives. The higher a firm's tolerance, the weaker will be the strength of its selection mechanisms.

Search behavior may also be considered a negative feedback loop when a discrepancy detected between desired and actual performance triggers expanded search and strategic

---

[16]More precisely, we can define positive and negative feedback as processes in which, respectively,

$$\frac{d\dot{x}}{dx} \rangle 0 \text{ and } \frac{d\dot{x}}{dx} \langle 0,$$

where $\dot{x}$ the derivative of x with respect to time, $\frac{dx}{dt} = \dot{x}$ (Richardson, 1995).

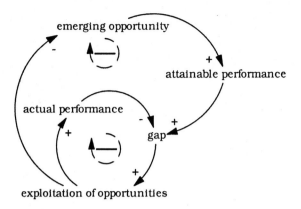

Figure 4: Business-level negative feedback loops.

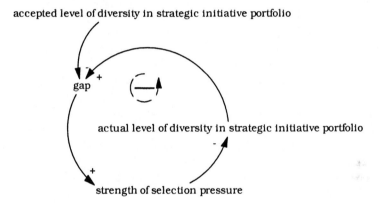

Figure 5: Corporate-level Selection Negative Feedback.

initiative selection criteria are relaxed to encourage new initiatives intended to bring performance back at desired levels.[17]

In real firms, just as in the model described in Figure 3, negative feedbacks are interconnected with positive feedbacks, so that it is often not easy to foresee what kind of behavior will emerge within the firm under different conditions.

It is generally the case that the effects of the gap closing mechanism described above will be countered or even overpowered by an interconnected positive feedback loop. For example, when performance objectives are based upon past performance, if current performance goes up, future performance objectives go up as well, thereby maintaining an ongoing performance gap and fostering continuous corrective actions. As illustrated in Figure 6, the effect of corrective actions is to increase performance, which leads in

---

[17]The search might lead to counterinuitive and undesired results but still it represents a goal-oriented or gap-closing behaviour whose purpose is the improvement of the current situation of the firm.

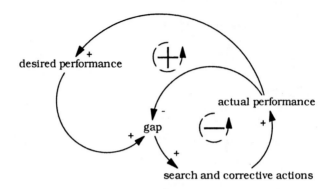

Figure 6: Corporate-level Search Negative Feedback with Connected *Superstitious Learning* Positive Feedback.

turn to further raising of performance targets and an upward spiral of increasing performance.

The spiral effect can also work the other way around, however, with low performance leading to lowering of performance targets, reduced perception of need for corrective action, and resulting lower performance. This working of the positive feedback loop leads to a downward spiral of worsening performance. This pathological inability of a firm to improve its performance is also the consequence of the positive feedback between historical performance and performance targets which compromises the ability of a negative feedback loop to work properly.

In Figure 3 it is possible to highlight other positive feedbacks. Figure 7 identifies three nested positive feedback loops that constitute self-reinforcing engines driving the growth of a firm's strategic initiatives. First, a positive feedback loop links resource-stocks with performance and with asset accumulation routines. Indeed, from a resource-based perspective, one might expect that the stronger a firm's resource position, the higher the firm's performance will be (Link 17). Higher performance leads to increases in financial resources that can be allocated to resource accumulation (Link 10). In addition, as the tangible resource base enlarges, the intangible resources knowledge and experience grow, contributing to improvements in a firm's resource deployment capabilities.

A second positive feedback loop connects performance, the structural context determination rate of change, resource-stocks in the structural context box, selection of resources, and resource-stocks in the asset position box. If we consider, for example, strategic initiatives like the development of a new product, some capital will be allocated through the resource accumulation routines in order to acquire the resource-stocks needed to pursue the initiative (Link 6). If the initiative is successful and generates adequate competitive performance (Link 17), the structural context determination rate of change will work to update the relative performance track records of different strategic initiatives in the corporate portfolio (Link 4). As a consequence, the resource-stocks in the structural context will be adjusted to reflect the results of the new strategic initiative and will re-orient the decision-making routines in the selection mechanism (Link 11). Further initiatives dealing with the same kind of successful product or other initiatives backed by the same successful

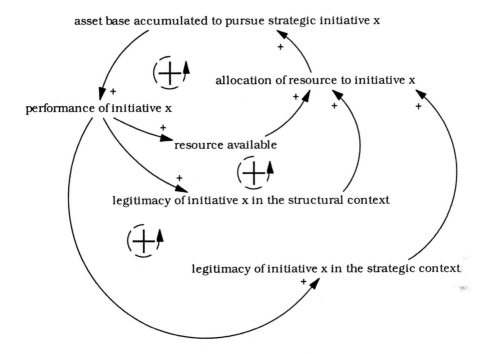

Figure 7: Corporate and Business-level Positive Feedback: Engines of Growth for Strategic Initiatives.

managers will have increased likelihood of being accepted, and as a consequence the selection mechanism will allocate even more capital to successful initiatives and managers. In this process, the faster firms adjust their structural context determination rates, the stronger is the positive feedback. By contrast, inertia in updating resource-stocks in the structural context reduces the strength of the positive feedback.

Finally, a third, more complex positive feedback loop couples resource-stocks in the asset position box, competitive performances, strategic context determination, resource-stocks in the strategic context box, the structural context determination, resource-stocks in the structural context box, the asset accumulation routines in the selection mechanism, and the resource-stocks in the asset box. Suppose that a new strategic initiative like an investment in a new business has been selected and has shown positive performance. Such a result will mould the concept of strategy (Link 5) to include the new business in the perceived action domain. This change will be transmitted through the Link 12 to the resource-stocks in the structural context box and will influence corporate selection behavior. The selection mechanism will now include the new business among those in which the firm operates, and therefore it will be easier for further strategic initiatives in the new business to be legitimized, positively selected, and assigned further capital in order to build resource-stocks to compete and generate performance. How frequently and quickly a firm updates its strategic context determination rate determines the strength of this positive feedback loop.

Linking the positive and negative feedbacks described above leads to complex behaviors of the system. On the one hand, the positive feedbacks represent the mechanism through which variation in resource accumulation routines can be supported, leveraged, and eventually find its way through the selection mechanism of the organization. In this way, positive feedbacks can generate the necessary momentum for a new initiative to achieve legitimacy in the firm. On the other hand, positive feedbacks are also the cause of increasing inertia when they generate a spiral of deepening commitment towards current courses of action and create "lock-in" into sub-optimal competitive positions (Arthur, 1989), in effect fostering "core rigidities" (Leonard-Barton, 1992).

In general, gap-closing mechanisms (Sanchez & Heene, 1996, 1997) in the form of negative feedback loops work to control the trajectory of an organization and guide the "teleonomic" (Van de Ven & Poole, 1995) behaviors of firms. Mechanisms in the form of positive feedback loops are mechanisms that push organizations away from their current trajectories towards new paths of evolution. In this light, positive feedback loops can be seen as the "exciters" that drive the variation, selection, and retention in the evolution of organizational behavior.

In the strategic management literature, a number of scholars have tried to explain the emergence of processes that lead to order or disorder by looking at the feedback structure of change mechanisms. This research generally associates positive feedback loops with disorder-generating processes and negative feedback with order-maintaining processes (Burgelman, 1983b; Van de Ven & Poole, 1995). What is suggested in this paper, however, is that to fully understand strategic behavior and resource position evolution, it is essential to study the functioning of *inter-connected* positive and negative feedback loops.

If we consider the organizational selection mechanism alone, it has predominantly negative feedback loop properties. By eliminating strategic initiatives which deviate from the currently accepted concept of strategy, the selection mechanism controls the degree of variation in the population of strategic initiatives. In this way, negative feedback loops act to keep a desired level of autonomous strategic initiatives in place. The selection mechanism, acting alone, seems to increase the homeostatic tendencies of an organization through negative feedback loop processes, but when it is coupled with the organization's retention mechanism, the two (positive and negative) feedback loops acting jointly might result in positive feedback that can move the organization away from its current trajectory of activities. By producing a successful track-record, selected strategic initiatives may tilt internal selection in their favor, thereby leading to resource allocations that further improve performance (Noda, 1994; Noda & Bower, 1996). In this case, an initial event (a new selection and resource allocation) is endogenously amplified by a self-reinforcing retention mechanism which seeks further success from successful initiatives,[18] thereby originating a new trajectory of evolution. On the other hand, by amplifying the success of a new strategic initiative, positive feedbacks in the retention mechanism are likely to create increasing commitment to such initiatives and to inhibit the growth of other strategic initiatives by lowering their relative attractiveness.

---

[18] See Senge's "success to the successful" archetype in Senge (1990).

The feedback view of organizational evolution elaborated here suggests a number of propositions that may support development of better theory about competence building and adaptation.

(1) Successful firms create competences by using internal selection mechanisms based on negative feedback loops to direct human and financial capital allocation to strategic initiatives that promote accumulation of particular kinds and combinations of resources.

(2) Successful firms avoid core rigidities by allowing a number of deviant strategic initiatives to be undertaken, thereby maintaining a certain level of disorder, experimentation, and disequilibrium in the organization. Deviant strategic initiatives depend upon and promote accumulation of resources that are qualitatively different from the organization's current resource endowments.

(3) Successful firms regulate their level of experimentation by defining a particular level of tolerance to deviant initiatives, and by doing so moderate the "narrowing" tendency of the corporate selection process as a negative feedback loop (see Figure 5).

(4) Successful firms avoid core rigidities by maintaining both corporate and business level negative feedbacks in the form of "nurturing" gap-closing behaviors. "Nurturing" negative feedback loops are implemented at business level by front-line managers who respond to perceived opportunities in the environment (see Figure 4), and at corporate level by top and middle managers who expand their search behavior and increase their tolerance for deviant strategic initiatives (see Figure 6).

(5) Successful firms avoid core rigidities by maintaining positive feedback loops that give momentum to deviant strategic initiatives (see Figure 7). At the same time, successful firms control positive feedbacks to prevent uncontrolled escalation of commitment to new trajectories of competence evolution.

(6) Failures in building and adapting firms' competences can be studied and interpreted as the undesirable emergent behavior of an organization's feedback systems. Poor performing or failing firms do not properly understand how to manage the feedback structure that drives the intra-organizational evolution of the firm and its choices of strategic initiatives.

Conclusions

Corporate strategy-making and the evolution of a firm's resource positions can be investigated by modelling firms as complex and dynamic *resource accumulation systems*. Such systems are populated by locally and boundedly rational actors whose inter-connected decision-making may generate causally ambiguous (Dierickx & Cool, 1989) and uncertainly imitable (Lippman & Rumelt, 1982) resource accumulation behavior that may therefore be capable of producing Schumpeterian rents.

The model developed here is aimed at contributing to strategy studies in two ways. First, following the line advanced by Sanchez, Heene, and Thomas (1996), the model tries to overcome the long-standing dichotomy in the strategy field between content- and process-oriented studies (Mahoney & Sanchez, 1996) and, by extension, the dichotomy between strategy- and structure-oriented studies.

Drawing on Burgelman's work (1983c, 1991), a model is presented in which strategy-making (i.e., resource accumulation decisions) follows from structure (accumulated resource-stocks), because strategic decisions of managers are based on information they have about the resource-stocks (state variables) of the firm. At the same time, structure (accumulated resource-stocks) follows from strategy (resource accumulation decisions) because human and financial capital allocation decisions lead to accumulations of stocks of resources.[19] Therefore, this work interweaves content — and process-oriented views to develop the concept of firms as *information-feedback systems* that drive the accumulation of resources.[20] Such human systems are termed here *resource accumulation systems*.

The model presented here also tries to overcome the dichotomy between goal-oriented/ teleonomic representations of firm behavior and evolutionary/self-organizing system perspectives. Drawing on evolutionary theories of change, the model emphasises the role of random variations in generating new patterns of behavior and the importance of retention of history in shaping future behavior. Drawing also on behavioral decision-making, the model stresses the role of goal-oriented behavior in triggering search routines which generate variation.

In addition, this model illustrates how a complex feedback structure can generate strategic behavior and how a firm's competence evolution can be explored as the emerging dynamic properties of such a feedback structure. In this light, negative feedbacks are considered as incorporating goal-oriented/teleonomic mechanisms of control, whereas positive feedbacks lead resource accumulation systems towards new behaviors.

The interactions of positive and negative feedbacks generate apparent causal ambiguity, so that an organization's resource position evolution may often be surprising and unintended, even to the organization's managers. Therefore, depending on the relative strength and the polarities (positive or negative) of the feedbacks involved, emergent strategic behavior may become largely disconnected from the original purpose and motives for an initiative, making the relation between top management's strategic intent and realized resource accumulation behavior to some extent unpredictable (Hannan & Freeman, 1984). In this sense, not only can firm behavior be seen as locally and boundedly rational, but it also becomes apparent that firm-level behavior emerges from the self-organizing behavior of locally and boundedly rational decision-makers. This representation provides an intra-organizational dimension to the Schumpeterian idea that competitive position evolution is generated by waves of creative destruction. Firms may create temporary competitive advantages by exploiting new combinations of resources, but to do so they must also suffer the "destruction" activities brought about by "self-organizing" aggregate behavior produced by the structure of inter-linked resource-stocks and resource accumulation routines.

Finally, this paper contributes to the strategy literature and to suggestions for further research by delineating the potential for cross-fertilization between strategy studies and feedback approaches in the analysis of the behavior of complex and dynamic social

---

[19]This interdependency of content and process and strategy and structure provides further illustration of the fundamentally inseparable "end-means" interrelationships in human systems (Heene & Sanchez, 1997).

[20]It is useful to recall here that *an information-feedback system exists whenever the environment leads to a decision that results in action which affects the environment and thereby influences future decisions* (Forrester, 1961).

systems (Forrester, 1961, 1968, 1969, 1973, 1992). Such fertilization may take at least two directions.

First, a key system characteristic of management processes is that managers generally seek to maintain a balance between use of negative feedback loops to achieve rigorous homeo-static control over strategic initiatives in the face of exogenous disturbances, on the one hand, and the preservation or development of the firm's capability to explore new trajectories by riding positive feedbacks that push organizations away from their current trajectories, on the other. The model presented should provide a theoretically grounded framework for exploring ways to foster competence development without creating core rigidities.

Based on the conceptualization of firms as resource accumulation systems, further work could investigate how to define, manage, and calibrate the level of tolerance to the deviant initiatives needed to sustain competence building and evolution. In addition, studies could explore how to calibrate the strength of reinforcing mechanisms in leveraging competences to avoid developing core rigidities. These investigations may be supported by using computer simulation studies to represent, to investigate, and eventually, to design organization feedback structures.

In a more theoretical vein, investigating the effects of non-linear relations among variables can help to develop new insights into counterintuitive and chaotic organizational behavior, multiple equilibria, and bifurcations of competitive positions. Models of non-linearities in a dynamic system can help to reveal the relative strengths of an organization's positive and negative feedback loops and therefore the dominant polarity of the organization as a system.

The potential gains from a systems and feedback interpretation of evolutionary dynamics has been suggested by Weick (1979). Weick linked the study of evolutionary dynamics to the feedback view by developing a feedback-based interpretation of how a structure of inter-linked variables could generate a particular evolutionary path. This research suggests that feedback structures and their relation to emerging behavior of a system provide critical new systems concepts and methodological tools for developing new organization and strategy theory.

References

Amit, R,. & Schoemaker, P. J. H. (1993). Strategic assets and organizational rent. *Strategic Management Journal, 14*, 33–46.

Arthur, B. (1988). Self-reinforcing mechanisms in economics. In P. W. Anderson, K. J. Arrow & D. Pines (eds) *The Economy as an Evolving Complex System*. Reading, MA: Addison-Wesley.

Barney, J. B. (1986). Strategic factor markets: Expectations, luck, and business strategy. *Management Science, 32(10)*, 1231–1241.

Barney, J. B. (1991). Firm resources and sustained competitive advantage. *Journal of Management, 17(1)*, 99–120.

Baum J. A. C., & Singh, J. V. (1994). Organizational hierarchies and evolutionary processes: Some reflections on a theory of organizational evolution. In J. A. C. Baum & J. V. Singh (eds), *Evolutionary Dynamics of Organizations*. New York: Oxford University Press.

Bower, J. L. (1970). *Managing the Resource Allocation Process: A Study of Corporate Planning and Investment*. Boston, MA: Harvard University Press.

Burgelman, R. A. (1983a). A process model of internal corporate venturing in the diversified major firms. *Administrative Science Quarterly, 28*, 223–244.

Burgelman, R. A. (1983b). Corporate entrepreneurship and strategic management: Insights from a process study. *Management Science, 29*, 1349–1364.

Burgelman, R. A. (1983c). A model of interaction of strategic behavior, corporate context, and the concept of strategy. *Academy of Management Review, 8(1)*, 61–70.

Burgelman, R. A. (1991). Intraorganizational ecology of strategy making and organizational adaptation: Theory and field research. *Organization Science, 2*, 239–262.

Burgelman, R. A., & Mittman, B. S. (1994). An intraorganizational ecological perspective on managerial risk behavior, performance, and survival: Individual, organizational, and environmental effects. In J. A. C. Baum & J. V. Singh (eds), *Evolutionary Dynamics of Organizations*. New York: Oxford University Press.

Carlsson, B. and G. Eliasson (1994). The nature and importance of economic competence. *Industrial and Corporate Change, 3(3)*, 687–711.

Chandler, A. D., Jr. (1962). *Strategy and Structure*. Cambridge, MA: MIT Press.

Conner, K. R. (1991). A historical comparison of resource-based theory and five schools of thought within industrial organization economics: Do we have a new theory of the firm? *Journal of Management, 17(1)*, 121–154.

Cyert, R. M., & March, J. M. (1963). *A Behavioral Theory of the Firm*. New Jersey: Prentice-Hall.

Dierickx, I., & Cool, K. (1989). Asset stock accumulation and sustainability of competitive advantage. *Management Science, 35(12)*, 1504–1511.

Fombrun, C. J. (1994). Taking on strategy 1-2-3. In J. A. C. Baum & J. V. Singh (eds), *Evolutionary Dynamics of Organizations*. New York: Oxford University Press.

Forrester, J. W. (1961). *Industrial Dynamics*. Cambridge, MA: Productivity Press.

Forrester, J. W. (1968). *Principles of Systems*. Cambridge, MA: Productivity Press.

Forrester, J. W. (1969). *Urban Dynamics*. Cambridge, MA: Productivity Press.

Forrester, J. W. (1973). *World Dynamics*, Cambridge, MA: Productivity Press.

Forrester, J. W. (1992). Policies, decisions and information sources for modeling. *European Journal of European Research, 59*, 42–63.

Foss, N. J. (1995). The resource-based perspective and three economic approaches. Working Paper, Institut for Erhvervs-og Samfundsforskning Handelshojskolen i Kobenhavn.

Ghemawat, P. (1991). *Commitment: The dynamic of strategy*. New York: Free Press.

Ginsberg, A., & Baum, J. A. C. (1994). Evolutionary patterns of core business change. In J. A. C. Baum & J. V. Singh (eds) *Evolutionary Dynamics of Organizations*. New York: Oxford University Press.

Goshal, S., & Moran, P. (1996). Value creation by firms. SRLP Working Paper 11/1996, London Business School.

Grant, R. M. (1991). The resource-based theory of competitive advantage: Implications for strategy formulation. *California Management Review*, 114–133.

Hall, R. (1992). The strategic analysis of intangible resources. *Strategic Management Journal, 13*, 135–44.

Hall, R. (1993). A framework linking intangible resources and capabilities to sustainable competitive advantage. *Strategic Management Journal, 14*, 607–18.

Hamel, G. (1994). The concept of core competence. In G. Hamel & A. Heene (eds) *Competence-based Competition*. Chichester: John Wiley & Sons.

Hannan, M. T., & Freeman, J. (1984). Structural inertia and organizational change. *American Sociological Review, 49*, 149–64.

Hannan, M. T., & Freeman, J. (1989). *Organizational Ecology*. Cambridge, MA: Harvard University Press.

Helfat, C. E. (1997). Know-how and asset complementarity and dynamic capability accumulation. *Strategic Management Journal, 185,* 339–61.

Heene, A., Sanchez, R. (1996). *Competence-based Strategic Management.* Chichester: John Wiley & Sons.

Holland, J. H. (1975). *Adaptation on Natural and Artificial Systems.* Ann Arbor, MI: University of Michigan Press.

Homans, G. C. (1974). *Social Behavior: Its Elementary Forms.* New York: Harcourt, Brace.

Kuhn, T. (1970). *The Structure of Scientific Revolutions* (2nd ed.). Chicago: University of Chicago Press.

Lant, T. K., & Mezias, S. J. (1992). An organizational learning model of convergence and reorientation. *Organization Science, 3(1),* 47–71.

Leonard-Barton, D. (1992). Core capabilities and core rigidities: A paradox in managing new product development. *Strategic Management Journal, 13,* 111–125.

Levinthal, D. A. (1991). Organizational adaptation and environmental selection — interrelated process of change. *Organization Science, 2,* 140–45.

Levinthal, D. A. (1994). Surviving Schumpeterian environments: an evolutionary perspective. In J. A. C. Baum & J. V. Singh (eds) *Evolutionary Dynamics of Organizations.* New York: Oxford University Press.

Levinthal, D. A. (1995). Strategic management and the exploration of diversity. In C. A. Montgomery (ed.), *Resource-based and evolutionary theories of the firm: towards a synthesis.* Kluwer Academic Publishers.

Levitt, B., & March, J. G. (1988). Organizational learning. *Annual Review of Sociology 14,* 319–40.

Lippman, S. A., & Rumelt, R. P. (1982). Uncertain imitability: An analysis of interfirm differences in efficiency under competition. *The Bell Journal of Economics, 13,* 418–453.

Machlup, F. (1983). Semantic quirks in studies of information. In *The Study of Information.* New York: John Wiley.

Mahoney, J. T., & Sanchez, R. (1996). Competence theory building: Reconnecting management research and management practice. In A. Heene & R. Sanchez (eds), *Competence-based Strategic Management.* Chichester: John Wiley & Sons.

Mansfield, E. (1975). *Microeconomics: Theory and Applications.* New York: W. W. Norton & Company.

March, J. G. (1991). Exploration and exploitation in organizational learning. *Organization Science, 2(1).*

March, J. G., & Simon, H. A. (1958). *Organizations.* New York: John Wiley.

McKelvey, B. (1982). *Organizational Systematics: Taxonomy, Classification, Evolution.* Berkeley, CA: University of California Press.

Metzias, S. J., & Glynn, M. A. (1993). The three faces of corporate renewal: Institution, revolution, and evolution. *Strategic Management Journal, 14,* 77–101.

Miller, D., & Friesen, P. H. (1980a). Archetypes of organizational transition. *Administrative Science Quarterly, 25,* 268–99.

Miller, D., & Friesen, P. H. (1980b). Momentum and revolution in organizational adaption. *Academy of Management Journal, 22,* 591–614.

Miner, A. S. (1994). Seeking adaptive advantage: evolutionary theory and managerial action. In J. A. C. Baum & J. V. Singh (eds) *Evolutionary Dynamics of Organizations.* New York: Oxford University Press.

Monod, J. (1970). *Les Hasard et la Necessite.* Paris: Le Seuil.

Montgomery, C. (ed.) (1995). *Resource-based and Evolutionary Theories of the Firm: Towards a Synthesis.* London: Kluwer Academic Publishers.

Nelson, R. R. (1995). Recent evolutionary theorising about economic change. *Journal of Economic Literature, 33*, 48–90.

Nelson, R. R., & Winter, S. G. (1982). *An evolutionary theory of economic change.* Cambridge, MA: The Belknap Press of Harvard University Press.

Newell, A. & Simon, H. A. (1964). Information processing in computer and man. *American Scientist, 52(3)*, 281–300.

Noda, T. (1994). Intra-organizational strategy process and the evolution of intra-industry firm diversity: A comparative study of wireless communications business development in the Seven Bell regional holding companies. Doctoral Dissertation, Harvard University Graduate School of Business Administration.

Noda, T., & Bower, J. L. (1996). Strategy making as iterated processes of resource allocation. *Strategic Management Journal, 17*, Special Issue, 159–192.

Penrose, E. (1995). *The Theory of the Growth of the Firm.* New York: Oxford University Press.

Peteraf, M. A. (1993). The cornerstones of competitive advantage: A resource-based view. *Strategic Management Journal, 14*, 179–191.

Prahalad, C. K., & Hamel, G. (1990). The core competence of the corporation. *Harvard Business Review, 90(3)*, 79–91.

Reed, R., & DeFilippi, R. J. (1990). Causal ambiguity, barriers to imitation and sustainable competitive advantage. *Academy of Management Review 15*, No. (1), 88–102.

Richardson, G. P. (1991). *Feedback Thought in Social Science and System Theory.* Philadelphia, PA: University of Pennsylvania Press.

Richardson, G. P. (1995). Loop polarity, loop dominance, and the concept of dominant polarity. *System Dynamics Review, 11(1)*, 67–88.

Rubin, P. H. (1973). The expansion of the firm. *Journal of Political Economy, 81*, 936–949.

Rumelt, R. P. (1995). Inertia and transformation. In C. A. Montgomery (ed.), *Resource-Based and Evolutionary Theories of the Firm: Towards a Synthesis.* London: Kluwer Academic Publishers.

Schendel, D. E. (1994). Introduction to competitive organizational behavior: Towards an organizationally-based theory of competitive advantage. *Strategic Management Journal, 15* (Special Issue), 1–4.

Sanchez, R. (1997). Managing articulated knowledge in competence-based competition. In R. Sanchez & A. Heene (eds), *Strategic Learning and Knowledge Management.* Chichester: John Wiley & Sons.

Sanchez, R., & Heene, A. (1996). Competence-based strategic management: Concepts and issues for theory, research and practice. In *Competence-based Strategic Management* A. Heene & R. Sanchez (eds), Chichester: John Wiley & Sons.

Sanchez, R., & Heene, A. (1997a). Reinventing strategic management: New theory and practice for competence-based competition. *European Management Journal, 15(3)*, 303–317.

Sanchez, R., & Heene, A. (1997b). A competence perspective on strategic learning and knowledge management. In R. Sanchez & A. Heene (eds) *Strategic Learning and Knowledge Management.* Chichester: John Wiley & Sons.

Sanchez, R., Heene, A., & Thomas, H. (1996). Towards the theory and practice of competence-based competition. In R. Sanchez, A. Heene, & H. Thomas (eds), *Dynamics of competence-based competition: Theory and practice in the new strategic management.* Oxford: Elsevier Science.

Selznick, P. (1957). *Leadership in Administration: A Sociological Interpretation.* Harper & Row.

Senge, P. M. (1990). *The Fifth Discipline.* New York: Doubleday.

Simon, H. A. (1947). *Administrative Behavior: A Study of Decision-making Processes in Administrative Organization.* New York: Macmillan.

Simon, H. A. (1955). A behavioral model of rational choice. *The Quarterly Journal of Economics, 69*, 99–118.

Simon, H. A. (1985). *The Science of the Artificial.* Cambridge, MA: MIT Press.

Sterman, J. D. (1985). The growth of knowledge: Testing a theory of scientific revolution with a formal model. *Technological Forecasting and Social Change, 28(2)*, 93–122.

Teece, D. J., Pisano, G., & Shuen, A. (1990). Firm capabilities, resources and the concept of strategy. Working Paper, University of California at Berkeley.

Tversky, A., & Kahneman, D. (1986). Rational choice and the framing of decisions. *Journal of Business, 59*, S251–S278.

Van de Ven, A. H., & Poole, M. S. (1995). Explaining development and change in organizations. *Academy of Management Review, 20(3)*, 510–40.

Weick, K. E. (1970). *The Social Psychology of Organizing.* Reading, MA: Addison-Wesley.

Wernerfelt, B. (1984). A resource-based view of the firm. *Strategic Management Journal, 5,* 171–180.

Wernerfelt, B. (1989). From critical resources to corporate strategy. *Journal of General Management, 14(3)*, 4–12.

Winter, S. G. (1987). Knowledge and competence as strategic assets. In D. J. Teece (ed.), *The Competitive Challenge: Strategies for Industrial Innovation and Renewal.* Cambridge, MA: Ballinger Publishing Company.

Winter, S. G. (1994). Organizing for continuous improvements: Evolutionary theory meets the quality revolution. In J. A. C. Baum & J. V. Singh (eds) *Evolutionary Dynamics of Organizations.* New York: Oxford University Press.

Chapter 7

From Resources to Processes in Competence-Based Strategic Management

Philippe Lorino and Jean-Claude Tarondeau

Introduction

The field of strategic management has been influenced by theories which try to explain differences in firms' performances by the composition of their portfolios of resources. Although these theories exist in embryonic form in the works of Chamberlain (1933) and Penrose (1959), their development is relatively recent, beginning with the publication of Wernerfelt's well-known paper in 1984. Since this time, resource theories have been extended, modified, and refined in many ways, but have until recently generated little if any empirical work.

The lack of empirical research may be due to the characteristics of the concepts mobilized in these theories. The strategic resource concept has often been a "catch all" concept that includes human or physical assets, tacit or codified knowledge, scientific or empirical knowledge, and information. In this ensemble, however, it is often difficult to identify assets that can be characterized as "strategic," and to predict the effects of specific resources on the performance of a firm. In general, in resource-based research observation of a firm's successful performance leads to a search for strategic resources that could explain it. The scientific validity of such explanations for a firm's success is problematic to establish, however, because in dynamic environments, ex-post explanation of the strategic importance of some resources in the past does not enable one to infer the future strategic value of those resources. Furthermore, many resource-based explanations of past performance are simply tautological: some observed good performance is assumed to result from some specific assets a firm has and thus those assets explain the observed performance.

The lack of credible empirical work may also be due to certain postulates stemming from the concept of resource barriers developed by Wernerfelt (1984) and subsequently taken up by many authors in the resource-base stream of research. For a resource to be strategic, it must be rare and difficult to imitate or to replace. Tacit knowledge satisfies these conditions, for example, but the identification and observation of tacit knowledge is highly problematic. Such an intangible strategic asset is essentially unobservable, and thus the role it plays in value added or contribution to performance would be problematic to investigate.

Systems Perspectives on Resources, Capabilities, and Management Processes, pages 127–152.

Solutions to these conceptual problems must be found, so that the role of resources in strategy can be researched and explanations of performance based on resources can be verified. To overcome the shortcomings of resource-based theory, we develop the concept of *strategic process*,[1] in which resources of a firm are put into *action* and produce some specific *output* which brings value to external clients. We propose that this concept can serve as the basis for scientific analysis and observation of resource-based strategies. As we will show, processes are identifiable and observable, they can be rare and difficult to imitate or replace, and they create value more directly than the resources used in processes.

A case on Port Express illustrates our concept of strategic process and its application in both strategy research and practice.

A Critical Approach to Strategy Theories Based on Resources

During its existence, strategy has undergone substantial development in its concepts, definitions, and theoretical frameworks. Initially based on military strategies and principles of warfare, company strategy was first conceived as the art of doing battle on the field of competition. Strategy was designed to obtain an advantage over one or more competitors through maneuvers (confrontation, sharing, dissuasion, or avoiding the battle) and positioning (choice of terrain, timing, opponents, allies, and type and size of resources allocated to maneuvers). Strategic decisions depended on the types of competition between belligerent parties and on the type and quantity of resources that adversaries had at their disposal. The resources available to a firm could enable them to act quickly or to defer action, to strike hard at a given point or to increase the number of less-significant actions, to form alliances to increase available resources, to cooperate rather than fight, or to discourage action in order to avoid doing battle. In the 1990s, the dominant conception of strategy has shifted to the acquisition and control of resources that enable a firm to differentiate itself from its competitors, to innovate, or to have sufficient flexibility to adapt to environmental developments or to competitors' strategies. In both perspectives (position and movement *versus* resources), strategy is conceived as proactive and deliberate, a set of decisions or intentions which can be expressed and identified: "*A set of broad commitments made by a firm that defines and rationalizes its objectives and how it intends to pursue them*" (Nelson, 1991).

The Origin of Strategies Based on Resources and Competences

Resource-base theoreticians portray each firm as possessing a specific resource endowment which provides advantages in the implementation of certain strategies. By contrast, competition theoreticians represent all firms in a given industry (or in a strategic group) as homogeneous and subject to the same "structural factors" that in turn lead to similar

---

[1] We draw the reader's attention to the meaning of "strategic process" here: it does not particularly point to the process of building the strategy of the firm, but rather to any organized combination of activities which produces an output contributing to customer's value.

behavioral patterns. Resource theoreticians, however, regard industries as heterogeneous, since firms are characterized as consisting of specific combinations of resources. In this context, for a given firm developing a strategy means choosing a set of actions which acquire resources and best exploit the specific features of its resource endowment. Competition between firms in the industry takes place through the deployment of resources, but each firm is protected from competition to some extent through the idiosyncrasy of its resource portfolio and through its capacity to maintain this idiosyncrasy over time. Resource heterogeneity creates monopoly areas in which each firm can determine its behavioral patterns. According to this point of view, a firm should differentiate itself from its competitors to acquire freedom and mobility of action. In order to do this, it must strive to accumulate a resource portfolio which is valuable in the competitive context where the firm operates and which creates differentiation and makes competitive advantages sustainable. Many authors have previously stressed the importance of a firm's idiosyncratic resources in order to explain its performance level (Selznik, 1957; Chandler, 1962; Learned, Christensen, Andrews & Guth, 1969; Rumelt, 1974). But Penrose (1959) and Wernerfelt (1984) are generally considered to have started the current line of thinking that links a firm's performance to its resource portfolio.

A New Theory of the Firm?

Basing the study of the firm upon resources can be considered a new theory of the firm since it explains the existence and the boundaries of the firm without any reference to previous theories (Conner, 1991). However, although presented as a new theory of the firm, resource-based theory can only establish superiority over previous theories by providing better explanations of actual phenomena. We next consider whether this is the case. Strategy and firm theories based upon the heterogeneity of resource portfolios have numerous limits which reduce their potential for generating normative theory: (1) imprecision and (2) unobservability of the concepts of resources, (3) circular or tautological explanations of performance levels, and (4) value paradox. Let us consider each of these problems.

Imprecision in the Concept of Resources. Resources are commonly defined by listing the various factors that may contribute to the creation of value. For Wernerfelt, resources may be anything that is a source of competitive strengths or weaknesses of the firm. This definition does not bring much new light to the "strengths-weaknesses/opportunities-threats" model. Other proposed lists are not more illuminating. Barney (1991) places resources in three categories: physical capital resources (technologies, equipment), human capital resources (training, experience, judgment, intelligence of people), and organizational capital resources (structures, planning/control methods, coordination systems, informal relationships between groups). Although it is undeniable that each of these resource categories may influence the value created by the firm, none of them can claim such an influence by itself, independent of contributions from and interactions with the others (Sanchez & Heene, 1997c). Grant differentiates resources, which by themselves are rarely productive, from capacities, which are defined as a set of resources enabling an activity. "Whereas the resources are the source of a firm's capacities, its capacities are the main source of its competitive advantage" (Grant, 1991). Henderson & Cockburn, (1994) differentiate resources from "architectural competences," which are defined as capacities to integrate basic resources. More generally, Sanchez, Heene, and Thomas (1996) define competences as the ability of an organization to sustain coordinated deployments of resources. The distinction between resources and competences is essential in under-standing value creation and the achievement of competitive advantage. Value creation and competitive advantages can only be achieved by building competences in using resources.

The Unobservability of Strategic Resources. A fundamental axiom of resource-based theories is that the more a resource is protected by imitation barriers (i.e., it is not identi-fiable or observable), the more it can be a source of sustainable competitive advantage. "Due to its very construction, it is impossible to observe … a non-observable construct" (Godfrey & Hill, 1995). Since resources do not have any value independent of their use in a given context, they cannot be directly compared from one firm to another. Qualita-tive measures specific to each firm to portray the existence or non-existence of a resource or a capability can be imagined (Black & Boal, 1994), but no absolute measure of inten-sity or quantity is conceivable.

Circular or Tautological Explanations of Performance Levels. By working back up causality chains or by breaking down resources to basic elements of knowledge, there is a risk of breaking down the sources of competitive advantages ad infinitum and ultimately of being unable to draw any conclusion at all from such analyses (Collis, 1994). As Conner asks somewhat bluntly, how can we know why and when resources are strategic? "At some level, everything in the firm becomes a resource and hence resources lose explana-tory power" (Conner, 1991).

Value Paradox. Resources are strategic assets when they are inimitable, unobservable, and unavailable on a market. Tacit, intangible, or uncodified resources generally meet these criteria. But in order to extract its full potential value, a resource needs to be codified, deployed, and put into action in processes. Thus, there is a paradox of resource value, because a resource remains strategic (i.e., potentially valuable) only when it is not observed and imitated by competitors (Boisot, Griffiths & Moles, 1997).

Process-Based Strategic Management Theory

In order to overcome the aforementioned difficulties and limits of resource-based theories, rather than observing the stock of resources controlled by a firm at a given moment, we observe the value creating *processes* in which resources are brought into action. As we try to show theoretically and empirically, a focus on processes can overcome some of the logical difficulties and conceptual limits encountered in strategic analyses based on resources (Sanchez & Heene, 1997). The process concept involves:

- the way in which the value chain is organized and responds to competitive challenges;
- the actions in using resources that lead to capabilities, the framework in which organiza-tional learning takes place and a firm's competences develop;

- the socialization processes through which dispersed elements of knowledge, often possessed by individuals, are combined in collective operations to create competences of an organization.

Process, Value Creation, and Response to Competitive Challenges

Process in organizations has been defined and studied by many authors (Davenport & Short, 1990; Lorino, 1995a; ISO/DIS 8402). We adopt the following definition for our research:

> *A process is a set of coordinated activities combining and implementing resources and capabilities in order to produce an output which, directly or indirectly, creates value for an external client.*

Processes are thus the way a firm interacts with its environment. Confronted with threats or opportunities, a firm's responses necessarily take the form of action processes. To respond to a threat or to exploit an opportunity requires coordinated actions in using resources to implement a process for organizing, managing, and acting. In complex and tumultuous environments, where it is essential to anticipate and adapt quickly, firms increasingly pursue competitive advantages that require innovation or flexibility in cross-functional or cross-departmental processes. Processes ultimately determine expression of how an organization creates value through deployment and coordination of its resources (Sanchez, Heene, & Thomas, 1996).

To understand how the activity system of the firm produces responses to external demands, it is essential to analyze firms in terms of processes. "*When described as a bunch of processes, the activity system of the firm is viewed from the customer and external requirement perspective, based on the outputs and the fulfilled demands*" (Lorino, 1995). Processes respond to customer needs or, more generally, the requirements of the environment, as seen and assimilated by the firm. Processes organize the firm's activities according to its strategic logic of value creation, through "*... actions which are always local, but capable of producing a result which is globally viable and consistent*" (Martinet, 1993).

The vision of the firm as a set of processes is not new. It is in a basic sense the practical implementation of the value chain concept (Porter, 1986). The process-based approach is also central to modern management theories like "reengineering" (Hammer & Champy, 1993), continuous improvement (Imaï, 1989), and total quality management (Hurdiburg, 1993).

Process as the Visible and Observable Demonstration of Competence

Resources and Capabilities. As it is used by resource theoreticians, the resource concept has a fundamental conceptual imprecision, because it groups together two entities that are quite different. Our focus on processes helps to clarify the essential difference in these two entities. A process uses two types of inputs:

- *Resources*, in the sense of economic "factors" of the production function, which may be subject to transactions as described by the transaction-based economic theories (Williamson, 1986);
- *Capabilities*, which cannot be directly exchanged and thus are not subject to transactions (it is not sufficient for a firm to purchase an efficient machine or even to recruit skilled personnel to acquire the corresponding capability and to create a competence).

Some resource theoreticians have indirectly recognized this important distinction between capabilities and resources, without necessarily using these terms, when they differentiate between resources which cannot be sources of sustainable competitive advantages, because they can be imitated, are not path-dependent, are static, can be more or less inferred from the context, and are transferable. For this type of entity, we will retain the term "resource" because it is quite similar to the concept of "resource" in economic theory.

Resources that can be sources of sustainable competitive advantages, since they cannot be directly imitated, are based upon specific experience and background, and are complex, context-dependent, and permanently changing. In our conceptual framework, capabilities have these properties.

Competence has been defined as the ability to combine resources in order to implement an activity or a given action process:

> *"Competence is not a state of a person or a given knowledge which one owns. It is not reduced either to knowledge or to know-how. There is no competence except competence in action. Competence does not reside in resources (knowledge, aptitudes ...) to be mobilized, but in the very mobilization of these resources. The competence concept refers to a dynamic reality, a process of action. Competence proves itself in action"* (Le Boterf, 1994).

This view of competence is consistent with the concept of competence in competence-based management research (Heene & Sanchez, 1997; Sanchez & Heene, 1997a), which defines competence as *"an ability to sustain the coordinated deployment of assets in a way that helps a firm to achieve its goals"* (Sanchez, Heene, & Thomas, 1996).

Thus, resource, competence, and capability may not be lumped together as in the resource-based view. It is not sufficient to have resources in order to be able to implement a process. Capability based on experience must be combined with resources to create processes that give rise to competences. Experiences, in turn, are anchored in informal know-how of individuals and in specific contexts. Due to their historical nature and their specific context, both competence and capability are necessarily pragmatic and contingent concepts (i.e., they exist only in specific situations and through specific actions). As they are inseparably linked to action, one cannot consider competence and capability as special types of resources. Competence and capability thus are conceptually distinct from resources because they arise from the actions which mobilize resources, rather than intrinsically residing in the resources that are mobilized by action.

Competence is the source of sustainable competitive advantages. In this sense, resources, whether material or immaterial "objects" (equipment, personnel, formal theoretical knowledge, training courses, or books), are *a priori* exchangeable, and do not generally have intrinsic properties which prohibit their transferability, quite unlike production factors in economic theory. Competences and capabilities, on the other hand, are based on experience and on a mixture of explicit and tacit knowledge. Competences and capabilities then arise from a given cultural and social context (e.g., the cleverness of people from the Jura Mountains of Switzerland in the field of micro-mechanics) that is difficult to reproduce elsewhere and at another time. The collective nature of competence and capability, including division of work, coordination, and organization, brings historical, social, and relational characteristics into play, making them more difficult to imitate than resources.

Resources and Processes. A process mobilizes various types of tangible and intangible entities: machines, databases, space, the working time of individuals, their ideas, their energy, and their efforts. These things become useful as resources only when they are mobilized by a process and brought into relationship with other resources in order to fulfill a specific function. Although resource theoreticians have proposed some criteria for defining strategic resources, a process view makes it clear that no resource can have a strategic character per se. What makes a resource strategic is its mobilization, actual or potential, in one or more processes that are strategically motivated. Empirically, therefore, it follows that a researcher trying to explain the performance of firms must initially observe processes rather than resources, as observation of resources alone cannot reveal anything about a firm's sustainable competitive advantages.

Processes and Organizational Learning

The concept of competence helps one to see the essential link between action (i.e., the concrete action processes through which the organizational activities of the firm are executed) and learning — a link that is absent from resource-based strategic theories. Competence is the result of action. What has been demonstrated at the individual level, particularly by Piaget (1947), becomes even more apparent at the group level: There is no competence or capability without organized action. An orchestra has to rehearse in order to acquire the necessary mastery of a piece of music. It is not sufficient for musicians merely to possess a musical score or even to practice parts of the score individually. The score is a resource, but successful interpretation requires coordinated group action, generated by a rehearsal (repetition) process and by the experience (past action) of the group.

Because processes lead to capabilities and competences, they are the frames wherein both incremental learning (continuous improvement) and breakthrough learning (innovation) take place. Processes enable tacit knowledge and capabilities to be disseminated through interactions with and observation of others and through imitation in action.

Informal forms of knowledge are made explicit and codified (Sanchez, 1997) through processes of communication between parties involved or interested in the same process. Processes also allow different kinds of knowledge to be combined, resulting in new forms of knowledge, and new forms of knowledge to be assimilated through implementation and repeated practice within processes.

Processes constitute the four major stages of Nonaka's organizational learning model: socialization, explanation, combination, and internalization (Nonaka, 1994). By providing framework for organizational learning, processes enable competences to be dynamic. Far from being "static" resources, capabilities and competences are realized through action processes that usually entail learning and that therefore transform capabilities and competences. From the process perspective, competence emerges from purposeful action, including a continuous progression of the firm's cognitive base.

The learning effects of processes build up organizational memory. Processes give rise to experimentation through action, exchange, and interaction. Repeated action sequences that are subsequently evaluated modify and perhaps restructure an organization's operational memory. "*Setting up routines represents the most important form of storage of operational knowledge specific to an organization*" (Nelson & Winter, 1982). Organizations store acquired experience in the conscious or unconscious implementation of routines and thereby preserve accumulated learning or transfer it to new situations (Cohen & Bacdayan, 1994). Routines become the memory of actions.

The Process-Driven Learning Organization

New forms of process-based learning are now emerging to fulfill new types of performance requirements: those for which "*lateral coordination needs are more important than general benefits generated by the specialization of functions and individuals*" (Tarondeau & Wright, 1995). Such forms of process-based learning arise in managing total quality, logistics, product development, and in the overall process of responding to market needs.

The process approach to describing organization is reflected in psychological action theories (Weick, 1991). "*By analyzing organizations in terms of activity systems, one avoids to look at knowledge as independent of actors, as an objective resource like all the others, which would be built independently of the action, a product of speech and interpersonal communication only*" (Blackler, 1993). Psychological action theories assert that knowledge is created in action (Piaget, 1947).

Pragmatic philosophers such as Charles S. Peirce (Peirce, 1932) and John Dewey (Dewey, 1938) also share this view. John Dewey opposed the dualistic view of classical Logic, in which truth is an attribute of the logical structure of reasoning, independent of context, and in which the validation of truth depends on the conformity of the results of reasoning to some observation of reality. This duality places reality on one side and knowledge on the other side, as two separate and autonomous entities. John Dewey believed on the contrary that knowledge can only originate from bringing specific contextual inquiries to practical solutions. Within this view, action and knowledge are intrinsically interconnected. Knowledge is procedural. It is the result of experience, and the starting point for new experience. Capability and competence building appear as an on-going, iterative interaction between doing and thinking.

Processes, Individual Knowledge, and Organizational Competence

What we have been describing is a systemic view of the nature of competence as an integration of theoretical knowledge, practical knowledge, and social and relational aptitudes. These basic cognitive resources are carried by individuals. But obviously, competence does not result from the simple juxtapositions of individual knowledge. Competence emerges only with the socially-organized implementation of a combination of cognitive resources, with division of labor, coordination mechanisms, interpersonal exchanges, and use of routines, undertaken in the framework of social processes of action. That is why process plays a double role of conversion and integration. Conversion transforms the simple juxtaposition of basic knowledge forms into an action-based competence arising from an organized *system* of knowledge. Through integration of cognitive resources, process "validates" knowledge and generates competence. Conversion also transforms individual action into a social-organizational basis for competence. By integrating individual actions, process gives competence a social foundation.

Research on Strategic Processes

Processes are the conceptually essential "unit of analysis" for competence-based management theories (Sanchez and Heene, 1997). Thus, the strategic processes of a firm must be identified, and the way they secure advantages for a firm must be analyzed.

Strategic Processes as Subjects of Research

As we have argued, by themselves resources cannot be strategic. Resources become strategically important only when they are used in processes and only in a specific context of action. Competences can therefore be indirectly observed in concrete ways through observation of an organization's systemic processes of action. Since processes and activities produce observable effects, the strategic significance of processes can be more feasibly researched than any resources and capabilities that they mobilize.

In order to identify strategic processes in an organization, it is necessary to define the limits or boundaries of a system studied and to observe the contributions each system makes through its processes. Analyzing an organization's value chain helps to identify strategically important processes. In identifying processes considered as strategic, process analysis and strategic analysis are necessarily intertwined. We may consider as strategic those processes which modify the firm's relation to its environment in ways that secure competitive advantages.

Observing processes, whether or not they are strategic, requires observing and describing activities or actions in a precise way. Describing a process may require the researcher to study both the process itself and the way it is represented by the actors (Johnson, 1992; Davenport, 1993; Hammer & Champy, 1993; Buckler, 1998). Research points to the importance of actors' interpretation in process analysis and collective learning (Weick, 1993; Lorino, 1995b, 2001).

To study the strategy-performance relationship, it is more useful to analyze strategies by observing processes than by observing structures or resources. A process directly generates performance whose value can be assessed by an observer outside the studied system, given a firm's strategic objectives. The causal link between resources and performance is usually ambiguous. The breakdown of an organization's resource-performance linkages into less complex, more direct links can reduce causal ambiguity (Mosakowski & McKelvey, 1997). The links between resources and processes (mobilization of resources by a process, influence of resources on the process) and the links between processes and strategic objectives (influence of processes on the firm's strategic performance) are more observable and analyzable than the indirect links between resources and performance. Trying to explain performance directly in terms of resources ignores the way resources must be deployed and coordinated, even though resources are also needed to explain performance (Lorino, 1995a).

Value Creation and Strategic Processes

Because processes combine tangible, codified resources and tacit resources which are not easily transmissible, and because they mobilize and generate specific competences and group learning, processes are even more idiosyncratic than any of the resources they combine. For a process to be a source of sustainable competitive advantage, two conditions must be satisfied.

First, strategic processes or sets of processes must have a substantial impact on some aspect of strategic performance. In other words, they must play an important definable role in taking advantage of an opportunity or warding off a threat. Such processes can then be said to be *critical*. Let us take the example of an industrial firm producing plastic parcels for the frozen food industries. Suppose this firm considers it could gain five percent market share by guaranteeing delivery in less than 48 hours. In fact, given the perishable nature of foods, frozen food companies cannot risk an interruption in the supply of packages, as this would oblige them to stop their automatic freezing equipment. Short delivery lead-time for plastic film therefore enables reducing their packaging inventories without risk of major disturbances in operations and thus of losses due to spoiled foodstuffs. In order to deliver in less than 48 hours, it is necessary for a packaging firm to reach high performance-levels in its logistics process (management of flows between orders and deliveries) and in its production process (transformation of materials and components into finished products). These two processes have major, direct, observable consequences for the delivery lead-time to the customer. In addition, the process for maintaining equipment has an indirect impact since equipment breakdowns could cause delivery delays. Three processes are therefore critical in successfully responding to this opportunity to gain market share by differentiating oneself from competitors through improved response times.

Second, strategic processes must be able to create value on a sustainable basis. For any competitive advantages obtained to be sustainable, the critical processes which generate advantages must not be replaceable by another set of processes accessible in an open market and must be difficult to imitate. Applying these criteria enable us to determine which critical processes are also *strategic*. For example, a process to develop new products might be a source of sustainable competitive advantages if it cannot be replaced by contracting with product engineering subcontractors who are also accessible to competitors. In order for a critical process to be strategic, it must be difficult to imitate. Mosakowski and McKelvey (1997) suggest using value and rarity of the outputs generated by processes to determine whether those processes are imitable and thus whether they are strategic or not. Therefore sustainable competitive advantage arises when a critical process (a process with substantial consequences for a firm's competitive position) mobilizes resources held or accessed by the company, and the output of this mobilization is difficult to replace and difficult to imitate. As we argued earlier, in most cases process-based competences are the source of strategic advantages rather than simple resources.

In the plastic packaging firm mentioned above, the logistics process mobilizes the following resources:

- A manufacturing resources planning (MRP) software. It is true that some software is better than others, but competitors can secure it without any difficulty;
- Market data. These data are supplied by professional data banks to which every firm can gain access;
- Packaging equipment and carrier services that are available on the open market.

Clearly, none of these market accessible resources can alone provide a sustainable competitive advantage. On the other hand, when using this fairly common portfolio of resources, a firm may be able to draw on its experience to integrate these resources into an effective value-adding logistics process which may be difficult to imitate. For instance, professional data banks are an accessible resource, but knowing which data to use in what way is not obvious and thus is difficult to imitate. Knowing which equipment, services, and software to access and how to combine them requires experience and is also difficult to imitate. It is the repetition, the experience, the know-how, the formal and informal mutual adjustments (whether conscious or unconscious), the individual and group behavioral dispositions, the repetitive scenarios absorbed into collective routines, the specific languages, and so on, which are collectively the source of the firm's "inimitable Just-in-Time" advantage.

Another possible source of sustainable competitive advantage is the competence acquired by a firm through processes involving partnerships with third-party logistics companies. These processes require integration of information systems via electronic mail and, above all, integration of organizations, communication languages, and operating methods, including coordination of scheduling procedures. Competitive advantage thus depends on a complex set of individual and group interactions developed throughout past history, and materialized in an action process that goes beyond the firm's boundaries to include partners.

The Analysis Model

Analysis consists of identifying in what ways a firm has sustainable competitive advantages and what processes are critical and contribute directly to those advantages. Sustainable competitive advantage can be established at three distinct levels of organizational action and process analysis: individual activities, processes consisting of organized sets of activities, and a firm's overall value chain as a set of coordinated processes. To perform this analysis, we will use the following definitions:

- An activity is a combination of elementary tasks (movements, speeches, signs) which provides some identifiable (tangible or intangible) output and requires identifiable skills (for instance, "machining," "negotiating a supplier's contract");
- A process is an organized set of activities which provides some identifiable output and requires more than one kind of skill (for instance, "producing," "developing new products," "preparing technical and commercial proposals to prospects");
- A value chain is a coordinated set of processes able to create value by providing a set of outputs responding to specific customer requirements and preferences.

We may now see that sustainable competitive advantage may arise in several ways, at three levels in a firm's processes.

(1) A sustainable competitive advantage may stem from a firm's advantage in a *specific key activity within a process* based on very local skills or capabilities.
    Example: A firm producing microprocessors has made substantial advances in using its photo-lithography machines and obtains yield rates substantially higher than those of its competitors. Such an advantage can have a major impact on the cost and quality position of the firm relative to competitors.
(2) Competitive advantage may stem from a firm's control of an entire process, including the general organization of the process and coordination between activities within the process.
    Example: Concurrent engineering methods involve all aspects of the product development process, encompassing a complex set of activities: training, information processing activities, technological development activities, prototype production. Effective coordination of these activities may enable an automobile group to develop its new products faster and at lower cost than its competitors, and thus to renew its range more frequently and at a lower cost.
(3) Finally, competitive advantage may result from a superior approach to designing the structure of processes in the firm's overall value chain, from the way distinct processes are connected to each other, and from achieving and maintaining control of the system as a whole.
    Example: The Japanese firm National Bicycle has reduced its production lead-times to less than two weeks and can now produce and sell made-to-order bicycles, whereas its competitors with longer production lead times are obliged to produce bicycles to inventory. National Bicycle completely integrates sales, distribution,

and manufacturing-to-order for its high-range bicycles. Thanks to its fast response and direct relation with customers, National Bicycle can now test new product designs in "real time" (Sanchez & Sudharshan, 1993) and can more quickly discover market changes and develop new versions of its basic lower-range products (Kotha, 1995).

Depending on whether the advantage resulting from a firm's system of processes is based on innovation and breakthrough (giving the firm exclusive control over a capability or a competence) or on accumulated experience and continuous improvement (giving the firm an advantage in a craft-capability), six types of sustainable competitive advantages can be identified.

Table 1: Sustainable Competitive Advantage Types.

	Differentiation based on acquired experience (continuous improvement)	**Differentiation based on innovation (breakthrough)**
advantage based on the performance of a specific activity in a process	Creation and maintaining of a local, distinctive capability (pertaining to a specific activity) through the accumulation of experience in this activity (local experience path).	Creation and maintaining of a local, distinctive competence (pertaining to a specific activity) through innovation (local experimentation program).
advantage based on the performance of a process	Creation and maintaining of an organization and integration capability (pertaining to the configuration of activities within a process), through the accumulation of experience (targeted organizational experience path).	Creation and maintaining of an activity organization and integration capability (pertaining to the configuration of several activities within a process) through innovation (targeted organizational experimentation program).
advantage based on the overall design and coordination of the process organization of the whole value chain	Creation and maintaining of methods for organizing, integrating, and coordinating processes in the overall configuration of the value chain, through the accumulation of experience (overall experience path).	Creation and maintaining of methods for organizing, integrating, and coordinating processes in the overall configuration of the value chain, through innovation (overall experimentation program).

The Port Express Case

Overview of the Company

A large French firm, which we shall call Port Express,[2] was founded in the 1960s. It expanded quickly by taking from French postal authorities the major part of the market for express transport of small parcels (pickup one day after 4:00 p.m. with delivery the next day before 7:00 a.m., 9:00 a.m., or 12 noon, depending on the type of service requested). At that time, the express transport of small parcels appeared to be an up-market product that the Post Office could not undertake. The major foreign express carriers — such as Fed Ex, UPS, and DHL — were barely present in the French market. Thus, for a long time, Port Express was able to establish a leading position in this type of service in France and was very profitable, since customers were ready to pay for reliability and speed.

Port Express was able to create advantage in this situation by setting up an efficient transportation network that was very reliable (less than one percent late deliveries and unexpected incidents). Moreover, its sales representatives were able to establish good relationships with customers based on trust. Today, Port Express has a turnover of two billion French francs and employs 2400 people, with consolidated profits of 160,000,000 French francs in 1996 and a high self-financing level.

The Structure of the Express Transport Value Chain in Port Express

Port Express has built up a transportation business in which the actual transport operations, whether interurban transport or local pickup and distribution, are completely subcontracted to truck carriers, which can be either firms or owner-operators. This enables Port Express to benefit from the low prices of French road haulage and to have considerable flexibility to respond to variations in its business situation. Increasing requirements for greater reliability, quality, and service nonetheless led Port Express to gradually transform its relation with subcontracting carriers from a pure market relationship based on the negotiation of prices into a partnership relationship in which various technical and administrative cooperation aspects play an important role. Thus Port-Express accesses and integrates resources which are not owned but rather are *firm-addressable* (Sanchez & Heene, 1997c).

Under this strategy, (Sivula *et al.*, 1997), Port Express has acquired valuable knowledge about both national road haulage (interurban links) and local haulage (pickup and delivery of parcels), and now plays a leading role in the ongoing transformation of this sector.

The main processes in the express transport value chain as practiced by Port Express are the following:

(1) Flow scheduling and optimization;
(2) Real-time monitoring of flows;

---

[2] The name of the company has been changed for confidentiality reasons.

(3) Partnership management on the national level;
(4) Partnership management on the local level;
(5) Processing of late deliveries and incidental situations;
(6) Interurban transportation of parcels;
(7) Package pickups;
(8) Package deliveries;
(9) Loading, unloading and sorting of parcels in branch-offices;
(10) Promotion and sale of services with firms;
(11) Invoicing and debt-collection;
(12) Definition, production, and supply to customers of customized economic and logistics information on their flows;
(13) Technical analyses for the design, standardization, and improvement of methods.

In this market, the key performance requirements are reliable delivery time and low cost. Five of the company's processes are considered especially critical, since they have a direct and decisive influence on the reliability of delivery time and on cost, and consequently have a decisive influence on value creation:

(1) Flow scheduling and optimization;
(2) Real-time monitoring of flows;
(3) Partnership management on the national level;
(4) Partnership management on the local level;
(5) Special processing for late deliveries and incidental situations.

In the overall processes of Port Express, how can the five processes in Table 2 be identified not just as critical, but as *strategic* in the firm's value chain? Why not processes six, seven, eight, and nine, which physically handle the parcels? Analysis suggests that process nine is fairly simple to perform, generates few errors, and is not seen as a major cost issue. The reliability and costs of processes six, seven, and eight (subcontracted transport) are actually mostly determined by processes two and three (partners' quality assurance and cost optimization) and by processes one, four, and five (planning and control of the transport network). Thus, the processes in Table 2 are "spanning" management processes that assure the coordination and performance of other more focused, critical activities. These five processes, which are the observable, assure the creation of value through several interrelated key capabilities:

- A thorough knowledge of the road haulage sector on the national level, acquired over years of negotiating and subcontracting, enabling a build up of the carriers' reliability and optimization of cost structure. (Port Express has gradually acquired a respected position as controller, auditor, technical advisor, and management assistant with many of its carrier partners);
- A thorough knowledge of the road haulage sector at the local level, based on the same types of capabilities as on the national level, but supported by local agencies;
- An ability to control a complex logistics network in real time, with support of electronic control devices (technical communication and localization tools such as mobile radio

Table 2: Strategic Processes and Objectives.

	Delivery lead-time reliability	Cost
planning and optimization of parcel flows	• rapid adaptation of transport capacities to demand • optimization and consolidation in delivery lead-times for haulage runs	• optimized cost-efficiency of the haulage runs
real-time monitoring of parcel flows	• immediate and reliable identification of positions (traceability) • capability for rapid redeployment of equipment and for adapting haulage runs (fast reaction times)	• reduction of late deliveries and the corresponding penalties
management of partnerships on the national level	• obtaining national carrier loyalty	• negotiation of transport prices
management of partnerships on the local level	• obtaining local carrier loyalty	• negotiation of transport prices
processing of late deliveries, emergencies and incidental situations	• limitation of the impact of incidents on delivery lead-times through rapid actions	• reduction of late deliveries and the corresponding penalties

communications, location determination via satellite, bar-code reading of parcels, etc.), real-time data processing and monitoring systems (development of a very efficient computerized system for real-time control of the logistics network), and adequate organization forms (emergency round-the-clock stand-by support, good communication channels, and a responsibility and accountability scheme which is clear and carefully followed by the relevant parties);

• A capability to model, plan, and control a complex logistics network, with the ability to simulate and adapt transport capacities to varying requirements, to make haulage-runs reliable and to cost optimize them, and to optimize the locations of branch offices. The experience acquired in this area has created some key assets: (1) a substantial database on haulage-run times, loading methods, routes, and traffic patterns, (2) methods for optimizing the branch offices network, and (3) the gradual improvement and "fine-tuning" of the network's computerized control model;

• A capability to rapidly mobilize mechanical and logistics assistance in case of problems such as accidents or breakdowns (breakdown assistance service, emergency stand-by equipment) particularly through a network of branch offices covering all of France and, increasingly, all of Europe, and through the development of efficient emergency procedures (driver training, workers' acceptance of heavy job schedules, quick response to unexpected situations, and organization of emergency round-the-clock stand-by support).

As a consequence of the above capabilities working together in a coordinated way, Port Express has achieved a highly reliable and cost-efficient system for the collection, transport, and delivery of goods. These five critical processes in this coordinated system can therefore be considered as strategic, since the experience acquired by Port Express enables the firm not only to implement these processes efficiently, but also to create sustainable competitive advantages in terms of reliability and cost. Port Express' competence as an organization thus results from this complex network of multiple activities, resources, and skills.

Response to New Strategic Data

After its significant initial successes, Port Express' profit margins in the express parcel transport market, while very substantial previously, began to decline under the effect of:

- Increasing availability of express parcel transport provided by other French companies, with intensifying price competition;
- Increasing competitive pressure of foreign firms which set up business in France, as well as subsidiaries of state-owned French companies such as the French Railways and the Post Office which launched the same kind of service at a lower price, although delivery reliability was not quite comparable to that of Port Express;
- General increase in the price sensitivity of customer firms, who became increasingly willing to trade lower cost for decreased reliability, thereby decreasing the strategic value of the high reliability of the Port Express network.

Because of these developments, Port Express' system became in some ways a too-high-quality infrastructure for the "standard" segment of the express transport market. As a result, the former strategic processes gradually ceased to be strategic, since the market value of offering high reliability began to decline, and since the express transport service became commonplace and virtually a commodity product. Reduced reliability, substantial volumes, and economies of scale became a new approach to the market that enabled certain operators to market a basic express transport service at a low price, against which Port Express' highly reliable system was less competitive. There remained a "top-range" market in which service quality remained a substantial differentiation factor, but a problem arose as to how to define and isolate this service from the run-of-the-mill fast-growth lower-price segment.

The New Port Express Strategy: A "Grafting" and "Daisy" Strategy

In response to these market developments, Port Express has adopted a new strategy based on the simultaneous pursuit of reductions in costs and a clear differentiation of its services.

The processes previously described as "strategic" are gradually ceasing to be strategic for the basic express transport mass market, but they may still be used within the new strategy. Port Express now tries to increase the value it can provide by developing services which are more sophisticated than mere transport, but that use efficient express transport as one major input. When integrated into expanded value-adding services, the five processes described in Table 2 could remain strategic and continue to provide competitive differentiation. In effect, by using existing processes to create value in new ways, Port Express is following a "process-based value-differentiation" approach to strategic differentiation.

To achieve this approach, it is necessary to identify and develop other processes which, when combined with the five previous strategic processes, will enable Port Express to design new value chains other than those of "commodity" express transport. Nonetheless, these new value chains must be based on the express transport know-how that Port Express has acquired. In effect, the previous strategic processes serve as a "trunk" on which the firm can graft new "branches." Those new processes have to do with traceability management, network engineering studies, inventory and logistics management, and handling exceptionally urgent deliveries. Information processing systems must be developed to support customization and increased differentiation of the service provided, in order to offer a more diversified and more sophisticated product range.

In order to slow down the commercial decline in its standard express transport, however, Port Express continues to control and reduce costs in its basic transport business. In that business, cost optimization has now become a major strategic issue. Processes that consume the greatest amount of resources must now receive more attention. Since major expenses are incurred by subcontracted transport and by in-house labor costs for sorting operations, cost control now is focused on productivity improvement efforts in the physical flow processes six to nine (interurban transportation, pickups and deliveries, loading, unloading, and sorting). These are fairly repetitive processes, rather similar to mass manufacturing, and cost reduction is now sought in a "Taylorian" approach by increasing standardization to obtain economies of scale (standardization of working methods and tools, development of management standards for times and costs, actual-standard variance control). As a secondary effect, the cost optimization of basic express transport activities will contribute to the cost-competitiveness and profitability of Port Express' new "value-adding" services.

In summary, Port Express' new strategy now must combine and coordinate increased customerization and differentiation in "new services" with increased standardization and repetitiveness in basic express transport. In order to make service differentiation and standardized logistics compatible, Port Express has developed a "daisy" strategy (see Figure 1): a "heart" made of standardized basic processes (mainly processes involving physical transport and handling), and "petals" made of differentiated services (some additional logistics services such as exceptional deliveries by taxis, specific labeling to meet customer requirements, inventory services, and above all information and logistics management services).

Implementation Policies

Port Express is endeavoring to capture new emerging markets, in which attributes such as "transport reliability," "parcel traceability," and "fast and reliable processing of logistics

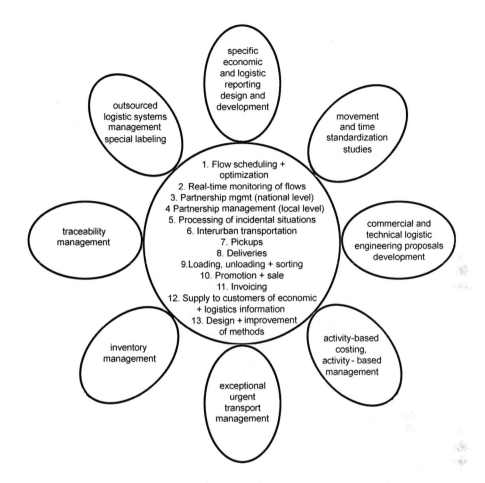

Figure 1: Port Express' Daisy Strategy for Integrating Standard and Customized Service Activities.

information" have strategic value. This new focus requires satisfying markets with more elaborate logistics needs than simple express transport. Newly targeted customers include:

- Industrial companies that want to subcontract (outsource) all of their logistics (stock control and logistics flow management). These customers are being served through a new subsidiary called Logistics Network Management;
- Industrial companies, mainly in professional data processing and electronics sectors, that want to subcontract their time-critical maintenance logistics (primarily urgent delivery of spare parts). These customers are being served through a subsidiary called Maintenance and Spare Parts Management Company;
- Industrial companies, mainly in the professional components sectors, that want to subcontract the design, implementation, and management of their logistics networks.

These customers are being served through the subsidiary Logistics Engineering Company;

- Industrial companies that want to outsource the management of logistics with high traceability requirements (for example, pharmaceuticals). The Economic Flows and Traceability subsidiary serves these customers.

However, combining processes "to be standardized" and processes "to be customized" raises some delicate issues:

- **Cultural issues.** It is necessary to develop a mass-manufacturing culture for basic logistics processes without losing a customized service culture in those areas where it is essential;
- **Technological issue.** How can the information system be designed to support the combination of customized and standard processes?
- **Organizational issues.** Given the contrast of cultures and operating methods required, Port Express decided to develop new services through subsidiaries, while keeping standardized processes for express transport in the parent company. Will this organizational scheme be the best approach to managing both emphases in the new strategy?
- **Management issues.** The combination of standardized and customized processes could lead to substantial distortions and cross-subsidies in the allocation of resources and costs, particularly in allocating volume-based costs (specific to standardized processes) and complexity-based costs (specific to customized processes). Traditionally, Port Express costs are allocated to orders and customers on the basis of volume (number of parcels). But a large part of logistic and economic information processing cost is driven by the number of transactions (inventory transactions, orders). Urgent parts deliveries, for example, require specific activities and costs (specific order management) which are driven by the number of urgent deliveries. The management cost of outsourced inventory is partly driven by the number of inventory locations and partly by the number of stocked references (types of articles). Customer administrative interface cost (customer account management, billing) is mostly driven by the number of customers and the number of orders. If the traditional volume-based cost management system were kept, complex customers with many different types of articles, numerous small orders, scattered inventory locations, or frequent urgencies would be subsidized by volume-oriented customers that move a large quantity of parcels in repetitive flows and generic configurations. Such cross-subsidies would give a distorted view of the costs related with different types of customers and market segments, and could lead Port Express to drop profitable large volume customers or to underprice complex customers. So it has become even more important for Port Express to implement activity and process-based management systems, particularly Activity Based Costing, that are more capable of capturing the specific costs of complexity and differentiation and of measuring the performance levels of the firm's various processes.

New Comparative Advantages, New Strategic Competences

In the segments where added value is more substantial, Port Express can create sustainable competitive advantage by leveraging the high reliability and cost performance of the transport network it has built up over the years (corresponding to the five prior strategic processes and competences), including the following type three advantages from Table 1:

- A thorough knowledge of national and local carriers, the working out of partnership relationships and technological integration within them (through Electronic Data Interchange and adoption of equipment designed and certified by Port Express). This has been achieved through long experience and is difficult to imitate and replace;
- A high level of process control achieved through an efficient data processing system for modeling, scheduling, and real-time monitoring of package flows. This system is based on long and difficult development and customization work, and on the accumulation of a vast information base which has been validated by experience;
- Efficient teams that have been trained to work quickly under emergency situations and under strict time constraints, and the implementation of early warning procedures to minimize emergencies.

Thanks to these process-based capabilities, Port Express has considerable subcontracting flexibility, parcel traceability, real-time control of the network, and rapid resolution of incidental situations. But Port Express managers are aware that leadership in the control of transport processes alone will not be sufficient to ensure a sustainable competitive advantage in more sophisticated logistics services. In these sectors, logistics information processing capability is decisive. Additionally, management information (knowledge and analysis of logistics costs, inventory values, the economic optimization of inventories and flows, Activity-Based Costs, and cost driver measurements) that is relatively unimportant in standard parcel transport becomes essential in more integrated and customized logistics services. Given the high integration level between logistics information (volumes, times, dates) and economic information (costs, inventory, and flow values), the substantial experience of Port Express in managing logistics information may develop into a competitive advantage in compiling, using, and providing economic information.

Port Express therefore decided to speed up development of sophisticated management information systems in order to fulfil the information and management requirements of its new markets. For instance, the firm decided to provide logistics customers with regular statistical information on their inventories flows and to meet specific information requirements such as informing the customer firm in real time of the situation of a given shipment.

Customer loyalty tends to be strong in these new services, since a customer's logistics information systems (inventory, order, delivery, and invoice management systems) become partially integrated with the information system of Port Express. Without becoming totally captive, it is nonetheless in a customer's best interest to avoid breaking off relations with Port Express, as this would incur significant switching costs to partly rebuild the logistics information system which they have outsourced to Port Express. It is therefore essential to be able to design commercial proposals that are adapted to the specific needs of major customers, that is, to supply logistics-engineering services for customers that until now had been reserved for Port Express' in-house needs.

These new orientations expand the web of interrelated processes that may be considered as strategic, including one previously not identified: Process 14 for the design of proposals to major customers for advanced logistics services (including a technical and economic analysis, project planning, and budget estimates). In addition, some processes previously considered as less important now become strategic. These include Process 12 for the production and supply to customers of customized economic and logistics information on their parcel flows, and Process 13 for the technical analyses of the design, standardization, and improvement of logistics work methods.

Finally, some innovations which are strictly "local" (relating to specific activities) may eventually develop into potential sources of sustainable competitive advantage, such as development of on-site automatic counting and recording systems for unloading and sorting activities. Additional synergetic effects between different processes also become important. For instance, synergy between real-time control of flows and managerial information is realized when the automatic counting of flows and parcel types provides volume, cost driver, and routing keys for "real-time" cost management.

The Learning System

As the foregoing analysis of Port Express illustrates, the process-based analysis of value chains is a powerful tool for defining the strategic challenges and opportunities that a firm faces (in this case, differentiation of services and cost reduction of transport network). But process analysis also helps to translate these challenges into specific in-house capabilities and precise actions needed to create and implement them.

Process analysis therefore enables one to orient and target priorities in an organization's collective learning effort, and to make its learning practical. Learning leads to standardization of methods for highly structured processes (transport and sorting) and development of capabilities in design, engineering, and flexible adaptation for less repetitive processes (customized proposals, network engineering, design of customized information reports). Learning methods also differ between these two types of processes, especially in their analysis and representation methods as recent research indicates (Lerch, 1998). Structured logistics processes lend themselves to a standard representation by functional activity combinations (activities defined by their outputs). Less structured and less repetitive engineering and customized information processes, on the other hand, lend themselves to representations by the type of capabilities that they mobilize and develop, by the general objectives they can pursue, and by their knowledge requirements (Lerch, 1998). In other words, a strict Taylorian approach to activity analysis will be more or less applicable according to the type of activity at issue.

Port Express' "daisy" strategy, once analyzed and described in terms of processes, enabled the firm to configure a consistent and apparently efficient learning system. The development of new logistics services provides volume for the Port Express basic transport network. A standard Taylor-type learning process (with a focus on volume, repetition, scale and learning curve effects, and improvement of standards) can then be applied to some processes that previously were addressed on a purely local level, which led to different organization designs for local branches, no standardization of sorting, loading, and unloading operations, and no time standards or controls. At the same time, developing sales of customized logistics services provides growing experience that improves Port Express' capabilities to analyze customer requirements, design and develop solutions, and "fine-tune" information system services. Customized services lead to expansion of the field of experience, development of new tools and methodologies, understanding of "how to investigate" procedural standardization, and specific configurations of standard elements. This form of learning leads to economies of scope by applying new knowledge and capabilities in serving a range of market needs.

Final Perspectives on the Port Express Case

The new Port Express subsidiaries have grown rapidly. To consolidate this growth, the firm's managers face a number of challenges. Management must ensure that the Activity-Based Costing and Management system (ABC/ABM) is continually adapted to quickly provide direct and clear links between the firm's new strategic orientations and its processes for day-to-day cost and revenue control. Managers must achieve the effective and synergistic combination of standardization and customization processes. Here the challenge is to continuously define and control the boundaries between the processes for each of these two approaches, because these boundaries will vary over time. Managers must also ensure the continuous increase in the competences of carrier partners, especially with respect to cost reduction through efficiency improvement and reliable, fast data capture through information systems. The firm must also seek to internationalize key processes at least on a European scale, since the French market alone is too limited to justify substantial investments in the development of new logistics services.

As we have seen, in the case of Port Express, the joint process-based modeling of strategic issues, management control systems (cost-revenue-profit), and operational management systems (inventory-flow-time) has supplied the firm with a shared tool for understanding the origins of good performance and for improving decision-making that targets key activities for focused learning.

Conclusions

In our theoretical analysis and our discussion of Port Express, we have proposed that process-based definition and analysis of the strategy of a firm clarifies its strategic intent and makes it more amenable to empirical and managerial observation. Strategic processes require the combination and coordination of a number of goal-oriented actions (Sanchez & Heene, 1996). These actions must be organized according to policies intended to modify and improve the firm's position in its environment and to act advantageously in its interactions with its environment.

Using strategic processes as the framework of analysis makes it possible to translate threats and opportunities a firm faces in its environment into activities to be carried out throughout the whole organization. Process analysis, in effect, provides a means to directly connect an organization's internal structures with the external challenges it must face. Strategic processes provide a useful framework for managing learning, both reactively and proactively. Thus, a process view of strategy is exceedingly important when a firm's environment is complex and dynamic. With a process orientation, strategy becomes a theory of action in an uncertain environment.

By repeatedly combining resources and capabilities in action, strategic processes are fields for experimenting by managers and for building organizational memory. Processes are the source of competence dynamics and ensure competence validation through experience. As contexts for experimenting and adding to memory, processes animate the learning of organizations.

Our process-based perspective on strategy builds on resource-base concepts, but provides important conceptual clarifications and further development, lending specifically to the important distinctions between resources, capabilities, and competences. Processes that create competences define the context of essential actions and specific relationships that make a resource "strategic." Processes mobilize and combine numerous resources. An organization's approach to practical implementation of resources (combination, coordination, synchronization, testing, and adaptation) makes each firm's processes firm-specific and thereby limits the risks of diffusion and imitation of its process-based knowledge and capabilities.

Finally processes are identifiable and observable — as to their results, the activities which comprise them, and inter-activity links. Process is thus an essential conceptual midground between resources and strategic performance. Adopting processes that operate on resources as the unit of empirical and managerial analysis is the means to reduce causal ambiguity in explaining the sources of firm performance (Sanchez & Heene, 1997c).

References

Amit, R., & Schoemaker, P. J. H (1993). Strategic assets and organizational rent. *Strategic Management Journal, 14(1)*, 33–47.

Barney, J. (1986). Types of competition and the theory of strategy: Toward an integrative framework. *Academy of Management Review, 11(4)*, 791–801.

Barney, J. (1991). Firm resources and sustained competitive advantage. *Journal of Management, 17(1)*, 99–121.

Black, J., & Boal, K. (1994). Strategic resources: Traits, configurations and paths to sustainable advantage. *Strategic Management Journal, 15*, 131–149.

Boisot, M., Griffiths, D., & Moles, V. (1997). The dilemma of competence: Differentiation versus integration in the pursuit of learning. In R. Sanchez & A. Heene (eds) *Strategic Learning and Knowledge Management*. Chichester: John Wiley & Sons.

Buckler, B. (1998). Practical steps towards a learning organization: Applying academic knowledge to improvement and innovation in business processes. *The Learning Organization*, Vol. 5 (No. 1), pp. 15–23.

Conner, K. E. (1991). A historical comparison of resource-based theory and five schools of thought within industrial economics: Do we have a new theory of the firm? *Journal of Management, 17(1)*, 121–155.

Davenport, T. H. (1993). *Process Innovation: Reengineering Work Through Information Technology*. Boston: Harvard Business School Press.

Davenport, T. H., & Short, J. E. (1990). The new industrial engineering: Information technology and business process redesign. *Sloan Management Review, 31(4)*, 11–28.

Dewey, J. (1938). *Logic: The Theory of Enquiry.* Henry Holt.

Dierickx, I., & Cool, K. (1989). Asset stock accumulation and sustainability of competitive advantage. *Management Science, 35(12),* 1504–1514.

Hammer, M., & Champy, J. (1993). *Reengineering the Corporation: A Manifesto for Business Revolution.* New York: Harper Business.

Heene, A., & Sanchez, R. (eds), (1997). *Competence-based Strategic Management.* Chichester: John Wiley and Sons.

Imaï, M. (1989). *Kaizen: la Clé de la Compétitivité Japonaise.* Paris: Éditions Eyrolles.

Johnson, H. T. (1992). *Relevance Regained.* New York: The Free Press.

Kotha, S. (1995). Mass customization: Implementing the emerging paradigm for competitive advantage. *Strategic Management Journal, 16,* 21–42.

Le Boterf, G. (1994). *De la Compétence, Essai sur un Attracteur Étrange.* Paris: Éditions d'Organisation.

Lerch. C. (1998). Une nouvelle représentation du contrôle organisationnel; le pilotage des processus. Management Science Doctoral Thesis, Université Louis Pasteur, Strasbourg.

Lorino, P. (1995a). Le déploiement de la valeur par les processus. *Revue Française de Gestion, 104,* 55–71.

Lorino, P. (1995b). *Comptes et Récits de la Performance.* Paris: Éditions d'Organisation.

Lorino, P. (2001). A pragmatic analysis of the role of management systems in organizational learning. In R. Sanchez (ed.) *Knowledge Management and Organizational Competence.* Oxford: Oxford University Press.

Lowendahl, B., & Haanes, K. (1997). The unit of activity: A new way to understand competence building and leveraging. In R. Sanchez and A. Heene (eds), *Strategic Learning and Knowledge Management.* Chichester: John Wiley and Sons.

Martinet, A. C. (1993). Stratégie et pensée complexe. *Revue Française de Gestion, 93,* 67.

Mosakowski, E., & McKelvey, B. (1997). Predicting rent generation in competence-based competition. In A. Heene & R. Sanchez (eds) *Competence-based Strategic Management.* Chichester: John Wiley & Sons.

Nelson, R. R. (1991). Why do firms differ, and how does it matter. *Strategic Management Journal, 12,* 61–75.

Nelson, R. R., & Winter, S. (1982). *An Evolutionary Theory of Economic Change.* Belknap Press.

Nonaka, I. (1994). A dynamic theory of organizational knowledge creation. *Organization Science, 5(1),* 14–38.

Peirce, C. S. (1932–1954). *Collected Papers of C.S. Peirce.* Boston: Harvard University Press.

Peteraf, M. A. (1993). The cornerstones of competitive advantage: A resource-based view. *Strategic Management Journal, 14(3),* 179–192.

Piaget, J. (1947). *La psychologie de L'intelligence.* Paris: Armand Colin.

Porter, M. (1986). *L'avantage Concurrentiel.* Paris: InterEditions.

Prahalad, C. K., & Hamel, G. (1990). The core competences of the corporation. *Harvard Business Review, 68(3),* 79–92.

Reed, R., & De Fillipi, R. J. (1990). Causal ambiguity, barriers to imitation and sustainable advantage. *Academy of Management Review, 15(1),* 88–103.

Sanchez, R. (1997). Managing articulated knowledge in competence-based competition. In R. Sanchez, & A. Heene (eds) *Strategic Learning and Knowledge Management.* Chichester: John Wiley & Sons.

Sanchez, R., & Heene, A. (eds) (1997a). *Strategic Learning and Knowledge Management.* Chichester: John Wiley and Sons.

Sanchez, R., & Heene, A. (1997b). A competence perspective on strategic learning and knowledge management. In R. Sanchez & A. Heene (eds) *Strategic Learning and Knowledge Management.* Chichester: John Wiley and Sons.

Sanchez, R., & Heene, A. (1997c). Competence-based strategic management: Concepts and issues for theory, research and practice. In A. Heene & R. Sanchez (eds), *Competence-based strategic management*. Chichester: John Wiley and Sons.

Sanchez, R., Heene, A., & Thomas, H. (eds) (1996). *Dynamics of Competence-based Competition*. Oxford: Elsevier Science.

Sanchez, R., & Sudharshan, D. (1993). Real-time market research: Learning by doing in the development of new products. *Marketing Intelligence and Planning, 11(7)*, 29–38.

Selznick, P. (1957). *Leadership in Administration*. New York: Harper & Row.

Sivula P., van den Bosch, F. A. J., & Elfring, T. (1997). Competence-building by incorporating clients into the development of a business service firm's knowledge base. In R. Sanchez & A. Heene (eds) *Strategic Learning and Knowledge Management*. Chichester: John Wiley and Sons.

Tarondeau, J. C., & Wright, R. W. (1995). La transversalité dans les organisations ou le contrôle par les processus. *Revue Française de Gestion, 104*, 112–121.

Weick, K. (1993). Organizational redesign as improvisation. In G. P. Huber & W. H. Glick (eds), *Organizational Change and Redesign*. Oxford: Oxford University Press.

Wernerfelt, B. (1984). A resource-based view of the firm. *Strategic Management Journal, 5(2)*, 171–181.

Williamson, O. (1986). *Economic Organization, Firms, Markets and Policy Control*. Brighton: Wheatsheaf Books.

Winter, S. G. (1987). Knowledge and competence as strategic assets. In D. J. Teece (ed.) *The Competitive Challenge: Strategies for Industrial Innovation and Renewal*. Cambridge, MA: Ballinger Publishing Company.

PART III

Systems Concepts and Models for Improving Management Decision Making

Chapter 8

Cognitive Complexity in Decision Making and Policy Formulation: A System Dynamics Perspective[1]

J. Michael Spector and Pål I. Davidsen

Introduction

Managing dynamic complexity is a significant challenge in every sector — private, public, academic, and industrial. A growing array of computer-based technologies, tools, and methods are now available to help managers learn to manage complexity and improve decision making. This discussion focuses on one such methodology — system dynamics — and its implementation in computer-based decision support systems and learning environments. Our primary concern here is to help achieve *consistent* success in designing effective system dynamics-based learning environments and decision support systems, and to establish reliable indicators of the effectiveness of such environments.

We first consider the nature of complexity from a cognitive perspective. In so doing, we identify characteristics of decision-making situations in domains that are good candidates for system dynamics-based support. Having identified those characteristics, we then apply established principles from cognitive science to suggest a general framework for the conceptualization of system dynamics-based support systems. Once that framework has been elaborated, we consider implications for the design of support environments using system dynamics models and simulations. We identify relevant cognitive theory, elaborate its relevance to learning about and decision making in complex and dynamic systems, and suggest relevant systems design principles.

Improving cognitive processes for managing complexity is a central concern in competence-based management. The discussion of competence in the competence-based management literature includes aspects that are clearly dynamic and complex (for example, Sanchez, Heene & Thomas, 1996). Competence domains often span across businesses, products, and markets, may persist and evolve through periods of change, usually involve organizational and collective learning, and deepen the understanding of a business

---

[1]This chapter is based on a presentation at the Fourth International Conference on Competence-Based Management, held at Oslo, Norway, 18–20 June, 1998. The authors thank the reviewers for many helpful improvements.

enterprise (Rumelt, 1994). In short, the competence-based perspective is centrally concerned with processes for managing the dynamic, systemic, cognitive, and holistic aspects of complex domains (Sanchez & Heene, 1997). In essence, if an organization is to develop competences, it must learn to manage complexity.

Our focus here on the cognitive aspects of complexity investigates how cognitive complexity might be better managed in a system dynamics-based learning environment. In the model of the firm as an open system, managers must devise a strategic logic for deploying and coordinating firm-specific and firm-addressable assets and capabilities in the pursuit of the firm's goals (Sanchez & Heene, 1997). This essential strategic management task is fundamentally a cognitive process, leading to the characterization of competence-based competition as "a contest between managerial cognitions" (Sanchez, Heene & Thomas, 1996) in setting goals, deciding deployments of resources, and designing processes for coordinating resource flows within the firm as a system. System dynamics can provide a powerful framework both for modelling and researching managerial cognitive processes and for investigating alternative approaches to managing the complexity of strategic decision making and policy formulation within firms.

Types and Sources of Complexity

To make progress in modeling complex domains, one must manage two types of issues: (1) recognizing — and focusing managerial attention on — complex issues, and (2) developing and testing techniques and tools to support human sensemaking activities in complex domains. The nature of complexity has been investigated and analyzed by biologists, computer scientists, educational researchers, linguists, management theorists, mathematicians, philosophers, physicists, psychologists, and system dynamicists. As Crutchfield (1992, 1993) and others suggest, investigations into complex systems have generated substantial literatures in several disciplines, but there remains ample opportunity to build on prior work.

The literature on complexity suggests at least three approaches to the analysis of complexity: (1) in terms of aspects of the *external* situation (e.g., the number of factors or variables that influence parts of a problem); or, (2) in terms of *internal* individual perceptions (e.g., the existence of perceived uncertainties or fuzziness in various problem states). Of course, these two perspectives are usually related. For example, as aspects of an external situation became more numerous, dynamic, or diverse, problem solving becomes increasingly difficult and challenging (see, for example, Crutchfield, 1992, 1993; Pylysyhn, 1984). (3) A third, *socially-situated* perspective places emphasis on societal or cultural concerns (see, for example, Merry, 1995).

Problem-solving complexity is a function of a number of factors, including the following:

- the number and diversity of input factors to a problem situation;
- the number and diversity of processes involved in solving the problem;
- the number and diversity of the output factors associated with the problem;
- the degree of specificity and certainty of inputs, processes, and outputs;
- the degree to which factors change and interact with each other;

- the level of expertise of human agents in the problem situation;
- the stability of relevant assumptions.

These and other elements of a theory of complexity have been elaborated in various places, including Pylyshyn (1984), Sahal (1976), and Simon (1992). Inevitably, both internal and external elements come into consideration, as suggested by the list above. Compatible with the second approach (internal emphasis) are efforts to examine how individuals construct representations of situations that would be considered complex with respect to one or more of the above dimensions. This is essentially how many cognitive psychologists view learning — namely, as the acquisition of expertise (see, for example, Ericsson & Smith, 1991). Using techniques such as cognitive mapping, for example, one can represent how experts view various problem situations. Such models can then be compared with models used by novices in representing the same situations. Differences in these representations can be identified and used to guide the construction of various learning support mechanisms and to assess learning progress.

Our approach to designing systems for supporting decision making and learning in complex domains draws on both external and internal perspectives. However, we emphasize internal cognitive aspects since these must be well understood in order to improve decision making and learning. The perspective of socially situated learning therefore provides a useful structural mediation between the external and internal perspectives (Collins, Brown & Newman, 1989; Vygotsky, 1978). As a consequence, our perspective on managing complexity, especially with regard to improving decision support and learning, builds on the *socially-situated* perspective.

A Cognitive Orientation

Within the cognitive perspective, an individual human can be thought of as an information processor, with internal information processing mechanisms (Resnick, 1989; Tennyson, 1994). In order for a human information processor to operate efficiently and effectively, inputs to his or her processing must be as noise-free and unambiguous as possible. The task of filtering inputs to achieve efficient information processing can be viewed as a complexity reduction task. How and to what degree complexity can and should be reduced depends partly on the perceptual and cognitive mechanisms available to problem solvers and decision makers, and partly on cultural and social support mechanisms in the environment.

In order to receive and process a large variety of impressions, our perceptual mechanisms must generate a corresponding variety of internal signals. To comprehend and order a large variety of impressions, we must internally generate a variety of initial representations and then perform various filtering and categorization tasks. In order to understand and control a system (like an organization) that exhibits a rich variety of behaviors, we must generate a correspondingly rich variety of internal representations that can later be associated with appropriate actions. Matching levels of external and internal variety in this way is the essence of Ashby's Law of Requisite Variety (Ashby, 1956).

The cognitive challenge in processing information, however, is not just to meet variety with variety, although an important part of training for complex environments certainly involves exposure to a rich variety of situations. The more difficult challenge is to arrive at an *appropriate* response for a particular situation or challenge. A simple analytic approach identifies essential aspects and characteristics of a problem and then searches for a one-to-one mapping to a possible response or solution. If a uniquely effective one-to-one mapping is found, the response may be considered a good match for the problem or challenge at hand. In solving some complex problems, such an analytic approach may prove inadequate for finding a good match. A significant benefit of the analytic approach, however, is to generate initial relevant considerations and identify important aspects of acceptable solutions. Other aspects and considerations, however, may well emerge only as alternatives are explored.

A "perfect match" between situation and response may not always be obtainable. A "perfect match" may not be obtainable because of intrinsic characteristics of the problem, or because of our limited mental and physical response span and rate, or because of other resource constraints, such as time. Due to our limited information processing capacity, we often "cluster" variety to form categories of entities and events. Each cluster can then be matched so that information variety is reduced to the variety exhibited between and within clusters. Clustering depends on filtering techniques that allow us to concentrate on significant signals and ideas and to ignore residual variety. This kind of cognitive clustering and focusing can improve learning and decision making under conditions of complexity. In so doing, we apply a "metacognitive" strategy that combines responses to limit variety contexts and create a general capability to respond within a larger domain. Such "chunking" is a natural human capability and can be improved with coaching and practice (Ericsson & Smith, 1991). With improved clustering and filtering capabilities, humans may benefit by developing "combining" or matching relationships in many information intensive domains.

A combination of clustering and combinatorial techniques is often applied in many computer-based solutions to complex problems, beginning with early work in applying artificial intelligence to chess (Ericsson & Smith, 1991). A simple example is the clustering of attributes along a set of dimensions. Such a clustering allows us to generate a high variety of attribute combinations by sampling from the relatively low variety of attributes along each axis. Modern evolutionary algorithms are examples of this mode of abstraction (Biethahn & Nissen, 1995).

In many complex problems, the various sources of variety do not act completely independently. The interdependencies between sets of sources of variety constitute the structure that underlies complexity. Acting together, sources and structure constitute a *system*. It is the interactions of the sources of variety within a structure — especially within a structure that may itself change over time — that present particularly challenging and complex problems for decision makers.

An example may serve to bring together these preliminary remarks about complexity and the need for cognitive support in decision making under complexity. Consider a large project, consisting of perhaps fifty persons working on several hundred tasks over a period of a few years. The manager of such a project is likely to be confronted with many complex decisions, including allocating expertise and other resources, maintaining quality and motivation, and delivering products within appropriate time and budget constraints. The cognitive act of describing the manager's tasks as we have just done illustrates one kind of clustering. This might help to simplify a manager's job, but for a moment, let us think in the opposite direction. What are some of the sources of variety that generate complexity in such situations? There are, for example, a variety of employees with various backgrounds, interests, experience, etc. Simply keeping these people focused on a task and motivated may require considerable skill. Now add the fact that some decisions will have effects on employees' performance. Overtime may be required to stay on schedule, or perhaps lay-offs may need to be made to stay within budget. Other projects may also be competing for the same expertise and funding, calling for decisions about prioritization in allocating resources. High-level corporate policy makers may want immediate indications of progress at the same time that a critical learning curve is just beginning, implying that gains in productivity may be slowed if resources are diverted from production to reporting about production.

Even more subtle than these sources of complexity may be the structure that links these variables within the project. Indeed, managers may not immediately perceive this environment or situation as comprising a structure. The very process of recognizing structural relationships and interdependencies is a serious cognitive challenge for project managers. It is tempting to make facile simplifying assumptions which would make the structure, and thereby the *system* underlying the project, more cognitively accessible. For example, a manager may consciously choose to ignore motivational concerns, reasoning that employees are adult professionals who are not subject to significant fluctuations in levels of motivation. If true, this assumption may make it easier to make decisions. If false, the consequences of those decisions might be suboptimal and surprising results.

When and Why System Dynamics Models are Appropriate

System dynamics is a methodology for modeling systems that have the following characteristics (Forrester, 1961; Sterman, 1994):

- internal feedback mechanisms;
- delays;
- non-linearities;
- uncertainties;
- change in one or more of these characteristics over time.

Many systems have these characteristics, which arise from the interactions among a variety of elements — what we have called the structure of a system. We now consider more closely the notion of structure and how structures can be modeled in decision support and learning environments.

Structure limits variety and thereby fundamentally acts to constitute order. Thus, the human task of responding to a variety of inputs becomes more manageable if we can understand the structure that underlies and limits variety. This is why modeling, by which we mean the identification and representation of the content and structure of systems, plays a fundamental role in the many cognitive activities in our lives. Through helping us to determine and define the structure of complex situations, computer-based models can help us create mental models of the many complex situations and challenges we face.

The recognition of structure defines a framework of relationships in which we can begin to make inferences about one part of a situation based upon our understanding of other parts. We may thereby not only attain greater understanding of a given situation, but also may transfer and utilize that understanding purposefully in other domains and across time. To enable such cognitive transfers, we need to recognize structures, to filter complexity by means of abstraction, to compare situations through pattern recognition and analogy, and to act to test our generalizations. In these processes, computer-based modeling can be a powerful aid.

Models, when built properly, represent a well-defined system. In effect, reality is represented in a form that reduces complexity in order to serve a particular purpose. When we validate a model through experience, we add support to the hypothesis that the model as an abstract representation serves its purpose to a satisfactory degree (Barlas, 1996). Such validation usually requires a large sample of observations of the system in question, and can lead to the recognition of general relationships that often constitute the fundamental structural elements of systems.

In understanding and managing systems that over time exhibit a variety of states (complex behavior), timing is often critical. If we perceive and represent a problem situation too slowly or generate a response too late, then the response may no longer be appropriate and may even be counterproductive. In a battlefield example, an opposing force may initially accumulate on one front quite slowly and be ignored. At some point, when a significant number of opposing forces are massed, their presence is noted as a problem and a response is seen as necessary. Responding with a sudden placement of a large army in opposition may only serve to initiate a battle which neither side really wanted.

On the other hand, when delays exist in dynamic systems, reactive responses can easily become exaggerated. For example, in a system for controlling the temperature of a large room, there is typically a delay between when a thermostat setting is made and when the room reaches the target temperature. If one does not understand the length of such delays, one may become frustrated with what is perceived as a lack of response and set the thermostat again, this time going too far in the desired direction because of the perceived lack of responsiveness. When the room becomes uncomfortably warm or cold, another setting is made, and again the delay may cause impatience and result in re-setting too far in the opposite direction. In this example, the reactive responses serve to create an oscillating and somewhat unstable situation. Computer-based decision support systems that recognize and incorporate response delays can help a decision maker to initiate responses of appropriate magnitude at the appropriate time. This is especially true when using networked systems that can take full advantage of the potential of distributed cognitive processes (Davidsen, 1996; Sterman, 1994).

Instead of a reactive approach to managing a situation, a proactive approach may be preferred, in which case some form of forecasting is required. Forecasting can only be used with predictable systems — that is, systems that exhibit recognizable patterns of behavior. There are two approaches to forecasting: behavior-oriented and structure-oriented. Behavior-oriented approaches are based upon recognition of patterns of behavior and the estimation of parameters that characterize the observable behavior exhibited by the system (Chatfield, 1989). Structure-oriented approaches require the identification of the system structure responsible for generating future behavior. The underlying assumption is that there is some continuity in the underlying structure, and that the structure for a system model can be identified and validated on the basis of historical data. This is not to say that the structure cannot change, but only that such changes will be insignificant over the historical forecasting period. A structure-oriented approach essentially generates a *theory* that *explains* the behavior of a system, rather than merely *describing* it (Barlas, 1996). Such a theoretical explanation is often a necessary foundation for the effective management and understanding of a dynamic system.

A variety of researchers have described these two types of approaches in surprisingly similar terms. Descriptive, behavior-based pattern recognition corresponds to "know-how" or practical understanding. Theoretical, structure-based pattern recognition corresponds to "know-why" or causal understanding (Sanchez, 1997; see also Anderson, 1983; Ryle, 1949; Tennyson, 1994).

The structure of a dynamic system may be quite stable, and yet it may still generate complexity so rich that it cannot be characterized as other than chaotic (Peitgen, Jürgens, & Saupe, 1992). Complex patterns of chaotic behaviors arise when an underlying structure contains non-linear relationships and feedback with delays. Such complex systems usually cannot be analyzed in closed mathematical form. However, computer models and simulations can be used to study the behavior of such complex systems. Thus, the power of computers helps us to formulate structural hypotheses and to study the variety of dynamic relationships in complex domains. McKelvey (1998) makes similar arguments for using computer models to support strategy development.

Decision Support Systems and Learning Environments

How might we use computer models most effectively to improve decision making and learning with regard to complex systems? We shall first distinguish decision support systems from learning environments and then show that the two types of environments pose different challenges for the designer of learning environments.

A decision support system tries to enhance human performance with regard to specific, complex, demanding tasks. Decision support systems are a kind of sophisticated job aid. The boundary between a simple job aid (e.g., calculators, checklists, etc.) and a decision support system is sometimes unclear, but the general notion is that a decision support system is intended to provide on-the-job support for a human confronted with a cognitively challenging decision. The kind of support provided can range from simple spreadsheet analysis to a simulation of the consequences of adopting a particular policy.

The primary challenge for the designer of a decision support system is to effectively reduce complexity as much as possible while still improving human performance in a targeted decision environment. The generic architecture for a decision support system is depicted in Figure 1. In decision support environments, the interface between the support system and the user of the system is a primary focus, because it is through the interface that the user inputs decision factors, gains access to information, and reaches a decision. Research in this area emphasizes the kinds of models and methods that work well in various decision making situations. (See the naturalistic decision making literature — e.g., Klein & Zsambok, 1991.)

A learning environment has a more complicated purpose than a decision support system. The goal of a learning environment is to foster a relatively permanent and stable change in beliefs about cause-effect relationships, in behavior, in attitude, or in ways of thinking in a particular domain. Such changes are commonly intended to persist long after exposure to the learning environment and to remain intact without further assistance from the learning support system.

The primary challenge for the designer of a learning environment is to foster these long term changes in beliefs, behavior, attitudes, and thinking. When a domain is complex, one strategy for improving learning within the domain is to "hide" some of the underlying complexity from learners early in their learning experiences so as not to overwhelm them with too many distracting details while they acquire a foundational conceptual framework for the domain. Figure 2 depicts a generic architecture for a learning environment that also recognizes the support one can derive from peers and tutors.

As learners progress and become more knowledgeable in a complex domain, it is important to progressively reveal complexity and to encourage learning about various aspects of complexity. Frequently, mastering a complex domain requires an ability to recreate complex models and to reason about their effects and behaviors in a wide variety of settings. Figure 3 depicts an architecture for a learning environment which provides access to and support for learning about the underlying structure and sources of complexities represented in the model.

Decision support systems aim to improve the efficacy of human decision making and are generally designed for continuing use. There is no expectation, however, that use of a decision

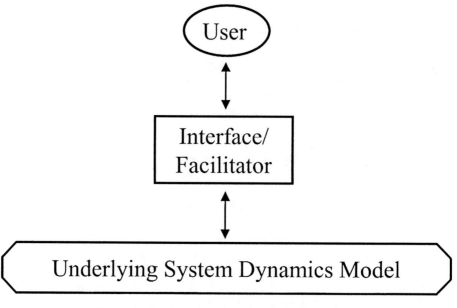

Figure 1: Decision Support System Architecture.

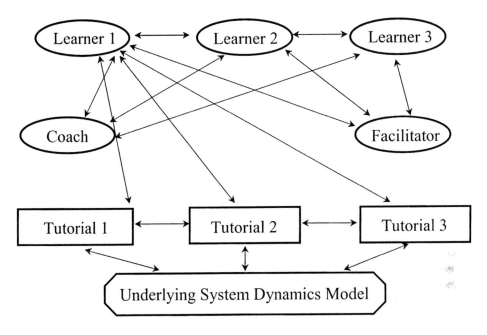

Figure 2: Black Box Architecture — no Access to the Underlying Model.

support system will lead to improved performance without the decision support system, although that may happen (Spector, Polson, & Muraida, 1993). The purpose of a learning environment, however, is to promote improved performance long after the user is no longer interacting with the system. Because this is a more serious challenge for designers, our remaining discussion focuses on the design of learning environments for complex learning environments. Many of these ideas can also be incorporated into the design of decision support systems, however, and it is often possible and desirable to develop a common kernel for a computer-based learning environment and a decision support system, in keeping with the general notions of object orientation and designing software components for reuse.

Implications for Design

The following discussion analyzes a project to plan and implement an interactive learning environment for instructional project management.[2] Analysis of our target domain

---

[2]Most of this section involves a description of the design implications for a learning environment. Much of what we say here applies as well to the design of a decision support system. Specifically, we advocate a strong cognitive orientation, especially in the needs assessment phase. It is possible to use an underlying system dynamics model, although high level understanding of and access to these models may be less necessary for decision support than it is for learning. In terms of Figure 3, a decision support system has no associated coaches, facilitators, or tutorials, and may not provide direct access to the underlying model. However, a common model can be used for both.

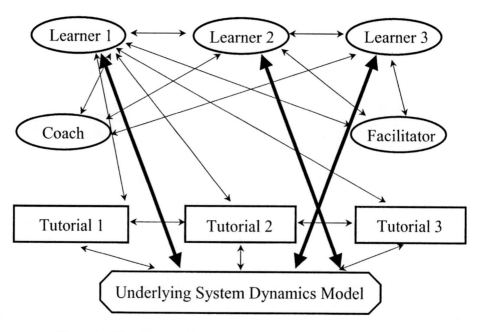

Figure 3: Glass Box Architecture — Access to the Underlying Model.

indicated that it was appropriate to use system dynamics modeling because instructional project management is a dynamic and complex process filled with uncertainties and feedback, not unlike (but somewhat more complex than) the domain of software project management. A pilot effort to build a model of the early phases of the instructional project was successful (Grimstad Group, 1995; Spector, 1996).

The analysis of the subject domain and target learners is part of well established instructional systems development practice (Tennyson, 1994) that occurs in the early phases of planning instruction. It involves an analysis of what the targeted learners are expected to do upon completion of the learning (that is, a needs assessment which might involve both job and task analysis). In addition, in planning a learning environment an analysis of what the learners might already know and be able to do or understand is critical. Finally, an analysis of the subject domain must identify key concepts, principles, procedures, and relationships. Most instructional system developers adopt a strong cognitive orientation in these analyses, especially when the domain is complex and the learning goals involve "deep" understanding of complexities in a domain (as opposed to simpler kinds of learning of facts, concepts, and straightforward procedures). The cognitive orientation in the analysis phase typically consists of a cognitive task analysis, which is distinct from a behavioral task analysis. A cognitive task analysis aims to understand how people are thinking when they perform complex tasks, whereas a behavioral analysis focuses on descriptions of externally observed aspects of tasks performed.

Dörner (1996) and others propose that it is important for learners to acquire an understanding of the structure of complex systems if the learning goal is to understand the behavior of such systems. In short, if learners are expected to reliably predict outcomes and make informed policy decisions, learners must acquire some reasonably accurate concept of relationships among key system variables and must develop an understanding of the most influential delays and feedback mechanisms in the system.

We have investigated successful uses of system dynamics-based learning environments, typically called "management flight simulators" (Sterman, 1988), in domains of similar complexity, such as software project management (Abdel-Hamid & Madnick, 1991). We found that many of the more successful simulators depended on an informed and insightful instructor to provide preliminary preparations and basic instruction prior to use of the simulator. In addition, learning effects, especially those involving transfer of learning, appeared highly dependent on follow-on discussion and exercise (cf., Sterman, 1994). These interactions were external to the computer-based learning environment. Most significant of all, we found almost a complete lack of measures of learning effectiveness.

These observations lead to the following critical insight: An interactive simulation is not the same thing as a learning environment, although many persons have and continue to confuse a simulator with a learning environment. For example, flight training in the United States Air Force is premised on the belief that building a physical flight simulator constitutes the creation of a learning environment. A simulator may be part of a learning environment, but for learning to occur, there must be more than simple user interaction with a simulation. Frequent and constructive feedback from a tutor, especially in the early learning stages, is also critical to learning (Collins, Brown, & Newman, 1989). Explicitly stated learning goals and mechanisms to facilitate progress towards those goals are also critical to learning (Gagné, 1985) — e.g., linkage to things already known, assessment of progress, guides to improving performance, etc.

We address these issues in the following ways. First, we use computer-based tutors that are *not* based in system dynamics for preliminary instruction (e.g., basic introduction to facts, concepts, relevant schema, etc.). This approach avoids the cognitive complexity inherent in a system dynamics-based simulator and complies with sound instructional design principles that emphasize: (1) using advance organizers to look ahead to more complex topics; (2) using graduated additions of complexity for teaching complex material; and (3) avoiding overloading the working memory of learners (Reigeluth, 1983; Spector, Polson, & Muraida, 1993; Sprio *et al.*, 1987). Second, we use learning effectiveness measures that are well established in cognitive science. Specifically, we use concept mapping and mental modeling techniques to establish reasonably robust models of expert thinking in a complex domain. We use the same techniques in pre- and post-test measures to determine effectiveness of the simulator. We assume, in effect, that learning is equivalent to acquisition of expertise (Ericsson & Smith, 1991).

While learning has also been characterized as becoming a participant in a recognized community (Safard, 1998), from the perspective of measuring progress in learning in and about complex phenomena, it is useful to adopt the expertise acquisition perspective. In many complex domains, it is possible to establish patterns of expert thinking (Jonassen *et al.*, 1993; Schvaneveldt *et al.*, 1985) using concept mapping. The simplest way to uncover a pattern of conceptual thinking is to ask subjects to indicate the relative nearness of paired concepts. A more sophisticated technique asks subjects to indicate the nature of the association as well as the nearness between pairs of concepts. If it happens that experts consistently group concepts in a certain way and novices group those concepts differently, then one way to assess progress towards acquisition of expertise is to determine whether a learner's concept maps are evolving towards an expert's pattern.

According to cognitive researchers (Ericsson & Smith, 1991; Spiro *et al.*, 1987), experts not only think differently from non-experts, but they also tend to think of a group of closely related concepts as a single intrinsically linked notion (i.e., they use the clustering or chunking of concepts we have discussed earlier). In addition, experts perform many actions automatically and also perceive actions in chunks. For example, to an expert technician, removing an engine from a vehicle may be perceived as a single action that is performed automatically, without hesitation or uncertainty. A less experienced person might regard that activity as a collection of steps and refer frequently to a technical manual or other job aid. When confronted with a novel problem or situation, experts most frequently spend a great deal of time analyzing aspects of the problem, searching their experience for a similar and relevant case (a partially constructed solution). By contrast, a novice will begin simple problem-solving procedures almost immediately, since there is little previous case experience to review for relevance.

It is possible to design a learning environment that takes into account these aspects of expertise, and to use these aspects of expertise to measure learning effectiveness. A causal loop diagram depicting how various parts of a complex system are related (nearness and quality of the relationship) can help less experienced learners link and cluster concepts in the same way that experts do. Because such diagrams are a result of a knowledge acquisition and structuring effort, they generally reflect expert thinking and are used in the creation of dynamic models. Giving learners access to such diagrams at appropriate points in learning environments provides support for an important form of acquisition of expertise. We refer to this as the design principle of *making the underlying model visible or transparent* to the learner. In other words, let the learner see how and why the model was designed as it was. Causal loop diagrams that depict how components are interrelated are thus a key learning support mechanism.

The next level of elaboration is to provide learners with a stock and flow diagram that shows whether components are variables, flows, or accumulators and also indicates exactly how the components are interrelated. A causal loop diagram can show that one component is causally related to another and that a change in the value of one component will tend to cause a change in the same direction in the value of another component. A stock and flow diagram can also indicate components that are variable flow rates, that are affected by various other parameters, and that cause increases or decreases in the accumulation of particular items according to a particular formula (which might be linear or non-linear). This additional representation is needed to capture more complex problems and to understand how a system as a whole functions.

The glass box architecture depicted in Figure 3 provides support for the acquisition of expertise by providing representations of expert thinking. It also provides opportunities for less experienced learners to gain problem-solving experience by working with partially constructed models to achieve specific goals, such as stopping a system from oscillating, finding a policy for managing a particular parameter to achieve a balance between certain components, and so on. The kind of access to the model provided to a learner depends on his or her learning progress and in general takes the form of a new causal loop diagram (to show a first level of elaboration) or a stock and flow diagram (to convey deeper levels of elaboration), as depicted in Figure 4.

Whether access is controlled by the learner or not also depends on a learner's experience. In general, as learners progress they should be given more control in learning environments, consistent with the principles of cognitive apprenticeship (Collins, Brown, & Newman, 1989). Consistent with both cognitive apprenticeship and cognitive flexibility (Collins, Brown, & Newman, 1989; Spiro *et al.*, 1987), learners should proceed from solving relatively simple, but realistically situated problems, to confronting more complex problems, with opportunities to formulate and test hypotheses about the complex domain and to construct new models and interpretations of the domain. These kinds of interactions are all possible with modern computer simulation tools and are consistent with the design architecture depicted in Figure 3.

It is important to provide learners with access to both types of explanatory frameworks depicted in Figure 4. Causal loop diagrams are useful to provide new learners with holistic and integrated causal views of a complex domain. The stock and flow diagrams provide more detailed support when learners are confronted with problem solving activities that involve interactions of multiple components. In advanced problem-solving settings, it is desirable to help learners generate and construct conceptual frameworks with variety and complexity comparable to the problem situation. In these settings, the stock and flow diagrams become a necessity. Both kinds of frameworks can be used to promote learner-learner and learner-tutor discussion and interaction.

Conclusions

We have argued that learning support in complex domains should take into account the types of complexity involved. A cognitive orientation in the task analysis phase of instructional design should provide insight into the kinds of explanatory support necessary for learners to begin to understand complex domains. Understanding how experts think about complex domains provides learning goals that can be operationalized in the form of concept maps and performance in complex problem-solving tasks.

Once one understands how experts think and work in complex domains, it is important also to realize that inexperienced learners cannot quickly or directly achieve such levels of performance or mastery of complexity. Rather a systematic approach to designing learning must be followed in these environments. First, one must provide learners with a sense of the scope of an entire complex domain to promote holistic understanding from the beginning. This can be accomplished with causal loop diagrams and perhaps also with associated scenarios and stories. Then, gradually introduce increasing levels of complexity and further forms of support for solving complex problems. Stock and flow diagrams are crucial in these stages, as is interaction with the simulation environment (e.g., letting learners experiment with various parameters, observe results, and analyze outcomes). Advanced learners may be challenged to reconstruct parts of a complex model. Finally, as is true in many complex domains, small group interactions can help to promote understanding, especially when supported by shared representations (i.e., causal loop and stock and flow diagrams).

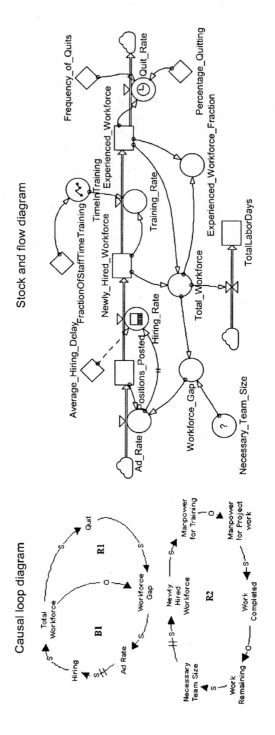

Figure 4: Causal Loop and Stock and Flow Diagrams.

We do not claim that this design approach will always be optimal. Long-term learning effectiveness studies must be conducted to determine whether this is the case, including implementing the same design approach in similar and eventually in less similar domains to ascertain whether ours is a truly generalizable approach.

What is clear, however, is that promoting learning and decision making through computer modeling is an important new approach to improving management processes. System dynamics can be used to improve both decision making in and learning about complex domains though a structured, "glass-box" approach that gradually makes complex models visible, accessible, and directly manipulatable by learners.

References

Anderson, J. (1983). *The Architecture of Cognition*. Cambridge, MA: Harvard University Press.

Ashby, W. R. (1956). *An Introduction to Cybernetics*. London: Chapman & Hall Ltd.

Biethahn, J., & Nissen, V. (eds) (1995). *Evolutionary Algorithms in Management Applications*. Berlin: Springer-Verlag.

Barlas, Y. (1996). Formal aspects of model validity and validation in system dynamics. *System Dynamics Review, 12(3)*, 183–210.

Chatfield, C. (1989). *The Analysis of Time Series* (4th ed.). London: Chapman & Hall.

Collins, A., Brown, J. S., & Newman, S. E. (1989). Cognitive apprenticeship: Teaching the crafts of reading, writing, and mathematics. In L. B. Resnick (ed.) *Knowing, Learning, and Instruction: Essays in Honor of Robert Glaser* (pp. 453–494). Hillsdale, NJ: Lawrence Erlbaum Associates.

Crutchfield, J. P. (1992). Knowledge and meaning: Chaos and complexity. In L. Lam and V. Naroditsky (eds), *Modeling Complex Phenomena* (pp. 66–101). Berlin: Springer.

Crutchfield, J. P. (1993). Observing complexity and the complexity of observation. In H. Armans-pacher (ed.) *Inside Versus Outside* (pp. 235–272). Berlin: Springer.

Davidsen, P. I. (1993). System dynamics as a platform for educational software production. In B. Z. Barta, J. Eccleston, & R. Hambusch (eds) *Computer Mediated Education of Information Technology Professionals and Advanced End-Users* (pp. 27–40). Amsterdam: North Holland.

Davidsen, P. I. (1994). The systems dynamics approach to computer-based management learning environments: Implications and their implementations in Powersim. In J. D. W. Morecroft & J. D. Sterman (eds) *Modeling for Learning Organizations* (pp. 301–316). Portland: Productivity Press.

Davidsen, P. I. (1996). Educational features of the system dynamics approach to modelling and simulation. *Journal of Structured Learning, 12(4)*, 269–290.

Dörner, D. (1996). *The Logic of Failure: Why Things Go Wrong and What We Can Do To Make Them Right* (R. Kimber & R. Kimber, Trans.). New York: Metropolitan Books. (Original work published in 1989.)

Ericsson, K. A., & J. Smith (eds) (1991). *Toward a General Theory of Expertise: Prospects and Limits*. New York: Cambridge University Press.

Forrester, J. W. (1961). *Industrial Dynamics*. Cambridge, MA: MIT Press.

Forrester, J. W. (1985). 'The' model versus a modeling 'process'. *System Dynamics Review, 1(1)*, 133–134.

Forrester, J. W. (1992). Policies, decision, and information sources for modeling. *European Journal of Operational Research, 59(1)*, 42–63.

Gagné, R. M. (1985). *The Conditions of Learning* (4th ed.). New York: Holt, Rinehart, and Winston.

Goel, V., & Pirolli, P. (1989). Motivating the notion of generic design within information processing: The design space problem. *AI Magazine, 10(1)*, 18–36.

Gonzalez, J. J., & Davidsen, P. I. (1995). Integrating systems thinking and instructional science. In R. D. Tennyson (ed.), *Automating Instructional Design: Computer-Based Development and Delivery Tools*. Berlin: Springer-Verlag.

Gonzalez, J. J., & L. Vavik (1994). Experiences and prospects derived from the Norwegian R&D project in automation of instructional design. In R. D. Tennyson (ed.), *Automating Instructional Design, Development, and Delivery*. Berlin: Springer-Verlag.

Grimstad Group (1995a). In R. D. Tennyson (ed.), *Automating Instructional Design: Computer-Based Development and Delivery Tools*. Berlin: Springer-Verlag. [The Grimstad Group consists of P. I. Davidsen, J. J. Gonzalez, D. J. Muraida, J. M. Spector, & R. D. Tennyson.]

Grimstad Group (1995b). Using system dynamics to model courseware development: The project dynamics of complex problem solving. In K. M. George, J. H. Carrol, E. Deaton, D. Oppenheim, & J. Hightower (eds) *Proceedings of the 1995 ACM Symposium on Applied Computing*. New York: ACM Press.

Grimstad Group (1995c). Applying system dynamics to courseware development. *Computers in Human Behavior, 11(2)*, 325–339.

Hannafin, M. J., & Hooper, S. R. (1993). Learning principles. In M. Fleming, W. H. Levie (eds) *Instructional Message Design: Principles from the Behavioral and Cognitive Sciences* (2nd ed.). Englewood Cliffs, NJ: Educational Technology Publications.

Jonassen, D. H., Beissner, K., & Yacci, M. A. (1993). *Structural Knowledge: Techniques for Conveying, Assessing, and Acquiring Structural Knowledge*. Hillsdale, NJ: Lawrence Erlbaum Associates.

Klein, G. A., & Zsambok, C. E. (1991). Models of skilled decision making. In M. Galer, S. Harker, & J. Ziegler (eds) *Proceedings of the Human Factors Society 35th Annual Meeting* (pp. 1363–1366). San Francisco, CA: ACM Transactions on Information Systems.

Mandinach, E. B., & Cline, H. F. (1994). *Classroom Dynamics: Implementing a Technology-Based Learning Environment*. Hillsdale, NJ: Erlbaum.

McKelvey, B. (1998). Can strategy be better than acupuncture? A realistic/semantic conception of competence-based research, presented at the Fourth International Conference on Competence Based Management, Oslo, Norway.

Mellar, H., Bliss, J., Boohan, R., Ogborn, J., & Tompsett, C. (eds) (1994). *Learning with Artificial Worlds: Computer Based Modelling in the Curriculum*. London: Farmer Press.

Merry, U. (1995). *Coping with Uncertainty: Insights from New Sciences of Chaos, Self-Organization, and Complexity*. New York: Praeger.

Morecroft, J. D. W., & Sterman, J. D. (eds) (1994). *Modeling for Learning Organizations*. Portland: Productivity Press.

Peitgen, H.-O., Jürgens, H., & Saupe, D. (1992). *Chaos and Fractals. New Frontiers of Science*. New York: Springer-Verlag.

Pylyshyn, Z. W. (1984). *Computation and Cognition*. Cambridge, MA: MIT Press.

Reigeluth, C. M. (ed.) (1983). *Instructional-Design Theories and Models: An Overview of Their Current Status*. Hillsdale, NJ: Erlbaum.

Resnick, L. B. (ed.) (1989). *Knowing, Learning, and Instruction*. Hillsdale, NJ: Lawrence Erlbaum.

Richmond, B. (1993). Systems thinking: Critical thinking for the 1990s and beyond. *System Dynamics Review, 9(2)*, 113–134.

Rowland, G. (1992). What do instructional designers actually do? An initial investigation of expert practice. *Performance Improvement Quarterly, 5(2)*, 65–86.

Rumelt, R. P. (1994). Foreword. In G. Hamel & A. Heene (eds) *Competence-Based Competition* (xv–xix). New York: Wiley.

Ryle, G. (1949). *The Concept of Mind*. New York: Barnes and Noble.

Sahal, D. (1976). Elements of an emerging theory of complexity per se. *Cybernetica, 19*, 5–38.

Sanchez, R. (1997). Managing articulated knowledge in competence-based competition. In R. Sanchez & A. Heene (eds) *Strategic Learning and Knowledge Management*. Chichester: John Wiley & Sons.

Sanchez, R., & Heene, A. (eds) (1997). *Strategic Learning and Knowledge Management*. Chichester: John Wiley & Sons.

Sanchez, R., Heene, A., & Thomas, H. (eds) (1996). *Dynamics of Competence-Based Competition: Theory and Practice in the New Strategic Management*. Oxford: Elsevier Science.

Schvaneveldt, R. W., Durso, F. T., Goldsmith, T. E., Breen, T. J., Cooke, *et al.* (1985). Measuring the structure of expertise. *International Journal of Man-Machine Studies*, *23*, 699–728.

Senge, P. (1990). *The Fifth Discipline: The Art and Practice of the Learning Organization*. New York: Doubleday.

Sfard, A. (1998). On two metaphors for learning and the dangers of choosing just one. *Educational Research*, *27(2)*, 4–12.

Simon, H. A. (1982). *Models of Bounded Rationality*. Cambridge, MA: The MIT Press.

Simon, H. A. (1992). *Economics, Bounded Rationality and the Cognitive Revolution*. Brookfield, VT: Elgar.

Spector, J. M. (1994). Integrating instructional science, learning theory and technology. In R. D. Tennyson (ed.), *Automating Instructional Design, Development, and Delivery*. Berlin: Springer-Verlag.

Spector, J. M., Polson, M. C., & Muraida, D. J. (eds) (1993). *Automating Instructional Design: Concepts and Issues*. Englewood Cliffs, NJ: Educational Technology.

Spiro, R. J., Vispoel, W., Schmitz, J., Samarapungavan, A., & Boerger, A. (1987). Knowledge acquisition for application: Cognitive flexibility and transfer in complex content domains. In B. C. Britton (ed.) *Executive Control Processes* (pp. 177–200). Hillsdale, NJ: Lawrence Erlbaum Associates.

Sterman, J. D. (1988). *People Express Management Flight Simulator*. Cambridge, MA: Sloan School of Management.

Sterman, J. D. (1994). Learning in and about complex systems. *System Dynamics Review*, *10(2–3)*, 291–330.

Tennyson, R. D. (1994). Knowledge base for automated instructional system development. In R. D. Tennyson (ed.) *Automating Instructional Design, Development, and Delivery*. Berlin: Springer-Verlag.

Wallace, W. A. (ed.) (1994). *Ethics in Modeling*. Oxford: Pergamon.

Vygotsky, L. S. (1978), *Mind in Society*. Cambridge, MA: Harvard University Press.

Chapter 9

Managing Speed in Competence-Driven Strategic Renewal

Volker Mahnke and John Harald Aadne

Introduction

Competence-based strategic management holds that competence is at the heart of competitive success (Hamel, 1990; Hamel & Prahalad, 1994; Sanchez & Heene, 1996, 1997). As firms compete to build new competences, creating situations of high market uncertainty and changing technological trajectories (d'Aveni, 1994; Volberda, 1996), firms face the dual challenge of proactively building new competences while maintaining and leveraging existing competences in efforts to sustain competitive advantage (Oliver, 1990). To assure their survival, companies need not only to avoid competence rigidities (Leonard-Barton, 1992; Barnett, Greve & Park. 1994) and competence traps (Levitt & March, 1988; Levinthal & March, 1993), but also to master competence-driven strategic renewal. Firms seeking growth cannot advance without managing the "dynamic process of building, accessing, and leveraging competences" (Sanchez, Heene & Thomas, 1996) in the process of strategic renewal.

While research has yielded insights into conditions under which competences lead to competitive advantage (Barney, 1991; Peteraf, 1993), how to manage the process of competence-driven strategic renewal has scarcely been addressed so far. The process of strategic renewal requires initiating, preparing, and building competences, maintaining existing competences, and managing the interactions and transitions between existing and emerging ones.

Existing theories of strategic renewal (e.g., Hambrick & Mason, 1984; Pettigrew, 1985; Quinn, 1980; Tushman & Romanelli, 1985; Strebel, 1992; Huff, Huff & Thomas, 1992; Hamel, 1996) start out from different, partly implicit assumptions about the triggers of strategic renewal (reactive vs. proactive), participation (top management vs. wider participation), and process (incremental adjustment vs. revolution, punctuated change). Taken together, however, these theories suggest two mutually dependent and equally important dimensions of strategic renewal: (1) strategic renewal aims at bringing the organization back into a situation of freshness and vigor in strategic thinking, and (2) transforming strategic thinking into coordinated strategic action is essential for successful strategic renewal. In this chapter we will argue that the systems view within the competence perspective sheds new light on the process of managing strategic renewal. We submit that the integrative power of the competence perspective (Sanchez

Systems Perspectives on Resources, Capabilities, and Management Processes, pages 173–195.
ISBN: 0-08-043778-8

& Heene, 1996, 1997; Sanchez, 1997a) provides a solid foundation for research on strategic renewal that is based on explicitly stated and practically relevant assumptions. In our discussion, we put a particular emphasis on the role of speed and timing in competence-driven strategic renewal.

This discussion is divided into five major sections. First, we briefly outline our assumptions, which are firmly rooted in the competence perspective, and draw implications for understanding the context and process of strategic renewal. We also contrast the concept of speed from a traditional management perspective with the notion of speed from a competence perspective. Second, we present a model of competence-driven strategic renewal. Third, we describe managerial variables relating to the management of speed and timing and identify potential sources of breakdown in competence-driven strategic renewal. Fourth, we discuss trade-offs in the management of speed when managers try to speed up or slow down the process of change. Finally, we present implications for further research within the competence perspective, and suggest managerial implications.

Strategic Renewal Through the Competence Lens

The competence perspective is based on four cornerstones (Sanchez, Heene & Thomas, 1996). It advocates a (a) cognitive and (b) holistic perspective, assumes (c) dynamic competence-based competition, and (d) pictures a firm as an open and complex co-adaptive system. Here we outline on a general level the implications of the competence perspective for understanding and managing strategic renewal as well as speed and timing within this process.

Cognitive Perspective

Stressing a cognitive perspective means taking the bounded rationality and limited cognitive abilities of managers seriously. To the extent that managerial perceptions and cognition are limited (Simon, 1958), individual managers will be limited in their abilities to identify sources of sustainable competitive advantage (Sanchez, 1997a). Thus, the competence perspective calls for a focus on *collective cognitive processes* within organizations — i.e., a dynamic process of organizational sensemaking (Weick, 1995). Consequently, we suggest that the essence of strategy renewal is less a question of finding the "right" strategy, and more the organizational cognitive process of imagining and developing the company's world view and strategy. The world external to a firm is viewed as an output of this cognitive process rather than an input (Hurst, Rush & White, 1989; Daft & Weick, 1984; Weick, 1979). From this perspective, perceived strategic "realities" in organizations are developed through complex interactions between an organization's collective cognitive processes and perceived elements in its environment (Hurst, Rush & White, 1989), from which emerges what Penrose (1959) has called the firm's "opportunity set."

Holistic Perspective

To be capable of systemic change, any organization engaged in competence-driven stra-tegic renewal must consider the diverse interests of internal and external participants (Sanchez, Heene & Thomas, 1996). Strategic renewal may require inviting new internal and external stakeholders (Hamel, 1995) into the renewal process and engaging them in new strategic conversations (von Krogh & Roos, 1996). But not all potential participants are equally qualified, and so various voices may have different importance in the conver-sation. Furthermore, participants in this conversation may have different stakes in both the past and the future of the company. Thus, to holistically balance the interests of various participants, while engaging a sufficiently diverse set of voices, is a major challenge for firms interested in competence-driven strategic renewal.

Conditions of Internal and External Dynamics

The dynamics of competence-based competition impose at least two conditions on proc-esses of strategic renewal. First, the bases of competitive advantage are constantly eroding, because expectations, competences, and relationships in the market place are subject to learning and change. When the structure of competition changes, so do the relative advan-tages among firms that drive market evolution (Nelson & Winter, 1982). Second, not only does the external firm environment emerge from the dynamic interplay between market participants, but the dynamic complexities of the internal environments of firms (i.e., existing capabilities, coordination mechanisms, pools of skilled people and their interac-tions) create a dynamic structure which acts as an "enabling constraint" (Giddens, 1993) for perceiving and responding to the external environment. Thus, the competence perspec-tive sees competition not as a given external reality, but as an evolving cognitive structure, which is driven by multi-actor processes of attention, interpretation, and learning (Pfeffer & Salancik, 1978; Daft & Weick, 1984; Smircich & Stubbart, 1985; Gorman, Thomas, & Sanchez, 1996). As a consequence, the competence perspective reconciles the "inside-out" orientation advocated in the resource-based view (e.g., Grant, 1991) and the "outside-in" orientation of prior strategy research (Porter, 1985).

Strategic Renewal in Open and Complex Co-Adaptive Systems

Finally, picturing a firm as an open, complex, co-adaptive system highlights the depend-ency of the firm on a constant flow of external and internal resources as inputs into the firm's internal and external co-adaptive processes. While recognition of valuable external inputs (e.g., in the form of access to external competences, transactions for resources, means for sensing opportunities and threats) is a necessary condition for the dynamic co-adaptation of the firm, a firm's internal co-adaptive processes shape recognition of poten-tially valuable external inputs. Because managers are guided by their own mental models (Porac & Thomas, 1990; von Krogh, & Roos, 1994), competence-driven strategic renewal begins with identifying and building new competences through co-adaptive processes of participation, strategic conversation (Westley, 1990), shared interpretation of strategic variables (Floyd & Wooldridge, 1992), and sharing experiences (Weick, 1995). Maintaining existing competences while managing transitions between existing and emerging competences also calls for recognizing the company's past in the development of renewal strategies for the future.

Speed in Competence-Driven Strategic Renewal

Several studies have emphasized the importance of speed as a strategic weapon and as a source of competitive advantage (e.g., Bourgeois & Eisenhardt, 1988; Eisenhardt, 1989; Judge & Miller, 1991; Smith, Grimm, Chen & Gannon, 1989; Stalk, 1988; Brown & Karagozoglu, 1993; Page, 1993; Smith & Reinertsen, 1992). For example, Eisenhardt emphasizes that "… most managers have recognized that speed matters. A slow strategy is as ineffective as the wrong strategy. So, fast strategic decision making has emerged as a crucial competitive weapon" (Eisenhardt, 1990).

Empirical studies have shown that reducing a firm's response time to a competitor's action leads to improved performance (e.g., Smith, Grimm, Chen, & Gannon, 1989). Porter (1980) argued that being the first mover in the market place results in competitive advantage in several industries. Moreover, being able to move quickly may create important options for further strategic actions in the market place (Sanchez, 1993). Many researchers emphasize the importance of speeding up operations to create fast-mover advantages in the market place (Lieberman & Montgomery, 1988; Porter, 1980) to accelerate the pace of time-based competition (Page, 1993) and to respond to rapidly changing business environments (Stalk, 1993; Stalk & Hout, 1990).

From a competence perspective, the perceived "strategic realities" in an organization are developed through the complex interactions between an organization's managers' cognitive processes and elements in the environment (Hurst, Rush & White, 1989). Moreover, Sanchez and Heene (1996) argue that "managerial cognition and managers' approaches to coordinating are harder to change than stocks of intangible resources like knowledge, stocks of tangible resources like machines and buildings, or the firm's operations and products." Thus, in time sensitive competitive processes, managers face a challenge in improving the speed and timing of their collective cognitive processes. In this discussion we focus on managerial processes for representing time as managers learn how to manage their own cognitive processes (Sanchez & Heene, 1996).

Time, in the competence perspective, is subjective and interacts with other subjectively perceived features of reality through processes of differentially distributed attention (Cyert & March, 1963) and perceptions of issue importance and issue urgency among participants in the strategic renewal process (Dutton & Duncan, 1987). Speeding up organizational processes in many organizations may require a new conception of time that is more closely pegged to clock-time or calendar-time (Das, 1991). For long-term strategic thinking and imagining future opportunity horizons, conceptions of time and speed seem to be highly dependent on individual subjectivity and psychological perceptions of time (Das, 1991; Hurst, Rush & White, 1989). Empirical research indicates that top managers significantly differ in their future time perspectives, and that individual

differences in future orientations influence their approaches to conducting strategy processes (Das, 1986; Sawy, 1983). As a consequence, differences in psychological
conceptions of the future among managers can have a critical influence on the way they
try to manage strategic renewal.

   Although a slow strategy might be as ineffective as a wrong strategy, a fast strategy is
no guarantee of effectiveness. Achieving first-mover advantage requires more than fast
decisions. For strategic action to be effective and fast, companies usually need to be able to
initiate strategic renewal by building on the competence-base they already have.
Purposeful management of speed and timing in the process of competence-driven strategic
renewal is essential in making possible the speedy execution of a new strategy. The next
section proposes a cognitive model of competence-driven strategic renewal based on
speedy strategic decision making and execution.

A Model of Competence-Driven Strategic Renewal

The following model presents an extension of our previous work on strategic renewal
(Aadne, 1996; Aadne & Mahnke, 1996, 1997).[1] Our model defines strategic renewal as the
process that translates (1) *strategic imagination* into (2) new *coordinated strategic action*,
through (3) developing a *common ground* that facilitates the transformation of strategic
imagination into coordinated strategic action. In the terminology of the competence
perspective, our model concerns: (1) *maintaining competence,* which sustains coherent,
intentional, and coordinated asset deployments, and (2) *building competence,* which
involves qualitative changes in existing assets and coordination capabilities needed to
create new strategic options (Sanchez, Heene & Thomas, 1996). Both processes depend on
the careful and purposeful management of speed to avoid potential breakdowns in the
different sub-processes of strategic renewal. Figure 1 below illustrates the main aspects of
our model.

   If strategic renewal is the overall process that translates strategic imagination into new
coordinated strategic action through developing a common ground, we then need to understand each of these three essential sub-processes of strategic renewal. In short, while
strategic imagination aims at identifying and initiating new competence, developing
common grounds prepares the organization for new competence while maintaining
coherence (Teece *et al.,* 1994) and establishing linkages to existing competences.
Coordinating strategic renewal requires managing these two processes while building new
competences.

---

[1]This research is partly based on a twelve-month action research project on strategic renewal in a newspaper
group. The newspaper group had a dominant position in its market, but facing blurring industry barriers and
fierce competition, the newspaper group realized that its future competitiveness could be threatened. In this
respect, one important aspect was the development of electronic media. The project was focused on developing a strategy for electronic media and on enhancing the general conduct of strategy in the organization.
The newspaper group has about 1,600 employees. All quotes from managers presented in this article are
collected from interviews and meetings during and after the strategy process studied during the research
project.

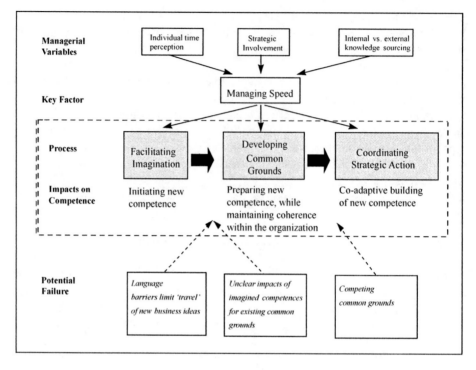

Figure 1: A Model of Competence-Driven Strategic Renewal.

Facilitating Strategic Imagination

Competence-driven strategic renewal involves the pursuit of new initiatives, like developing new product concepts, new markets, new technologies, or new processes (McGrath, MacMillan, & Venkataraman 1995). Strategic renewal therefore requires an ability and willingness to imagine and investigate a broad menu of potential competitive spaces. Developing new competitive strength depends on a company's ability to imagine products, markets, and opportunities that do not yet exist, and to see these possibilities before competitors see them (Hamel & Prahalad, 1991; Hurst, Rush, & White, 1989).

In companies, individuals and groups at several levels may produce ideas about the future. The vice president of development described the generation of ideas and beliefs in the Newspaper Group in the following way:

> "We can be very creative and innovative. We produce a lot of 'wild' ideas in this company. By wild, I mean good ideas, but also crazy and creative ideas. In general, we also have a high degree of openness towards new ideas. We have a fine-grained detector network making us very knowledgeable of new trends and new issues."

A company's opportunity horizon is not the responsibility of single individuals or the top management group alone, but depends on the collective imagination of the entire organization (Hamel & Prahalad 1991). A collective imagination involves many voices, at different organizational levels, with different knowledge and skills, taking part in idea generation and horizon scanning. A diversity of perspectives increases an organization's ability to create new knowledge (Nonaka & Takeuchi, 1995). Weick elaborates on this process in the following way: "The greater the variety of beliefs in a repertoire, the more fully should any situation be seen, the more solutions that should be identified, and the more likely it should be that someone knows a great deal about what is happening". Beliefs about possible future actions and opportunities can be characterized as purpose-based knowledge, or "know what" (Sanchez, 1997). Thus, strategic imagination is generating new ideas about what a firm could do, creating awareness of possible futures, and developing new approaches to markets. All three aspects are essential for imagining new competences an organization could build (Sanchez, Heene & Thomas, 1996).

Developing Common Ground

Collective organizational imagination can be seen as a repository of beliefs about opportunities, about possible problems to solve, and about possible solutions (Cohen, March & Olsen, 1972). Thus, imagination represents aspirations (Cyert & March, 1963) and possible futures, but is by nature more abstract than the direction and commitment needed to undertake concrete strategic action. To initiate timely actions, coherence in setting strategic priorities, goals, and strategies is essential (e.g. Floyd & Wooldridge, 1992; Dess & Priem, 1995). This implies a shift at some point in the strategic renewal process from imagining different possible futures to a focus on identifying an organization's most desirable and feasible futures. When the strategic renewal process shifts from efforts to imagine all possible futures to identifying specific futures the organization will prepare for, one approach to narrowing the variety of futures generated in the imagination phase is a process of *developing common ground* (Weisbord 1992; Weisbord and Janoff 1995). In our case study the sales and marketing director and project chairman emphasized the importance of establishing a common ground:

> "We need a common platform for our electronic media investments in attention, time and money. We've many opportunities and beliefs about electronic media. Possible partners also regularly take contact with us regarding everything from opinions to projects. You can say that our opportunity set is probably larger than most of our competitors. However, we've limited resources, and the uncertainty about the electronic media market is still very high. Thus, we need to develop a common platform and a strategy to extend and maintain our present strengths, and to develop the competences required for also leading in the future."

Through the process of developing common ground both the corporate direction and a framework for strategy-making in the organization are established (Aadne & Mahnke, 1997).

Creating common ground consists of at least three parallel activities: (1) sharing language and experience, (2) strategic agenda building, and (3) aligning past, present and future.

Sharing Language and Experience. Several authors have emphasized the importance of having a shared code for internally representing an organization's experience and knowledge (e.g., Kogut & Zander, 1992; Nonaka & Takeuchi, 1995). For example, a firm may develop its own vocabulary for describing opportunities and threats. Achieving collective action requires developing a shared vocabulary to facilitate sharing experiences (Czarniawska-Joerges, 1992). Storytelling is often the preferred form of spreading experience and developing shared knowledge within organizations (Boje, 1991). Storytelling about past strategies, competence developments, and prior strategic renewal figures prominently in the renewal process of organizations (Barry & Elmes, 1997). Thus, as a central part of the process of establishing a common ground for strategic change, people in an organization must intensively work on surfacing and sharing assumptions, commitments, expectations, experiences, and imaginations (Aadne & Mahnke, 1997). The sharing process, when successful, provides a group of people with a common platform for discussion, evaluation, and decision.

Building a Strategic Agenda. Through the process of sharing, awareness and understanding are developed, and some commonly held anchor points for future action are identified. Imagination is the starting point in the search for shared ideas about future competitive spaces, their characteristics, and strategies required. These elements are analyzed and evaluated, and a set of strategic issues is selected as constituting the strategic agenda (Dutton, Fahey & Narayanan, 1983). Developing common ground involves a collective search process directed towards putting together an overall picture of an organization's situation, identifying new directions, and discovering possibilities for synergy between new and old common grounds. As such, this process goes beyond mere formulation of a mission statement, goals, or strategies. Through the process of developing common ground both the direction and the framework for strategy-making in the organization are established (Aadne & Mahnke, 1997).

Aligning Past, Present and Future. History is a valuable asset in strategic renewal. Competences developed and deployed in the past may be sources of insights into potential sources of future success and failure (Brown & Duguid, 1991). An emerging strategic agenda and the new common ground it is based on will generally have important linkages to an organization's previous common grounds, strategic agendas, strategic actions, and competences. However, interpretations and wisdom that have developed over time may not always be accurate (Walsh & Ungson, 1991) or appropriate to support future action. Thus, another activity of the common ground process is to move the relevant past into the forefront and promote interpretations and re-interpretations that support an emergent strategic agenda and possible future actions. Cautious appreciation and re-interpretation of the past can enhance a perspective on the present decision situation (Walsh & Ungson, 1991), and facilitate organizational understanding of what is similar and different from previously communicated agendas and actions taken. In creating common ground, an organization prepares for new competences by selectively integrating prior beliefs, tasks, and intentions related to the futures perceived as most desirable. Creating a common ground that defines a shared view of the relationships between past, present and future competences prepares an organization for a unified, coherent process of competence-building.

In the common ground process, an organization prepares for new competences by integrating beliefs, tasks, and intentions related to its most desirable and feasible futures. In the process of sharing ideas, beliefs, and images, a collective understanding of essential new competences and the future value of current competences is developed as the new strategic agenda emerges. Here, the fundamental idea is to develop relationships between competence deployment in the past, competence maintenance in the present, and competence development for the future. To achieve this, storytelling — the sensemaking currency in human relationships — becomes a valuable instrument (Boje, 1991; Barry & Elmes, 1997). However, achieving coherence in future asset deployments requires more than just storytelling about the past. The development and deployment of competence in the past has to be carefully examined and re-interpreted to develop a collective awareness and understanding about how the past is relevant for building new competences and maintaining present competences.

Coordinating Strategic Action

Coherent strategic action does not take place automatically, and developing common ground in and of itself does not produce coherent strategic action (Johnson, 1992; Mintzberg & Waters, 1985). Value creation in firms does not result from resource endowments themselves; rather, new competence results from coordinated actions that lead to new deployments of resources (Løwendahl & Haanes, 1997). Coordinating strategic action is a continuous challenge that goes beyond "one time planning." It is an ongoing co-adaptive process. We suggest that coordinating strategic action includes two distinct activities: (1) developing a coherent project portfolio, and (2) constant organizational communication.

Developing a Coherent Strategic Project Portfolio. To translate ideas into actions it is essential to initiate and formulate projects that foster competence building. As the sales and marketing director in our case study explained:

> "It's important to formulate down to earth and concrete projects. People should nod approvingly to these projects (e.g., project on new electronic media) without any extensive discussion."

Based on the common ground developed, action planning should define concrete projects with specific plans, timelines, and responsibilities. These plans cover aspects like knowledge development, investment plans, or plans for specific departments or products. Several managers in our case study argued that two of the most serious challenges in building a coherent project portfolio were to terminate prior projects and to integrate new projects initiated at different points in time. Prior projects must be re-evaluated in the light of the new strategic agenda. While portfolio approaches introduced in the 1970s argued for balance as a key success factor (Mintzberg, 1990), our case study suggests that the most viable portfolio of projects is a coherent portfolio, which includes projects that are complementary to each other (Milgrom and Roberts, 1991). Thus, old projects must be terminated or re-defined to fit the new common ground and strategic agenda, and linked to existing projects whenever possible.

Constant Communication. Because individual projects are usually dispersed throughout an organization, it is important that project learning, failures, and advances are constantly communicated across projects. Communication is essential for achieving coordination (Grant, 1996) and co-adaptation between projects that contribute to competence building within a firm. Szulanski (1996) argues that developing shared understanding of actions facilitates coordination of action by making actions understandable, predictable (March & Simon, 1958; Nelson & Winter, 1982), and stable (Berger & Luckman, 1967). In this way, the co-adaptive process of coordinating strategic action contributes to the institutionalization of new competences and their deployments in the organization. Some of the issues to be communicated across projects are changes in organizational language and conversations (Ford & Ford, 1995), new key linkages between competences and future competitive advantage (Grant, 1996), and specific new actions to be undertaken.

Managerial Variables

Several variables under the control of managers can greatly influence the speed and timing of key transitions in the process of strategic renewal. These managerial variables include individual time perception, the degree of strategic involvement, and the degree of internal vs. external knowledge sourcing, all of which may facilitate or impede efforts to speed up or slow down competence-driven strategic renewal.

Individual Time Perception. Speed in strategic renewal depends on individual, subjective, psychological perceptions of time (Das, 1991; Hurst, Rush & White, 1989). Different individuals will not perceive time in the same way to the extent that experience, knowledge, and ideas about the future differ (Zakay & Lomranz, 1993, Flathery, 1991). For example, in our case study, two newspaper directors facing a competitor's e-commerce activities (e.g., on-line sales, web editions, internet sourcing of stories) may have quite different ideas about the time left before advertising revenues decline significantly. A newly hired director with little market experience but great career prospects in the company may feel like rushing to action to immediately respond to the threat. Another director with more experience may stay relaxed because he knows that several prior activities of competitors have failed.

Several aspects of individuals' experiences are likely to reinforce the variances of individual time perception in strategic renewal processes (Zakay & Lomranz, 1993). For example, managers who were involved in prior strategic renewal processes in an organization may consider time spent in building common ground as essential because they believe that rushing to action leads to high coordination costs and substantial rework later on. Other managers with no such experience, however, may feel an urgency to act, because they overestimate the value of fast action relative to deliberate speed in common ground processes. In addition, differences in education and knowledge influence time perception (Flathery, 1991). An IT director in a newspaper company may perceive the possibility of the internet as a distribution channel differently from a CEO who has been educated as a journalist. While the former may understand technology better, the latter may believe that good stories determine advertising revenue more than any technological means of distribution. These two managers will have a different sense of urgency about using the internet as a new distribution channel. Finally, individual stakes in the company's future can influence individual time-perceptions (Franks, 1985). The builders of a firm's current competences may feel little urgency to change, while others who are new to the firm may have strong interest in building new competences.

If time perceptions among managers differ significantly (Das, 1986; Sawy, 1983), and if there is diversity in the collective imagination of the firm, reaching agreement about strategic issue importance and urgency is unlikely to happen fast in the common ground process, and the identification and building of new competences through coordinated strategic action will become more difficult and will take longer. Furthermore, while participation of people with interests in current competences may be desirable in devising the transition between old and new common grounds, their participation may limit the speed with which strategic renewal can advance. Conversely, excluding the participation of such people may speed up the process, but may create distortion and lose important experience.

The greater the differences in time perceptions among participants, the greater the need for time-consuming integration in the process of strategic renewal. The diversity of time perceptions, however, can be managed in three ways. First, *ex-ante regulation of involvement* is needed to determine who should participate in which phases of the renewal process. Which builders of current and past competences need to be involved? Do they need to participate in all phases, or is it sufficient to invite their participation in the later phases only? Second, *ex-ante establishing relevant time perspective* may lead top management to declare that an issue is important and urgent. Finally, *ex-post matching of time perception* (in the form of explicit agreement on issue urgency and importance) determines when in the process involved participants should agree on the issue urgency, and whether and when participants should be excluded from the process when they impede such an agreement.

Strategic Involvement. The form and extent of strategic involvement influences speed in the process of competence-driven strategic renewal. Strategic renewal has often been viewed as a concern of top management (e.g., Hambrick & Mason, 1984). By contrast, in a future-oriented, idea-driven process, every member of an organization may contribute to new thinking and new ideas (Hamel, 1996). Only by inviting a wide range of voices into the strategy process is it possible to unleash this potential. As Hamel comments: "To invite new voices into the strategy-making process, to encourage new perspectives, to start new conversations that span organizational boundaries, and then to help synthesize unconventional options into a point of view about corporate direction — those are the challenges for senior executives ..." Seen from this perspective, strategic renewal ought to be a process with wide involvement throughout the organization. The vice president of development in our case study describes involvement in the following way:

> "In our department we had one 'table' where a small group of people actively discussed electronic media {...} However, the organizational effect would be limited. Thus, we had to establish several such 'tables' all over the organization having the responsibility of discussing different aspects of electronic media. Then suddenly, we have a possibility to achieve something."

Wide involvement can be regarded as beneficial in the common ground process when participation eventually leads to greater agreement on strategic direction (Floyd & Wooldridge, 1992). If agreement is based on a "wide-ranging sensing of the environment" (Huber, 1991: 97; Kiesler & Sproull, 1982) from a variety of perspectives, and if it results from an explicit strategic conversation (Westley, 1990, von Krogh & Roos 1995), developing strategic direction may have a better chance of avoiding rigidities and competence traps (Leonard-Barton, 1992; Levitt & March, 1988). By contrast, to the extent that different perceptions and underlying strategic assumptions of individuals are not articulated (Sanchez, 1996) within an organization and scrutinized in a common ground process, consensus formation among a small group of top managers may lead to increasingly narrow "group think" (Janis, 1982).

Wide organizational involvement in a common ground process should broaden managers' perceptions of external and internal environments (Sanchez, 1997; Bourgeois, 1985; Lawrence & Dyer, 1983), because scrutinizing, challenging, and negotiating each person's interpretations of strategic variables can lead to a constructive "cognitive dissonance" (Floyd & Wooldridge, 1992; Westley, 1990; Festinger, 1957). When individuals involved in a strategic renewal process seek to avoid or reduce inconsistency among their contradictory cognitions (Zimbardo & Leippe, 1991), they experience "an adverse state known as cognitive dissonance" (Kahle, 1984). Such a state may arise because of exposure to new information or simple disagreement in interpretation with other parties (Kahle, 1984). Cognitive dissonance generally motivates individuals to restore cognitive consistency by modifying their current ideas or adopting new ideas (Festinger, 1957), resulting in a critically developed interpretive framework that can guide managers' sensemaking (e.g., Gioia & Chittipeddi, 1991; Poras & Silvers, 1991). Wide organizational involvement can also trigger motivational mechanisms (Locke & Schweiger, 1979). While the cognitive mechanisms associated with involvement focus and refine managers' perceptions through exposure to different perspectives, motivational mechanisms increase individuals' readiness and openness for strategic change (Armenakis *et al.*, 1993*)*. For example, when individuals become involved in discussing the future direction of their company, they are usually more willing to contribute to achieving this future.

The involvement of different individuals or groups in the strategic renewal process may vary in form and extent during different sub-processes. Participation may be full-time or part-time. However, part-time participation in key sub-processes may slow down the renewal process by diluting managers' attention (e.g., Mabert *et al.*, 1992). Furthermore, not fully participating in a process-specific learning experience may lead to time delays when participants subsequently must engage in catch-up learning to avoid coordination failure (Mabert *et al.*, 1992; Zirger & Hartley, 1993). The vice president of development in our case study commented:

> "We're very good at initiating new projects. However, the efficiency is certainly questionable. Many projects move upwards in the organization, and are discussed at several levels. The answer from the Board is normally a whole set of new questions. Some projects move for years up and down in the organization."

Thus, the choice whether or not to invite wide participation of diverse groups (e.g., business unit expert groups, internal and external stakeholders) in the renewal process greatly impacts the speed of translating organizational imagination into the common ground process. While wide involvement may increase complexity and therefore lead to a slower process, too narrow participation may inhibit formation of common ground and may waste available but uninvited imagination. Selection of internal and external participants for strategic renewal processes should therefore be determined by essential functional expertise and important political considerations.

Internal and External Knowledge Sourcing. The speed of strategic renewal will vary with the extent of an organization's external vs. internal knowledge sourcing. Firms that pursue competence endowment too broadly become the masters of none. Yet focusing on "core" competences (Hamel & Prahalad, 1990) and mastering only a narrow range of activities may reduce diversity in the strategic orientation and knowledge bases available to the organization. Companies intending to build new competences may therefore seek external knowledge through interfirm cooperation (Badaracco, 1991; Hamel, 1991), by hiring external academics and consultants, or by bringing clients and other external stakeholders into the different phases of the renewal process (Meyer, 1993; Peters, 1987; Von Hippel, 1986). Through external knowledge sourcing, an organization's knowledge base may be broadened, and new external perspectives may lead to useful cross-fertilization of ideas in the strategic imagination process. Process knowledge provided by external advisers may also accelerate the speed and improve the quality of the renewal process. Sanchez and Heene (1996), taking a view of the firm as an "open system," propose explicitly using external knowledge inflows to challenge a firm's current cognitive frameworks. They note that "managers may try to overcome the constraints of their cognitive limits by hiring consultants". Managers must beware of overly extensive substitution of external wisdom for internal ignorance, which may reduce a firm's capacity for subsequent knowledge absorption (Cohen & Levinthal, 1991) and limit future competence development. Moreover, external consultants may lack knowledge of a company's past, which may limit their effectiveness in processes of building new common ground. In the process of strategic renewal, external wisdom should be "borrowed on time" and should not be seen as a substitute for a firm's own efforts to develop new competence. Unless external knowledge is internalized and used in building new competences during the strategic renewal process, apparent speed might be mistaken for real progress in the process of strategic renewal.

Potential Breakdowns in Strategic Renewal

Competence-driven strategic renewal is far from being straightforward or easy to achieve (Ford & Ford, 1995). Potential breakdowns of three types can occur within and during the transitions between each sub-process of strategic renewal: (1) Language barriers may prevent ideas from entering the common ground process. (2) The relation between an organization's imagination and its common ground is unclear. (3) Both a current and an emerging common ground exist, contradict, or compete with each other instead of complementing each other.

Language Barriers. Organizations are composed of different communities of specialization that effectively speak different languages when describing and coordinating their action (Brown & Duguid, 1991; Orr, 1996; Wittgenstein, 1952). Language communities result from shared functions or interests that lead to frequent interactions and creating the need for a common language. While development of a common language enables efficient coordination within a community, it may make communication between language communities quite difficult. The project manager for electronic media in our case study described the problem of achieving constructive communication in the following way:

> "It's just like the Editor-in-Chief and the Sales & Marketing Director are living in two totally different worlds. They're not only having different perspectives and priorities, they're not talking the same language either."

Especially when wider circles in the organization are included in strategic imagination, communication barriers may make it difficult to achieve successful competence renewal because they prevent new ideas from entering the process of common ground development. Furthermore, if language barriers are combined with high levels of uncertainty and a rush to action, misunderstanding is likely to increase. Participants in renewal processes who come from different communities within the organization may use the same words, but may mean quite different things (Knorr-Cetina, 1981). Some may express problems, for example, with the same words that others use to describe opportunities. Language barriers may be overcome by building a community of knowing (Boland & Tenkasi, 1995) based on articulating assumptions (Sanchez, 1997), establishing meaning of words by careful definitions, and using misunderstandings and communication break downs as a trigger for sensemaking (Weick, 1995). This can be a time consuming process, but inventing new language can give participants in renewal processes the means to talk about a not-yet-existing future. At the same time, the more such a new language develops, the more communication problems may occur among those who are participants in the renewal process and those who are not.

Unclear Relation between Imagination and Common Ground. When groups in an organization bring new imaginations into the process of competence building, managers often experience varying degrees of uncertainty, anxiety, and issue-urgency. Perceptions of the impact of new ideas on an organization's current common ground may vary between managers with their own sense of urgency, anxiety, and uncertainty (Dutton & Duncan, 1987). Managers may initially disagree whether or not new common ground needs to be established. Managers may question whether new ideas may be seen as refinements of existing common ground or as fundamental cognitive changes (March, 1991; Dutton & Duncan, 1987). In a discussion of possible levels of ambition, the production and service manager in our case study made the following statement:

> "We mainly focus our discussion on existing products and existing customers. If we want to develop an intellectual leadership in this area, we also have to imagine ourselves delivering totally new products to new

customer groups. We avoid challenges by defining new things as close as possible to the existing ones."

New ideas can be marginalized when observers characterize them using already existing concepts (Piaget, 1972). Excessive anchoring in current concepts contributes to conceptual stagnation in which new and promising distinctions are not noticed and the potential for building new competences and strategic renewal cannot be recognized (von Krogh, Roos, & Slocum, 1994).

Competing Common Grounds. As an overall picture of potential new strategic realities takes shape through increased understanding and sensemaking (Weick, 1995), competing common grounds may arise in the process of strategic renewal. The vice president of development in our case study described this situation in the newspaper group:

> "Each time we make a new comprehensive corporate level strategy process, we develop strategies and priorities for several particular matters, and we try to see these from a corporate level perspective. However, the problem is that each strategy process is seen as an isolated process. We're not very good at seeing new strategies in relationship with previous strategies. Thus, we have several strategies and strategy documents around which are still to some extent valid. They're at least not explicitly ruled out. As a consequence, we follow several more or less parallel strategies which can be both inconsistent and even contradictory."

Establishing common ground is a prerequisite for coordinated strategic action that turns new strategy into competitive reality. However, unless the relationship between old and new common grounds has been clarified in an organization, the existence of competing common grounds (new versus existing) may breed confusion, threaten organizational coherence (Teece *et al.*, 1994), and lead to disagreement in allocating resources.

Managing Speed

We now consider the implications of either low- or high-speed regimes in the process of strategic renewal, and the trade-offs and potential breakdowns an organization may face under low- or high-speed regimes in strategic renewal.

High-speed regimes are characterized by limited organizational involvement, limited expression of differences in time perception, high levels of external knowledge sourcing, an atmosphere of impatience, and a rush to action. Speeding up a strategic renewal process can be compared to driving a car to high speeds. As speed increases, the driver's field of vision progressively narrows, and the ability to recognize and consider a diversity of views along the periphery decreases. When the momentum in a renewal process is kept at a high level, it is difficult to bring in new perspectives, issues, or ideas.

In high-speed regimes, language barriers between different groups may simply exclude some members of the organization from full participation if they cannot learn quickly how to communicate. High-speed regimes therefore often come at the cost of decreased variety in the imagination that is brought to the common ground process. Consequently, high-speed regimes are more likely to rely on established thinking, agendas, interpretations, and arguments. Increasing divergence between a few activists leading the change process and the rest of the organization is likely to impede achievement of coordinated strategic action.

Low-speed regimes are characterized by relatively wide organizational involvement, clear expression of differences in time perception, low external knowledge sourcing, and an atmosphere of patience. Slowing down a strategic renewal process can be compared to decreasing the speed of a car before changing direction. As speed decreases, the field of vision widens. As a consequence, the ability to recognize a diversity of views along the way increases. Thus, when the strategic renewal process is slower, new perspectives and ideas have more time to enter the conversation. Wide participation in low-speed regimes may require greater efforts to overcome language barriers between different groups, and more imaginative contributions from diverse organizational groups may have to be evaluated. However, under low-speed regimes, competing common grounds are less likely to occur in the long run when new common ground is created through wide participation.

Managers of strategic renewal therefore face difficult trade-offs. On the one hand, speeding up the renewal process decreases variety in imagination brought to the common ground process, increases the tendency to subsume imagination to existing common grounds, and increases the likelihood of competition between existing and new common grounds that may prevent coordination of strategic action in new competence development. Thus, speeding up the strategic renewal process increases the likelihood that the process may fail altogether, either because the new competence developed does not provide enough variety, or the process of competence building fails to maintain adequate coherence to establish linkages between the company's past and future strategic moves. On the other hand, slowing down the process of strategic renewal increases the variety of imagination that can be brought to the common ground process, may allow for better common ground development, and increases the likelihood of achieving coordinated strategic action. However, slowing down the renewal process can increase the risk that the organization will become disadvantaged relative to faster acting competitors.

As the chairman of the newspaper group in our case study commented:

> "We are now really scratching the bedrock of our organization and business activities. We can't push this process. We have to take the time necessary to figure out our disagreements, and develop a common platform for future activities."

The essence of the challenge in finding the right speed for strategic renewal is thus a trade-off between the need to maintain adequate internal coherence and the necessity to keep pace with external competition.

Implications for Research

The model for strategic renewal outlined in this article has several implications for both research and practice. Scholars in the competence perspective have started to address problems related to strategic renewal (Volberda & Baden-Fuller, 1996; Volberda, 1996). Our model is complementary to their efforts but distinctive in its orientation, because we explicitly stress the role of managerial cognition in relation to time-sensitive processes — a theoretical and practical challenge identified by Sanchez and Heene (1996). Suggestions made in this paper therefore extend conceptually the descriptive literature on speed as a strategic factor (Bourgeois & Eisenhardt, 1988; Eisenhardt, 1989; Judge & Miller, 1991; Smith, Grimm, Chen & Gannon, 1989; Stalk, 1988). Working from the insights and assumptions of the competence perspective, we show that the careful management of speed and timing are essential to the success of strategic renewal processes.

Since time-sensitive cognitive processes are central to the process of competence-driven strategic renewal, managers need to understand how to manage speed and timing in several dimensions. We distinguish three crucial sub-processes — imagination, common ground development, and coordinating strategic action — and elaborate on their interactions. We identify several sources of breakdowns in the renewal process — language barriers, unclear contribution to common grounds, competing common grounds — which may impede the identification and building of new competences. We suggest how inappropriate management of speed in the strategic renewal process can lead to breakdowns in these sub-processes. Finally, we elaborate on several ways to improve speed and timing in the strategic renewal process and avoid sources of breakdowns. In essence, we have tried to elaborate a number of issues at the intersection of the systemic nature of organizations and the cognitive processes through which organizations may seek strategic renewal.

Our model also seeks to extend the strategic renewal literature, which thus far has mainly addressed the imagination dimension of competence renewal (e.g., Burgelman, 1983; Hamel, 1996). This literature has generally not addressed the need for coordination of strategic action or the processes through which imagination can be translated into coordinated strategic action. From a competence perspective, the integration of the three sub-processes of imagination, building common ground, and coordinated strategic action is essential in successfully managing strategic renewal. Thus, this model can be enriched and refined by further elaboration of processes for articulating and managing organizational knowledge (Sanchez, 1997b) and for competence building and leveraging through resource mobilization (Løwendahl & Haanes, 1997).

Our model of competence-based strategic renewal suggests several avenues for incorporating other disciplines and research perspectives. First, power and political processes are recognized as influential in organizational change processes (e.g., Pettigrew, 1973; Cyert & March, 1963). This research perspective focuses on the processes of bargaining, negotiation, and making trade-offs between different political interests. The role of political processes in competence building and competence-based strategic renewal has attracted limited attention so far. A useful area of research would be to develop a better understanding of the role of power in competence management in general, and more specifically in the strategic renewal activities outlined in this chapter. In particular, the influence of power relationships on speed and potential breakdowns is of central importance.

Second, research on organizational conversations (Barry & Elmes, 1997; Ford & Ford, 1995) and on communication between marketing departments and R&D departments in innovation processes (Dougherty, 1992) and in strategy formation processes (Franwick, Ward, Hutt, & Reingen, 1994) shed light on other important aspects of competence-driven renewal processes. Improved understanding of the role of language communities, the formation of new organizational language, the identification and overcoming of language barriers, and the interactions between speed and language development in competence management will require further research.

Third, we need better understanding of the contextual influences on the competence building processes and how they might be managed in the strategic renewal process. How are competence building processes influenced by competitive climate, various organizational characteristics, the history of renewal processes in the organization, and the dominant leadership style (as perceived by managers at different levels) in the organization? Better understanding of these contextual variables would help to improve the design of renewal processes.

Managerial Implications

Managers over the last decade have been told that being a first-mover and outpacing other firms in time-based competition are essential for competitive success in a changing and globalizing world. Perhaps as a result, managerial impatience in processes of competence-driven strategic renewal is becoming an increasingly common phenomenon in many top management teams. In this chapter, we argue that an impatient push for speed in strategic renewal and competence development may be a dangerous route that leads to neither near-term competitive success nor long-term strategic renewal. Competence-driven strategic renewal is fundamentally a cognitive process that requires mangers to take the time necessary to develop and gather beliefs about the future, to identify and agree on desirable future actions, to identify and develop new competences, to reinterpret and integrate past competence deployments with new competence development, to align perceptions of the past with current cognitions and imagined futures, and to define concrete steps for new coordinated strategic actions and competence deployments. A rush to action may undermine any or all of these essential steps.

This discussion also addresses the importance of recognizing and re-interpreting past competence leveraging. Without doubt, the history of a company and its top management — especially if previously successful — may be a major impediment to bold and successful strategic renewal (Hamel & Prahalad, 1994; Hamel, 1996). From a competence-driven strategic renewal perspective, however, past competence deployment may be both a vital source of experience and a useful facilitator of future coordinated strategic action. We therefore stress the importance of *both* imagining the future and seeing the relationships between an organization's past, present, and future competences. Management of an organization's cognitive continuity can greatly improve its prospects for achieving coordinated future strategic action.

Integrating competence building with the leveraging of existing competences through processes of imagining, creating common ground, and coordinating strategic action requires careful timing of the transitions between these three sub-processes. A hasty move from the imagination sub-process to trying to coordinate strategic action, without adequate building of common ground, is likely to seriously undermine strategic renewal. Managers involved in strategic renewal, therefore, have to meet the unique challenge of managing their own cognitive processes in managing these organizational phase transitions. It is here that external observers may provide valuable outside perspectives as correctives to a premature rush to action.

Conclusions

In this chapter the competence perspective's view of organizations as open systems governed by managerial cognitive processes provides a framework for investigating the process of competence-driven strategic renewal. It is now widely recognized that effective competence management is essential to developing and sustaining competitive advantage. However, successfully managing competence-driven strategic renewal processes still needs further theoretical scrutiny and research. Consistent with the competence perspective's emphasis on systems and processes as units of analysis in theory development and research, we have identified three sub-processes of imagining, creating common ground, and coordinating strategic action within the overall strategic renewal process. Our analysis leads us to a view of competence building in which strategic intentionality and goals are not assumed or decided ex ante, but rather emerge from a strategic renewal process with an organization as a cognitive system.

References

Aadne, J. H., & Mahnke, V. (1996). Managing strategy renewal: The role of language and speed, paper presented at the 16th Annual Strategic Management Society Conference, Phoenix, Arizona, November 10–13.

Aadne, J. H., & Mahnke, V. (1997). Managing strategy renewal: Sources of breakdown and trade-offs related to speed. Winning Paper at CEMS-conference 1998, Rotterdam, Netherlands.

Armenakis, A. A., Harris, S. G., & Mossholder, K. W. (1993). Creating readiness for large scale change. *Human Relations, 46*, 681–703.

Badaracco, J. L. (1991). *The Knowledge Link.* Cambridge, MA: Harvard Business School Press.

Baden-Fuller, C., & Volberda, H. (1996). Strategic renewal in large complex organisations: A competence based view. Management Report No. 267, Rotterdam School of Management.

Barney, J. B. (1991). Firm resources and sustained competitive advantage. *Journal of Management, 17(1)*, 99–120.

Barry, D., & Elmes, M. (1997). Strategy retold: Toward a narrative view of strategic discourse. *Academy of Management Review, 22(2)*, 429–452.

Berger, P., & Luckmann, T. (1967). *The Social Construction of Reality: A Treatise in the Sociology of Knowledge.* London: Penguin Books.

Boje, D. (1991). The storytelling organization: A study of story performance in an office-supply firm. *Administrative Science Quarterly, 36(1)*, 106–126.

Bourgeois, L. J. (1985). Strategic goals, perceived uncertainty, and economic performance in volatile environments. *Academy of Management Journal, 28*, 548–573.

Bourgeois, L. J. (1994). Commentary: Competitive agility — A source of competitive advantage based on speed and variety. In P. Shrivastava, A. S. Huff, & J. E. Dutton (eds) *Advances in Strategic Management.* Greenwich, Connecticut: JAI Press.

Bourgeois, L. J., & Eisenhardt, K. M. (1988). Strategic decision processes in high velocity environments: Four cases in the microcomputer industry. *Management Science, 34(7)*, 816–835.

Brown, W. B., & Karagozoglu, N. (1993). Leading the way to faster new product development. *Academy of Management Executive, 7(1)*, 36–47.

Cohen, M. D., March, J., & Olsen, J. P. (1972). A garbage-can model of organizational choice. *Administrative Science Quarterly, 17*, 1–25.

Czarniawska-Joerges, B. (1992). *Exploring Complex Organizations: A Cultural Perspective.* Newbury Park, CA: Sage Publications.

D'Aveni, R. (1994). *Hypercompetition.* New York: Free Press.

Das, T. K. (1986). *The Subjective Side of Strategy Making: Future Orientation and Perceptions of Executives.* New York: Praeger.

Das, T. K. (1991). Time: The hidden dimension in strategic planning. *Long Range Planning 24*, 49–57.

Dess, G. G., & Priem, R. L. (1995). Consensus-performance research: Theoretical and empirical extensions. *Journal of Management Studies, 42(4)*, 401–417.

Dougherty, D. (1992). Interpretive barriers to successful product innovation in large firms. *Organization Science 3* (May), 179–202.

Dutton, J. E., Fahey, L., & Narayanan, V. K. (1983). Toward understanding strategic issue diagnosis. *Strategic Management Journal, 12*, 307–323.

Eisenhardt, K. M. (1989). Making fast strategic decisions in high velocity environments. *Academy of Management Journal, 32*, 543–576.

Eisenhardt, K. M. (1990). Speed and strategic choice: How managers accelerate decision making. *California Management Review*, Spring, 39–54.

El Sawy, O. A. (1983). Temporal perspective and managerial attention: A study of chief executive strategic behavior, unpublished doctoral dissertation, Stanford University.

Festinger, L. (1957). *A Theory of Cognitive Dissonance.* Stanford, CA: Stanford University Press.

Flaherty, M. The perception of time and situated engrossment. *Social Psychology Quarterly, 54(1)*, 76–85.

Floyd, S. W., & Wooldridge, B. (1992). Managing strategic consensus: The foundation of effective implementation. *Academy of Management Executive, 6*, 27–39.

Ford, J. D., & Ford, L. W. (1995). The role of conversations in producing intentional change in organizations. *Academy of Management Review, 20(3)*, 541–570.

Franks, D. (1985). The self in evolutionary perspective. *Studies in Symbolic Interaction*, Supp.1, 29–61.

Franwick, G. L., Ward, J. C., Hutt, M. D., & Reingen, P. H. (1994), Evolving patterns of organizational beliefs in the formation of strategy. *Journal of Marketing*, April, 96–110.

Giddens, A. (1993). *New Rules of Sociological Method*, (2nd ed.) Stanford, CA: Stanford University Press.

Gioia, D. A., & Chittipeddi, K. (1991). Sensemaking and sensegiving in strategic change initiation. *Strategic Management Journal, 12*, 433–448.

Gorman, P., Thomas, H., & Sanchez, R. (1996). Industry dynamics in competence-based competition. In R. Sanchez, A. Heene, & H. Thomas (eds) *Dynamics of Competence-Based Competition: Theory and Practice in the New Strategic Management.* London: Elsevier.

Grant, R. M. (1996). Towards a knowledge based theory of the firm. *Strategic Management Journal,* *17*, 109–122.

Grant, R. M. (1991). The resource based theory of competitive advantage: Implications for strategy formulation. *California Management Review,* Spring, 114–135.

Hamel, G. (1996). Strategy as revolution. *Harvard Business Review,* July–August, 69–82.

Hamel, G., & Prahalad, C. K. (1991). Corporate imagination and expeditionary marketing. *Harvard Business Review,* July–August, 81–92.

Hamel, G., & Prahalad, C. K. (1994). *Competing for the Future.* Boston, MA: Harvard Business School Press.

Hamel, G., & Prahalad, C. K. (1996). Competing in the new economy: Managing out of bounds. *Strategic Management Journal, 17,* 237–242.

Hedberg, B. (1981). How organizations learn and unlearn. In P. C. Nystrom & W. H. Starbuck (eds) *Handbook of Organizational Design.* New York: Oxford University Press.

Huber, G. P. (1991). Organizational learning: The contributing process and literatures. *Organization Science, 2,* 88–115.

Huff, J. O., Huff, A. S., & Thomas, H. (1992). Strategic renewal and the interaction of cumulative stress and inertia. *Strategic Management Journal, 13,* 55–75.

Hurst, D. K., Rush, J. C., & White, R. E. (1989). Top management teams and organizational renewal. *Strategic Management Journal, 10,* 87–105.

Janis, I. R. (1982). *Victims of Group Think.* Boston: Houghton Mifflin.

Johnson, G. (1992). Managing strategic change: Strategy, culture and action. *Long Range Planning, 25(1),* 28–36.

Jones, J. W. (1993). *High-speed management.* San Francisco: Jossey-Bass.

Judge, W. Q., & Miller, A. (1991). Antecedents and outcomes of decision speed in different environmental contexts. *Academy of Management Journal, 43(2),* 449–463.

Kahle, L. R. (1984). *Attitudes and Social Adaptation: A Person-Situation Interaction Approach.* Oxford: Pergamon.

Kogut, B., & Zander, U. (1992). Knowledge of the firm, combinative capabilities, and the replication of technology. *Organization Science, 3,* 383–397.

Lawrence, P., & Dyer, D. (1983). *Renewing American Industry.* New York: Free Press.

Locke, E. A., & Schweiger, D. M. (1979). Participation in decision-making: One more look. In B. M. Staw (ed.) *Research in Organizational Behavior 1,* 265–339. Greenwich, CT: JAI.

Løwendahl, B., & Haanes, K. (1997). The unit of activity: A new way to understand competence building and leveraging. In R. Sanchez & A. Heene (eds) *Strategic Learning and Knowledge Management.* Chichester: John Wiley and Sons.

Mabert, V. A., Muth, J. F., & Schmenner, R. W. (1992). Collapsing new product development times: Six case studies. *Journal of Product Innovation Management, 9,* 200–212.

March, J., & Simon, H. (1958). *Organizations.* New York: John Wiley and Sons.

McGrath, G., MacMillan, L. C., & Venkataraman, S. (1995). Defining and developing competence: A strategic process paradigm. *Strategic Management Journal, 16,* 251–275.

McGrath, J. E., & Rotchford, N. L. (1983). Time and behavior in organizations. In L. L. Cummings & B. M. Staw (eds) *Research in Organizational Behavior, 5,* 57–101. Greenwich, CT: JAI Press.

Meyer, C. (1993). *Fast Cycle Time: How to Align Purpose, Strategy, and Structure for Speed.* New York: Free Press.

Mintzberg, H. (1994). The fall and rise of strategic planning. *Harvard Business Review,* January–February, 107–114.

Mintzberg, H., & Waters, J. A. (1985). Of strategies, deliberate and emergent. *Strategic Management Journal, 6,* 257–272.

Nelson, R., & Winter, S. (1982). *An Evolutionary Theory of the Economic Change.* Cambridge, MA: Belknap Press.

Nonaka, I., & Takeuchi, H. (1995). *The Knowledge-Creating Company.* New York: Oxford University Press.

Oliver, C. (1990). Determinants of interorganizational relationships: Integration and future direction. *Academy of Management Review, 15*, 241–265.

Orr, J. E. (1996). *Talking about Machines: An Ethnography of a Modern Job.* Ithaca: Cornell University Press.

Page, A. (1993). Assessing new product development practices and performance: Establishing crucial norms. *Journal of Product Innovation Management, 10*, 273–290.

Peteraf, M. A. (1993). The cornerstones of competitive advantage: A resource-based view. *Strategic Management Journal, 14*, 179–192.

Peters, T. (1987). *Thriving on Chaos.* New York: Knopf.

Pettigrew, A. M. (1973). *The Politics of Organizational Decision-Making.* London: Tavistock.

Piaget, J. (1972). *To Understand Is to Invent.* New York: The Viking Press.

Poras, J. I., & Silvers, R. C. (1991). Organization development and transformation. *Annual Review Psychology, 42*, 51–57.

Porter, M. E. (1980). *Competitive Strategy: Techniques for Analyzing Industries and Competitors.* New York: The Free Press.

Prahalad, C. K., & Hamel, G. (1994). Strategy as a field of study: Why search for a new paradigm? *Strategic Management Journal, 15*, 5–16.

Sanchez, R. (1997a). Strategic management at the point of inflection: Systems, complexity and competence theory. *Long Range Planning, 10(6)*, 939–946.

Sanchez, R. (1997b). Managing articulated knowledge in competence-based competition. In R. Sanchez & A. Heene (eds) *Strategic Learning and Knowledge Management.* Chichester: John Wiley and Sons.

Sanchez, R., Heene, A., & Thomas, H. (1996). *Dynamics of Competence-Based Competition.* Oxford: Elsevier.

Sanchez, R., & Heene, A. (eds) (1997). *Strategic Learning and Knowledge Management.* Chichester: John Wiley and Sons.

Smith, K. G., Grimm, C. M., Chen, M. J., & Gannon, M. J. (1989). Predictors of response time to competitive strategic actions: Preliminary theory and evidence. *Journal of Business Research, 18*, 245–258.

Smith, P. G., & Reinertsen, D. G. (1991). *Developing Products in Half the Time.* New York: Van Nostrand Reinhold.

Smith, P. G., & Reinertsen, D. G. (1992). Shortening the product development cycle. *Research Technology Management, 35(3)*, 44–49.

Stalk, G. (1988). Time — The next source of competitive advantage. *Harvard Business Review* July–August, 41–51.

Stalk, G. (1993). Time and innovation. *Canadian Business Review, 17(3)*, 15–18.

Stalk, G., & Hout, T. M. (1990). *Competing Against Time: How Time-Based Competition Is Reshaping Global Markets.* New York: Free Press.

Strebel, P. (1987). Organizing for innovation over an industry cycle. *Strategic Management Journal, 8*, 117–124.

Strebel, P. (1992). *Breakpoints: How Managers Exploit Radical Business Change.* Boston, MA: Harvard Business School Press.

Szulanski, G. (1996). Exploring internal stickiness: Impediments to the transfer of best practice within the firm. *Strategic Management Journal*, Winter Special Issue, 27–43.

Vinton, D. E. (1992). A new look at time, speed. and the manager. *Academy of Management Executive, 6(4)*, 7–16.

Von Hippel. E. (1986). Lead users: A source of novel product concepts. *Management Science 32*, 791–805.

von Krogh, G., & Roos, J. (1995). Conversation management. *European Management Journal 4*, 390–394.

von Krogh, G., Roos, J., & Slocum, K. (1994). An essay on corporate epistemology. *Strategic Management Journal 15* (Special Issue), 53–71.

Walsh, J. P., & Ungson, G. R. (1991). Organizational memory. *Academy of Management Review, 16(1)*, 57–91.

Weick, K. E. (1979). *The Social Psychology of Organizing*. New York: Random House.

Weick, K. E. (1995). *Sensemaking in Organizations*. Thousand Oaks, CA: Sage Publications.

Weisbord, M. R. (ed.) (1992). *Discovering Common Ground*. San Francisco: Berrett-Koehler Publishers.

Weisbord, M. R., & Janoff, S. (1995). *Future Search: An Action Guide to Finding Common Ground in Organizations and Communities*. San Francisco: Berrett-Koehler Publishers.

Westley, F. R. (1990). Middle managers and strategy: Microdynamics of inclusion. *Strategic Management Journal II*, 337–351.

Wittgenstein, L. (1953). *Philosophical Investigations*. Oxford: Blackwell.

Wooldridge, B., & Floyd, S. W. (1990). The strategy process, middle management involvement, and organizational performance. *Strategic Management Journal, 11*, 231–241.

Zakay, D., & Lomranz, J. (1993). Attitudinal identification, stimulus complexity and retrospective duration estimation. *Time and Society, 2(3)*, 381–397.

Zimbardo, P. G., & Leippe, M. R. (1991). *The Psychology of Attitude Change and Social Influence*. Philadelphia: Temple University Press.

Zirger, B. J., & Hartley, J. L. (1993). Accelerating product development: A conceptual model, paper presented at the annual meeting of the Academy of Management, Atlanta, GA.

Chapter 10

Systems Thinking in Managerial Decision Making

Jenshou Yang

Introduction

The dynamics and complexity of today's managerial environment require continual increases in the competence of a firm. Management must ensure not only that a firm's competences can be leveraged in the present, but that new competences are developed to meet the opportunities and needs of the future (Hamel, 1994). Thus, the ongoing challenge to top management is to achieve and maintain alignment between a firm's current competences and the changing demands of the external environment (Bogner & Thomas, 1994).

Recognizing the dynamic nature of competences, Sanchez and Heene (1996) outlined an open system view of organizations and their processes for building and leveraging competences. Sanchez and Thomas (1996) further proposed that managers must create a "virtuous circle" of competence building and leveraging in managing the firm as a system of resource stocks and flows. In the virtuous circle model, competence building brings a firm strategic options for action, while leveraging competence in effect exercises some of the firm's current strategic options. Exercising strategic options generates cash flows for the firm, which can then be allocated to further competence building and leveraging. The virtuous circle model suggests that both competence building and leveraging are systemic, complex tasks.

A firm's goal-seeking behavior is guided by the firm's *strategic logic*, which is the operative rationale within a firm for achieving its goals by applying available resources and capabilities (Sanchez & Heene, 1996). A firm's strategic logic determines what competences will be built and how existing competence will be leveraged through the firm's management processes. A second essential, ongoing task of top management is to improve their own cognitive frameworks by continually challenging the firm's strategic logic (Sanchez & Thomas, 1996). Therefore, when managing over a long time horizon, one of the essential challenges for managers is to learn how to manage strategic logic and management processes so as to build and leverage competences systemically. This capability for managing dynamic complexity falls within the perspective on managing characterized by Senge (1990) as a "systems thinking discipline."

Both laboratory and field studies show that people often do not manage dynamic decision tasks well, and sometimes cannot learn to improve. Senge (1990) claims that systems thinking

Systems Perspectives on Resources, Capabilities, and Management Processes, pages 197–214.
Copyright © 2002 by Elsevier Science Ltd.
All rights of reproduction in any form reserved.
ISBN: 0-08-043778-8

helps decision-makers to consider long-term rather than just short-term alternatives. A field study (Cavaleri & Sterman, 1997) showed that dynamic decision performance could be improved by rectifying managers' mental models with cognitive aids such as training in systems thinking. With appropriate mental models, decision-makers should be able to handle dynamically complex relationships better in both internal and external environments, and to improve their ability to select, build, and deploy competences to improve long-term success.

Researchers in the field of judgment and choice have shown that, as a rule, people tend to choose alternatives that result in more immediate outcomes even when payoffs are smaller compared to long-term outcomes (Herrnstein *et al.*, 1993; Rachlin & Green, 1972). Furthermore, Kudadjie-Gyamfi and Rachlin (1996) show that people may persist in making such biased choices even when cognitive aids are provided. One explanation for this may be that the value of longer-term outcomes is heavily discounted by decision-makers (Kudadjie-Gyamfi & Rachlin, 1996; Herrnstein *et al.*, 1993). These findings suggest that decision-makers are in general less likely to choose strategies focused on long-term achievement.

In the present study, we investigate whether decision-makers that explicitly use systems thinking will more readily select competence strategies focused on creating long-term success in a dynamically complex environment.

Competence-Based Management as a Dynamic Decision Task

Dynamic decision-making tasks arise when decisions will alter the state of a system in the present, and as a result will affect decision-making conditions in the future. Earlier decisions may lead to information feedback and consequently may lead to new decisions. Managing a firm's competence is an example of a dynamic decision-making context (Bogner & Thomas, 1994; Sanchez & Heene, 1996; Sanchez & Thomas, 1996). Managing interactions of technologies, organizational dynamics, and product markets in competence building involves multiple linked causalities, feedback loops, nonlinearities, and changing stocks and flows of tangible and intangible assets. Laboratory studies show that subjects have great difficulty managing dynamic and complex tasks, and tend to make significantly systematically dysfunctional decisions (Diehl & Sterman, 1995; Sterman, 1989a, 1989b; Paich & Sterman, 1993; Yang, 1996, 1997). Sterman (1989a, 1989b) attributes dysfunctional decision-making largely to misperceptions of feedback information. Decision-makers either fail to grasp the time delays between action and response, do not properly recognize outcomes that result from multiple feedback loops, or do not understand the non-linear behavior of a system. Under the circumstances, the mental models[1] that guide a person's decision-making are deficient, leading to poor performance.

Diehl and Sterman (1995) show that these modes of dysfunctional decision-making cannot be improved solely by providing decision-makers with outcome feedback. Sengupta and Abdel-Hamid (1993) observed, however, that subjects provided with

---

[1]Mental models represent human cognitive "maps" of a task. In a strategic decision-making context, these cognitive maps of key decision-makers shape an organization's strategic logic and the management processes used to carry out its tasks.

feedback identified as being about relationships among key decision variables were able to improve their decision-making performance significantly. Yang (1996, 1997) found that subjects who understood and accepted overall system goals generally developed more robust mental models and made fewer dysfunctional decisions than those who adopted only subsystem-level goals. In a field study, Cavaleri and Sterman (1997) provided both managers and non-managers with a series of training sessions in systems thinking. The result was that participants developed more effective mental models, policies were developed more systemically, and outcomes were improved.

In short, dynamic decision-making performance can be improved, but only when cognitive aids to support systems thinking are provided. These findings suggest that in their dynamic and complex decision environment, top managers can benefit from systems-oriented cognitive aids in deciding how to build and leverage competences.

Competence-Based Management as an Uncertain and Outcome-Delayed Decision Environment

Competence building involves managing qualitative changes in a firm's existing stocks of assets and capabilities to create new options for future action by the firm in pursuing its goals (Sanchez, Heene, & Thomas, 1996). Competence-building activities may face a wide range of uncertainties, and the outcomes of new competence-building actions taken are likely to involve significant time delays. Laboratory research suggests that subjects tend to be risk-averse and impulsive in uncertain situations, preferring "small-immediate-certain" (SIC) rewards to large-immediate-probabilistic (LIP) rewards, even when the expected value of the LIP is significantly greater (Rachlin & Siegel, 1994; Tversky & Kahneman, 1974). Some research (Herrnstein *et al.*, 1993; Rachlin & Green 1972) suggests that subjects even prefer a small-immediate-certain reward (SIC) to a large-delayed-certain (LDC) reward of greater amount. Kudadjie-Gyamfi and Rachlin (1996) suggest two explanations: (1) Those subjects who chose SIC over LIP alternatives may find probability a highly abstract concept and difficult to understand. (2) Those subjects who chose SIC over LDC alternatives might suffer from impulsive behavior, because such preferences reduce overall rewards.

Can decision-makers' preferences for SIC outcomes over LIP or LDC outcomes be reduced under certain circumstances? Herrnstein *et al.* (1993) found that subjects were less likely to choose LDC outcomes when the negative effects of SIC alternatives required more cognitive effort to detect. They also found that hints such as "choosing one alternative may increase or decrease future return" had no impact on LDC choice; however, stronger hints such as "choosing alternative *A* may increase future return, and alternative *B* vice versa" did have an impact. However, Kudadjie-Gyamfi and Rachlin (1996) found that hints were not effective in reducing the choice of SIC alternatives, and that impulsive behavior often limited the effectiveness of cognitive aids.

Building competence is time-consuming and uncertain, but it appears that human nature often prefers to choose short-term and certain benefits. Thus, cognitive aids to support more strategic thinking and appropriate designs of management processes can play an important role in competence-based management. Because each firm engages in a distinctive pattern of competence building and competence leveraging activities in pursuit of its specific set of goals, the goals a firm adopts will drive managerial allocations of a firm's resources to longer-term competence building *versus* shorter-term competence leveraging. Short-term oriented goals will lead decision-makers to allocate resources to SIC alternatives and discourage allocations to the sort of LIP or even LDC outcomes involved in competence building. In the present study, we investigate the hypothesis that decision-makers will more readily select a longer-term competence-building strategy when using a systems thinking aid and when pursuing more system-level kinds of goals in a dynamically complex environment.

Method

In order to test our general hypothesis, an experiment was set up in which factors of cognition and goal sets were manipulated. Decision making using three kinds of cognitive contexts was investigated: decisions made with no aids, with systems thinking aids, and with detailed-decision-rule aids. For goal sets, various degrees of short-term versus long-term performance pressure were used (null, ten percent, 50 percent, and 90 percent short-term performance pressure). A higher percentage of short-term performance pressure represents an incentive structure in which the decision-maker is rewarded mainly on the achievement of short-term performance goals instead of long-term ones.

Subjects

The three cognitive aids and four short-term performance pressure levels define twelve different decision-making conditions. Ten male and forty female undergraduate business students enrolled in an Organization Theory class were employed as subjects. Thirteen-subject groups were assigned to the null pressure and ten percent pressure conditions and twelve-subject groups to the 50 percent pressure and 90 percent pressure conditions.

Task

The decision-making task, shown in Figure 1, was based on Forrester's "market growth" model (Forrester, 1984). In the model, market growth is driven by long-term capital investment. The model is a "growth and under-investment" archetype (Senge, 1990) that simulates the growth behavior of a firm with very large potential market demand. In the model, the orders a firm receives drive revenues, earnings, and cash flow. If a manager decides to hire more salespersons, for example, orders, revenues, earnings, and cash flow will increase as a result. The order volume is not limited until it exceeds production capacity, which then causes delivery delays and imposes opportunity costs on customers left waiting for their orders to be filled. When this happens, some customers reduce their orders, leading to reductions in revenues, earnings, and cash flow. The firm is "operated" for eight quarters according to the resource allocation decisions of the subjects. Two decisions are made each quarter: (1)

the number of salespersons to hire (fire) to increase (decrease) the sales force, and (2) the amount of capital to invest in increasing production capacity.

The decision-making task in this model represents a simplified business situation in which a benign external environment is constant and advantageous to the firm. Management's only task is to coordinate organizational resource allocations. To meet this challenge, subjects must grasp the dynamics affecting the decision-making and form appropriate mental models to guide decision-making. Good decision-making in the task thus requires systems thinking that interrelates finance, market, and manufacturing factors.

The initial conditions of the simulated company are (1) production capacity is equal to order volume and (2) the initial cash endowment is not enough for investment to increase production capacity but is enough to hire more salespersons to increase orders. Future orders will decrease if subjects hire salespersons to increase orders at the beginning because shortages of product and delivery delays will result. A SIC choice means that subjects that decide to hire salespersons to increase orders will derive an immediate benefit that subsequently results in delivery delays and dramatic decreases in future orders.

In terms of competence-based management, the task represents a company that has built the competence to produce a unique product that is accepted by the market. The task of managers in the company is then to leverage competences so as to manage the company's

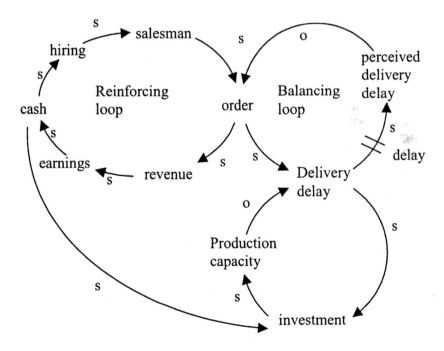

Figure 1: Causal Structure of the Decision Environment in the Experiment ("s" means that the two variables linked by an arrow will change in the same direction. "o" indicates that an increase in one variable will cause a decrease in the second variable and *vice versa.*).

existing stocks of assets and capabilities to achieve delivery of received orders and maintain the firm's market reputation. The management tasks include: producing the current product, managing the size of the sales force, accumulating cash for growth, allocating resources to increase production capacity and/or to hire salespersons, and coordinating manufacturing and sales volumes. Managers in this simulated company must develop a strategic logic for the firm through repeated trial-and-error decisions, eventually realizing that maintaining delivery performance and reputation is the dominant factor for success in this market. Subjects' discovery of this strategic logic and applying it in competence leveraging decisions are both affected by the kinds of cognitive aid provided to subjects and the degree to which short-term performance pressure figures in the incentive structure.

Manipulations

Types of Cognitive Context. As noted, there are three types of cognitive contexts: no aid, a task-specific systems thinking aid, and a task-specific detailed-decision-rule aid. The no aid condition provided only basic information such as performance measures and variables definition.

The systems thinking aid provided further guidance, stated as follows:

> "You must manage the system as a whole. There are three critical points you must be aware of. The first is the balance of order backlog and production capacity. Delivery delays can occur and lead to dramatic reductions in incoming orders. When the backlog exceeds capacity, orders are reduced to one twentieth of the original quantity. The system becomes inefficient when the capacity exceeds the backlog. The second critical point is financial support. You must acquire enough cash to invest in production capacity and then increase sales force to gain more orders. The third point is the delayed effect of delivery delay. After the fourth quarter, the negative effects of delivery delay on sales begin to occur."

The systems thinking aid provides a set of principles for managing the simulated company, along with an implicit warning that hiring more salespersons is an unwise decision in the first three quarters. If subjects fully comprehend the system management principles provided, they will limit the order growth rate and accumulate cash in the first three quarters to increase order growth and maximize cash accumulation in the remaining five quarters. If subjects do not fully grasp these principles and initially allocate resources to hire salespeople and increase orders, they will lose more than three quarters of order growth and end up with much less cash accumulation.

The detailed-decision-rule cognitive aid provides further guidance, including the obvious warning that hiring more salespersons is an unwise decision in the first three quarters, along with a detailed computation example as follows:

> "At the beginning, the firm starts with balanced production capacity and sales force. You can earn 120 units of cash in each quarter. However, the

endowed cash is not enough for a new investment in production capacity, which requires at least 600 units. Therefore, if you employ new salespersons to increase orders, delivery delays will occur. For example, if ten salespersons are employed in the first quarter, the backlog will increase from 400 to 600 but the production capacity remains at 400 due to the shortage of cash. In the following quarter, cash revenue reduces from 120 to 20 because of the increase of total salary expenditure. Thus it is even more difficult for you to accumulate enough cash to invest in production capacity. The best decision for the operation is, therefore, to employ no new salespersons in the first three quarters, until enough cash is accumulated to allow investment in capacity. The sales force can then increase."

If subjects follow the decision rule provided, they are unable to achieve a 50 percent order growth rate goal in the first three quarters, but are able to attain a 50 percent order growth rate goal in the remaining five quarters, as well as the largest cash endowment. If they are unable to follow the decision rule, subjects will not achieve either goal.

Short-Term Performance Pressure. Two types of goals, long-term versus short-term, are imposed on the subjects in the experiment. The long-term goal is to maximize total cash on hand after the game is finished. The short-term goal is to achieve at least a 50 percent growth rate of orders each quarter. If the growth rate fails to exceed 50 percent, the performance rating of the subject is reduced as a penalty. Thus, to maximize final cash on hand, order growth is necessary. On the other hand, increased orders leading to delivery delays will lose more orders in the future and result in substantial loss of cash. Therefore, subjects must learn that incurring a penalty for less than a 50 percent growth rate in the first three quarters is necessary to achieve success in the next five quarters and to accumulate the largest final amount of cash on hand.

Four levels of short-term performance pressure were imposed on subjects. In the first level, null pressure, a subject's performance was evaluated solely on the basis of long-term goal achievement. For the second level, ten percent pressure, the subject's overall performance was weighted ten percent on short-term goal achievement and 90 percent on long-term goal achievement. For the third level, 50 percent pressure, the subject's overall performance depended 50 percent on short-term goal achievement and 50 percent on long-term goal achievement. For the fourth level, overall performance depended 90 percent on the short-term goal and ten percent on the long-term goal.

Subjects in the first level were told that their scores depended on the final cash on hand compared to the achievement of other students. Subjects in the second level were told that 90 percent of their scores depended on their final cash on hand compared to the achievement of other students; the ten percent weighting for short-term performance was reflected in a loss of 1.3(=10points/8quarters) percentage performance points for each quarter in which the order growth rate was lower than 50 percent.

Procedure. Subjects were randomly assigned to the four groups facing the four pressure conditions. Before running the virtual business in the no aid condition, subjects were given a short briefing that described the decision variables, explained the two decisions of hiring and investing, and described the performance measurement structure. Subjects were then asked to manage the firm through the first eight quarters. Before the second eight quarters, the systems thinking aid was provided to subjects, and subjects were given information about task-specific systems thinking principles to use in managing the next eight quarters. In the third eight quarters, subjects were given the task-specific decision rules, and then managed the firm for a final (third) set of eight quarters.

Hypotheses

A number of hypotheses were formulated and tested through this experiment, as follows:

(1) Main effects:

H1.1: Short-term performance pressure encourages choice of SIC alternatives, so that subjects facing short-term performance pressure will choose SIC alternatives more often than those who face long-term performance pressure.

H1.2: Short-term performance pressure encourages choice of SIC alternatives, leading to lower long-term performance.

H2.1: Subjects who receive a task-specific systems thinking aid develop better mental models to guide decision-making and therefore will choose SIC alternatives less often than subjects who receive no aid.

H2.2: Subjects who receive a systems thinking aid develop better mental models to guide decision-making and therefore will achieve higher long-term performance than subjects who receive no aid.

H3.1: Subjects who receive a detailed-decision-rule aid develop better mental models to guide decision-making and therefore will choose SIC alternatives less often than subjects who receive no aid.

H3.2: Subjects who receive a detailed-decision-rule aid develop better mental models to guide decision-making and therefore will achieve higher long-term performance than subjects who receive no aid.

(2) Interaction effects:

H4.1: With no cognitive aid, short-term performance pressure results in a preference for SIC alternatives, and subjects with short-term performance pressure will choose SIC alternatives more frequently than subjects who do not face short-term performance pressure.

H4.2: With no cognitive aid, short-term performance pressure results in a preference for SIC alternatives, and subjects with short-term performance pressure will achieve lower long-term performance than those who face long-term performance pressure.

H5.1: With a systems thinking aid provided, subjects develop better mental models to guide decision-making and will choose SIC alternatives less often, even when they face short-term performance pressure.

H5.2: With a systems thinking aid provided, subjects develop better mental models to guide decision-making and will achieve higher performance, even when they face short-term performance pressure.

H6.1: With an optimal-decision-rule aid provided, subjects develop better mental models to guide decision-making and will choose SIC alternatives less often, even when they face short-term performance pressure.

H6.2: With an detailed-decision-rule aid provided, subjects develop better mental models to guide decision-making and will achieve higher performance, even when they face short-term performance pressure.

Results

Manipulation Check

Two sets of data were gathered to check the effects of performance pressure manipulation.[2] In the first set, subjects were asked to estimate the importance of the long-term goal achievement (on a scale of one to seven) in their decision making. The mean responses in relation to the four conditions (null, ten percent, 50 percent, and 90 percent pressure) were 6.5, 5.9, 5.5, 5.3, respectively. Subjects were then asked to estimate the importance in their decision making of achieving the short-term goal, again on a scale of one to seven. The means of estimates with respect to the four conditions were 4.2, 4.4, 5.6, 5.4, respectively. Statistical analysis[3] supports the hypothesis that subjects do respond strongly to short-term performance goal manipulation.

SIC Choice Behavior

(1) Main effects:

Table 1 reports the means of the subjects' choice frequency of SIC alternatives. It shows that null and ten percent weighting of short-term performance pressure have less SIC choice than 50 percent and 90 percent pressure conditions ($F(3, 46) = 6.475$, $p < 0.001$). By pairwise comparisons, the null pressure condition results in significantly less SIC choice than the 50 percent or 90 percent pressure conditions, ($F(1, 46) = 14.507$, $p < 0.0005$; $F(1, 46) = 4.510$, $p < 0.05$, respectively). The ten percent pressure condition also results in less SIC choice compared to the 50 percent or 90 percent pressure conditions ($F(1, 46) = 8.027$, $p < 0.01$; $F(1, 46) = 4.836$, $p < 0.05$, respectively). Hypothesis 1.1 is thus supported when short-term performance pressure is within the 50 percent and 90 percent weighting range.

---

[2]The cognitive aid manipulation was not checked because subjects kept the instructions and consulted them throughout the whole procedure.

[3]The total difference in the first estimates of importance of the long-term goal was marginally significant with the repeated measures ANOVA test ($F(3, 44) = 2.740$, $p < 0.1$). The total difference in estimates of importance of achieving the short-term goal was significant ($F(3, 42) = 3.232$, $p < 0.05$).

With regard to the three cognitive aid conditions, the detailed decision rule was effective in reducing SIC choices; however, the systems thinking aid was not. Table 1 shows that the no aid and systems thinking aid conditions have significantly more SIC choices than the detailed-decision-rule aid has (Wilks' Lambda = 0.2062, $F(2, 45)$ = 86.593, $p < 0.001$). By pairwise comparisons, only the detailed-decision-rule aid has significantly less SIC choices than no aid ($F(4, 46)$ = 17.762, $p < 0.0001$). Thus Hypothesis 2.1 is not supported whereas Hypothesis 3.1 is supported.

(2) Interaction effects:

The interaction effects between the two manipulations show that the effectiveness of the cognitive aids is moderated by short-term performance pressure (Wilks' Lambda = 0.6826, $F(6, 90)$ = 3.156, $p < 0.01$). As shown in Table 1 and Figure 2, the SIC choices decrease gradually from no aid to the systems thinking aid and the detailed-decision-rule aid under the no-pressure condition. However, this effect is less clear in the groups facing short-term performance pressure. Furthermore, in the no aid condition, the null and ten percent pressure groups have fewer SIC choices than the 50 percent and 90 percent pressure groups (null vs. 50 percent: $F(1, 46)$ = 7.546, $p < 0.01$; null vs. 90 percent: $F(1, 46)$ = 4.510, $p < 0.05$; ten percent vs. 50 percent: $F(1, 46)$ = 8.961, $p < 0.005$; ten percent vs. 90 percent: $F(1, 46)$ = 5.618, $p < 0.05$). In the systems thinking aid condition, the null pressure group has fewer SIC choices than the 50 percent and 90 percent pressure groups ($F(1, 46)$ = 8.544, $p < 0.01$; $F(1, 6)$ = 7.627, $p < 0.01$, respectively). In the optimal decision-rule-aid condition, all of the pairwise comparisons are insignificant at conventional levels. These results support Hypotheses 4.1 and 6.1, when short-term performance pressure is bounded

Table 1: SIC Choice Frequency.

Conditions of Pressure	Three Aid Modes			
	No aid	Systems thinking aid	Detailed-decision-rule aid	Aggregated mean
Null n=13	2.846 (2.248)	1.231 (2.258)	0.000 (0.000)	1.359 (2.178)
10% n=13	2.615 (2.132)	2.692 (2.126)	0.308 (0.606)	1.872 (2.090)
50% n=12	5.417 (2.178)	4.250 (2.919)	0.417 (1.115)	3.361 (3.066)
90% n=12	4.833 (2.409)	4.083 (2.564)	0.167 (0.373)	3.028 (2.891)
Aggregated mean N=50	3.880 (2.551)	3.020 (2.760)	0.220 (0.672)	2.373 (2.702)

Note: Standard deviations are in parentheses.

within 50 percent to 90 percent. Hypothesis 5.1 is not supported because the systems thinking aid could not lessen SIC choices under conditions of short-term performance pressure.

Performance

Table 2 shows that the null pressure group outperforms the ten percent, 50 percent and 90 percent pressure groups ($F(3, 46) = 3.168$, $p < 0.05$). By pairwise comparisons, the null pressure group significantly outperforms the ten percent, 50 percent and 90 percent pressure groups ($F(1, 46) = 4.335$, $p < 0.050$; $F(1, 46) = 5.717$, $p < 0.05$; $F(1, 46) = 7.903$, $p < 0.01$, respectively). Hypothesis 1.2 is thus supported.

Table 3 shows short-term performance expressed as the average quarter during which a 50 percent order growth rate was achieved. No significant differences were found among pressure groups. This indicates that the various weightings of short-term performance goals did not lead to performance differences in the long term.

Cognitive aids, however, were found to be beneficial in improving long-term performance. As shown in Table 2, the detailed-decision-rule group outperforms the systems thinking aid group and the systems thinking aid group outperforms the no aid group (Wilks' Lambda = 0.1763, $F(2, 45) = 105.134$, $p < 0.001$). Pairwise comparisons also confirm that the detailed-decision-rule group outperforms the systems thinking aid group ($F(4, 46) = 17.902$, $p < 0.0001$) and the systems thinking aid group outperforms the no aid group ($F(4, 46) = 4.440$, $p < 0.005$). These results support Hypotheses 2.2 and 3.2.

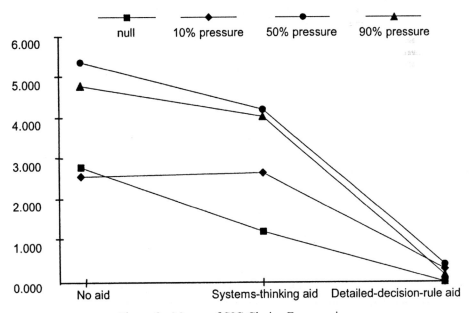

Figure 2: Means of SIC Choice Frequencies.

Table 2: Long-term Performance.

| Conditions of Pressure | Three Aid Modes | | | |
	No aid	Systems thinking aid	Detailed-decision- rule aid	Aggregated mean
Null n=13	281.4 (490.8)	1349.3 (1211.3)	2188.9 (854.9)	1273.2 (1192.6)
10% n=13	89.7 (581.7)	551.9 (1014.9)	1734.6 (733.9)	792.1 (1056.1)
50% n=12	54.7 (666.5)	366.3 (1041.8)	1706.8 (691.5)	709.3 (1087.7)
90% n=12	−82.1 (376.1)	128.1 (912.6)	1784.5 (316.4)	610.2 (1027.2)
Aggregated mean N=50	89.9 (555.1)	613.0 (1150.1)	1858.0 (712.8)	853.6 (1123.8)

Note: Standard deviations are in parentheses.

Table 3: Short-term Performance.

| Conditions of Pressure | Three Aid Modes | | | |
	No aid	Systems thinking aid	Detailed-decision- rule aid	Aggregated mean
Null n=13	0.538 (0.843)	2.231 (1.671)	3.462 (1.216)	2.077 (1.760)
10% n=13	0.769 (1.250)	1.538 (1.599)	3.077 (1.328)	1.795 (1.697)
50% n=12	1.000 (1.000)	1.417 (1.037)	3.417 (1.656)	1.944 (1.649)
90% n=12	0.833 (0.799)	1.667 (1.700)	4.167 (1.518)	2.222 (1.988)
Aggregated mean N=50	0.780 (1.006)	1.720 (1.563)	3.520 (1.486)	2.007 (1.783)

Note: Standard deviations are in parentheses.

Similar results were found with respect to groups facing high short-term goal pressure. As shown in Table 3, even under high short-term performance pressure, the optimal decision-rule group outperforms the systems thinking aid group, and the systems thinking aid group outperforms the no aid group (Wilks' Lambda = 0.2258, $F(2, 45)$= 77.126, $p <$ 0.001). Pairwise comparisons are all significant in confirming that the detailed-decision-rule group outperforms the systems thinking aid group ($F(4, 46) = 21.557, p < 0.0001$), and that the systems thinking aid group outperforms the no aid group ($F(4, 46) = 5.911, p <$ 0.001). These results strongly suggest that cognitive aids can be effective both in improving short-term performance and in sustaining performance in the long term.

Interaction effect tests showed that the short-term performance pressure moderated the effect of the systems thinking aid on performance, since as Table 2 and Figure 3 show, the null pressure group outperformed the other three pressure groups, especially when the systems thinking aid was used. Pairwise comparisons confirm that the null pressure group significantly outperformed the ten percent, 50 percent, and 90 percent groups when the systems thinking aid was used ($F(1, 46) = 3.427, p < 0.1; F(1, 46) = 4.999, p < 0.05; F(1, 46) = 7.716, p < 0.01$, respectively). The four pressure groups had nearly identical long-term performance when no aid or the detailed-decision-rule aid was used. The results thus do not support Hypotheses 4.2 and 5.2, but do support 6.2.

In terms of short-term goal achievement, Table 3 and Figure 4 show no statistically significant differences among groups using either the systems thinking or detailed-decision-rule cognitive aids. Heavy incentives for short-term goal performance, in other words, did not significantly improve short-term performance over the long term.

Discussion

Researchers and practitioners believe and have widely advocated that training in systems thinking is beneficial for decision-makers when developing strategies for long-term gains and overall systems performance (Senge, 1990; Cavaleri & Sterman, 1997). Sanchez and

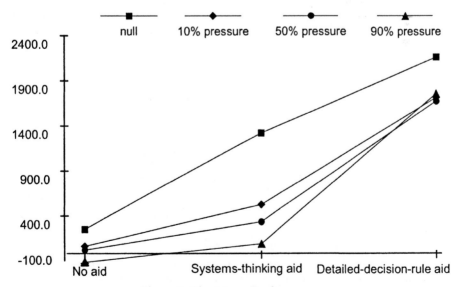

Figure 3: Short-term Performance.

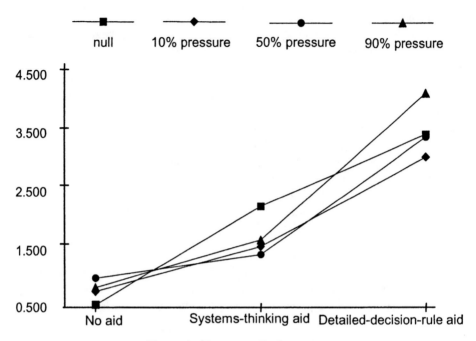

Figure 4: Short-term Performance.

Heene (1996) have further proposed that in understanding the management of compe-tences in dynamically complex situations, "incorporating the cognitive limits of managers acknowledges that causal ambiguity is also an internal condition of the firm and greatly affects the firm's decision process for selecting, acquiring, and using resources." The results of the present study support the view that — at least in the absence of pressure for short-term performance — systems thinking helps to ensure that fundamentally sound strategies are employed. Thus, improving managers' comprehension of systems thinking can be helpful in developing more effective strategic logics and management processes in competence-based management. However, the results of this study also suggest that the effectiveness of systems thinking can be diminished when performance measures strongly emphasize short-term goals.

There are four major findings of the present study that are relevant to understanding the cognitive dimensions of managing organizations as systems. First, when facing an unfa-miliar dynamic decision environment, decision makers are likely to prefer SIC alternatives to LDC alternatives and to perform poorly in the long term. In other words, they are likely to suffer the "growth and under-investment" problem described by Senge (1990). Second, the tendency to choose SIC outcomes can be reduced by systems thinking and detailed-decision-rule aids in the absence of heavy emphasis on short-term goals. Third, when short-term goal achievement is given 50 percent or more weightings in overall perform-ance measurements, however, the tendency to choose SIC outcomes is not likely to be moderated by a systems thinking aid. Furthermore, an emphasis on short-term goals may not lead to better short-term performance in the long term, even when systems thinking and detailed-decision-rule aids are provided. Fourth, the provision of detailed decision rules was beneficial in improving LDC choice and long-term performance, irrespective of the emphasis placed on short-term goals.

That subjects had their worst performance in the no aid condition in our experiments is not a surprising finding. Many previous studies have similar findings (e.g., Paich & Sterman, 1993; Sterman, 1989a, 1989b; Diehl & Sterman, 1996; Yang, 1996), confirming that dynamic complexity can easily challenge or exceed human cognitive capability, as asserted in the competence literature. Another possible explanation is that, in practice, the problematic nature of parameterizing and assessing higher order system elements (such as strategic logic and management processes) may lead managers to focus on ostensibly less ambiguous and more quantifiable system elements (Sanchez & Heene, 1996).

Given the present study's finding that a systems thinking aid may not improve SIC choice in the presence of significant short-term performance pressure, providing managers with some systemic managing principles may not provide enough information to stimulate what Argyris (1990) has called "double loop learning," in which people learn to adjust their mental models (Cavaleri & Sterman, 1997; Sengupta & Abdel-Hamid, 1993). Rather, appropriate emphasis must be made on long-term performance goals in order to stimulate decision makers to develop appropriate mental models for achieving better strategic logics and management processes. In other words, among people who have the same ability in systems thinking, individuals will make different choices between SIC and LDC alternatives depending on the degree of emphasis placed on short-term performance.

Kudadjie-Gyamfi and Rachlin (1996) and Herrnstein *et al.* (1993) were unable to explain their finding that cognitive aid is not sufficient to reduce SIC. The present study may shed light on this problem. In their studies, subjects received outcome feedback in the form of the reward they accumulated after each choice. This reward mechanism corresponds to short-term goal setting in the present study. Therefore, the effectiveness of the cognitive aid in guiding subjects to choose LDC outcomes was reduced in their studies, because the short-term rewards in their studies may have motivated subjects to choose SIC alternatives.

So, can the bias towards SIC choice be lessened? Kudadjie-Gyamfi and Rachlin (1996) provide a suggestion from a motivational perspective. Herrnstein *et al.* (1993) and the present study provide another suggestion from the cognitive aspect. Kudadjie-Gyamfi and Rachlin (1996) found that insertion of inter-trial intervals in series choices (or "temporal patterning") increased LDC choices significantly, in comparison to the condition where there were no such intervals. If people do have a natural tendency to make SIC choices impulsively, then temporal patterning may make the reward less immediate and thus provide a counterbalancing force. From the cognitive perspective, both Herrnstein *et al.* (1993) and the present study found that providing detailed decision rules significantly moderated the SIC bias. These findings suggest that intensive cognitive assistance can be effective, when both "how to do" (the principles for making decisions) and "what to do" (detailed guidelines for making each decision) are presented.

Implications

The findings of the present study have several implications for the theory of competence-based management.

First, it is often asserted that managers develop understanding of important causal relationships among phenomena through "learning by doing." In the present study, however, subjects did not learn very well simply by repeated decisions. These results suggest that "learning by doing" is not always an effective way to learn, not just in dynamically complex environments, but even when important causal relationships are not ambiguous. Factors that impede learning include not just human bounded rationality, but also the goals given to decision makers. People are rationally bounded in their understanding of multiple causal loops, particularly when delays are embedded in the causal loops. Goals, however, strongly direct attention in specific directions and lead to a lack of attention to the side effects of decisions.

Second, coordination mechanisms are essential in building and leveraging competences (Sanchez, Heene, & Thomas, 1996). The present study demonstrates that coordination can be difficult to understand even within a simple organization. The subjects in our simple experiment, for example, had difficulty in coordinating just manufacturing and sales levels. In real organizations, the coordination problem is accentuated when many decision-makers throughout a firm determine the resource flows that make up the firm's processes in the aggregate. Moreover, the performances of those decision-makers is usually evaluated on the basis of "uncoordinated" performance measures, creating incentive structures within an organization that make overall coordination even more difficult. Sanchez, Heene, and Thomas (1996) argue that a key challenge in competence-based management is to maintain organizational effectiveness by achieving consistency of strategic logic throughout the firm. To improve coordination within an organization, goals for performance measurement should be logically and consistently interrelated at the departmental and group levels. Interdependent performance measurements that cut across departments may also need to sustain a shared strategic logic among managers.

In terms of implications for competence-based approaches to management practice and managerial education, our study suggests that a group of strategic managers will be likely to fail if they try to manage a firm's strategic logic individually and heuristically. Collective learning and cognitive aids, such as tools for systems thinking, can be helpful and even necessary (Prahalad & Hamel, 1990; Klein & Hiscocks, 1994).

Second, any cognitive aids or acquired knowledge may not improve decision-making if top management lacks a shared knowledge, strategic logic, and vision of what competences to build and leverage, or if short-term performance pressures hinder consistent efforts to build and leverage those competences. Systems thinking approaches can serve as an organizational communication framework for reaching such consensus (Senge, 1990). This consensus is a prerequisite for undertaking the design of appropriate management processes.

Finally, the design of performance goals and measures should be undertaken with great care. Management processes like resource allocations and performance measures are necessary, but should have a long-term perspective and be holistically oriented if they are to build and leverage competences. When organizations become victims of short-term performance pressures, unwanted side effects may result, and inappropriate subsystem goals are likely to arise. If short-term goals predominate, neither synergy nor sustainable competitive advantage may be achieved.

In terms of future research, we have the following suggestions. First, studying the design of practical cognitive aids — to be used in addition to "learning by doing" — could greatly benefit strategic managers trying to formulate appropriate strategic logic and management processes. Second, for managers in the real world, short-term performance pressure is unavoidable. Thus, we need to understand better how organizations can incorporate the longer-term, holistic, systemic point of view into organizational incentive structures. Finally, there is a need to develop better theories that explicitly incorporate both reinforcing loops (positive feedback loops) and balancing loops (negative feedback loops), and their appropriate use by decision-makers. Previous researchers, such as Sanchez and Thomas (1996), have proposed that the dynamic processes of competence building and leveraging can become self-reinforcing. Negative feedback loops that act as balancing forces on competence building and leveraging also need to be recognized and understood.

References

Argyris, A. (1990). *Overcoming Organizational Defenses*. Boston, MA: Allyn and Bacon.

Argyris, A., & Schon, (1996). *Organizational Learning II: Theory, Method, and Practice*. New York: Addison Wesley.

Bogner, W. C., & Thomas, H. (1994). Core competence and competitive advantage: A model and illustrative evidence from pharmaceutical industry. In G. Hamel & A. Heene (eds) *Competence-Based Competition* (pp. 111–144). New York: John Wiley and Sons.

Bohm, D. (1996). *On Dialogue*. Cambridge, MA: Pegasus Communications.

Cavaleri, S., & Sterman, J. D. (1997). Towards evaluation of systems thinking interventions: A case study. *System Dynamics Review, 13*, 171–186.

Diehl, E., & Sterman, J. D. (1995). Effects of feedback complexity on dynamic decision making. *Organizational Behavior and Human Performance, 62(2)*, 198–215.

Forrester, J. W. (1984). Market growth as influenced by capital investment. In E. B. Roberts (ed.) *Managerial Applications of System Dynamics*. Cambridge, MA: The MIT Press.

Hamel, G. (1994). The concept of core competence. In G. Hamel & A. Heene (eds.) *Competence-Based Competition* (pp. 11–34). New York: John Wiley and Sons.

Herrnstein, R. J., Loewenstein, G. F., Vaughan, W. Jr., & Prelec, D. (1993). Utility maximization and melioration: Internalities in individual choice. *Journal of Behavioral Decision Making, 6(3)*, 149–185.

Klein, J. A., & Hiscocks, P. G. (1994). Competence-based competition: A practical toolkit. In G. Hamel & A. Heene (eds), *Competence-Based Competition* (pp. 183–212). New York: John Wiley and Sons.

Kudadjie-Gyamfi, E., & Rachlin, H. (1996). Temporal patterning in choice among delayed outcomes. *Organizational Behavior and Human Decision Process, 65*, 61–67.

Paich, M., & Sterman, J. D. (1992). Boom, bust, and failures to learn in experimental market, working paper 3441-92-BPS, Sloan School of Management, Massachusetts Institute of Technology.

Prahalad, C. K., & Hamel, G. (1990). The core competence of the corporation. *Harvard Business Review, 68(3)*, 79–91.

Rachlin, H. & Green, T. (1972). Commitment, choice, and self-control. *Journal of the Experimental Analysis of Behavior, 59*, 161–176.

Rachlin, H., & Siegel, E. (1994). Temporal patterning in probabilistic choice. *Organizational Behavior and Human Decision Process, 59*, 161–176.

Sanchez, R., & Heene, A. (1996). A systems view of the firm in competence-based competition. In R. Sanchez, A. Heene, & H. Thomas (eds) *Dynamics of Competence-Based Competition* (pp. 39–62). London: Pergamon.

Sanchez, R. & Thomas, H. (1996). Strategic goals. In R. Sanchez, A. Heene, & H. Thomas (eds), *Dynamics of Competence-Based Competition* (pp. 63–84). London: Pergamon.

Senge, P. M. (1990). *The Fifth Discipline: The Art and Practice of the Learning Organization.* New York: Doubleday Currency.

Sengupta, A., & Abdel-Hamid, T. K. (1993). Alternative conceptions of feedback in dynamic decision environments: An experimental investigation. *Management Science, 39(4)*, 411–428.

Sterman, J. D. (1989a). Modeling managerial behavior: Misperceptions of feedback in a dynamic decision making experiment. *Management Science, 35*, 321–339.

Sterman, J. D. (1989b). Misperceptions of feedback in dynamic decision making. *Organizational Behavior and Human Decision Process, 43*, 301–335.

Sterman, J. D. (1994). Learning in and about complex systems. *System Dynamic Review, 10*, 291–327.

Tversky, A., & Kahneman, D. (1974). Judgment under uncertainty: Heuristics and biases. *Science, 185*, 1124–1131.

Yang, J. (1996). Facilitating learning through goal setting in a learning laboratory. *Proceedings of the 1996 International System Dynamics Conference*, 593–596.

Yang, J. (1997). Give me the right goals, I will be a good dynamic decision maker. *Proceedings of the 1996 International System Dynamics Conference*, 709–712.

PART IV

Systems Concepts for Self-Managing Organizations

Chapter 11

Strategic Management at the Point of Inflection: Systems, Complexity, and Competence Theory[1]

Ron Sanchez

Introduction

Networking, reengineering, modular organizations, virtual corporations, perpetual enterprises, employee empowerment, stakeholder management.

The new vocabulary and preoccupations of managers are signalling both the emergence of new ways of thinking about the nature of organizations and the increasing appearance of new kinds of organization designs and management processes. As these changes progress, however, there are growing disparities between the traditional concepts of organizations underpinning most strategic management theory and the new organization concepts now evolving in strategic management practice. No surprise, then, that management conferences and journals are increasingly calling for new perspectives, concepts, and theory to give better insights into the developments now taking place in the practice of strategic management.

The emergence of new organizational forms and management practices in recent years has been paralleled, not coincidentally, by a growing interest among management researchers and practitioners in two theoretical perspectives — systems theory and complexity theory. Both theories offer frameworks for increasing our understanding of dynamic phenomena of all types, from the interactions of molecules to the struggle for survival of species to changes in the global ecosystem. In the following discussion, I suggest how some key insights of systems theory and complexity theory relevant to organizations are reflected in a new theoretical base for strategic management now being developed under the banner of *competence-based strategic management* (Sanchez, Heene, & Thomas, 1996a; Heene & Sanchez, 1997). I also suggest some ways in which systems and complexity concepts being incorporated in competence theory are leading to new insights into feasible organization designs and processes, to better understanding of the

[1]This paper was previously published under the same title in *Long Range Planning,* (1997), *30(6),* 939–946.

innovative kinds of organizations increasingly evident today, and to new principles for guiding strategic management in newly evolving kinds of organizations.

Incorporating systems and complexity concepts in competence theory has made evident that what have been widely regarded in strategy theory as fundamental concepts and general principles governing organizations in competitive environments are really only special cases in a larger scheme of possibilities. In the resource-base view in strategy theory, for example, a firm's resource endowments have been seen as the source of competitive advantages that lead to superior performance (Wernerfelt, 1984; Barney, 1991). The systems perspective incorporated in competence theory, however, suggests that a firm's current resource endowments are only one state of a firm that functions as an open system engaged in a dynamic process of *building, accessing, and leveraging resources and capabilities* (Sanchez & Heene, 1996). Thus, a more general theory of the role of resources in competitive advantage would have to include the processes by which firms identify and acquire strategic resources.

Similarly, while commitment has often been characterized as the essential "dynamic of strategy" (Ghemawat, 1991), in competence theory the complexity of the environment is presumed to create significant uncertainties for organizations, with the consequence that commitment is seen as only a final step in a more fundamental organizational process of *creating and exercising strategic options* (Sanchez, 1993, 1995; Sanchez & Thomas, 1996). Further, strategic management has traditionally been characterized as a centralized top-down planning, decision-making, and control-exercising function. In competence theory, however, strategic management is seen as a process of *designing organizations as adaptive systems*. As I will discuss below, the objective of this mode of strategic management is creating and supporting self-managing organizational processes that enable better interpretation of and faster response to complex, dynamic environments and their attendant uncertainties.

As the title of this paper suggests, the impact of incorporating systems and complexity concepts in a new theory of competence-based strategic management may be to bring strategy theory to an historic "point of inflection" — a point at which we see the beginning in competence theory of a major redefinition and expansion of the conceptual base of strategic management.

The first section of this discussion describes some key concepts common to both systems theory and complexity theory. Section 2 suggests how the interplay of systems and complexity concepts in competence theory is helping to shape a more *dynamic, systemic, cognitive, and holistic* representation of the task and processes of strategic management. Section 3 suggests several ways in which competence theory's broader view is expanding the theoretical base of strategic management. Section 4 concludes with some comments on the implications of systems and complexity concepts for the practice of competence-based strategic management.

The Common Conceptual Base in Systems Theory and Complexity Theory

Although some contemporary notions of the ways in which physical and social phenomena behave like systems appear as early as Alfred North Whitehead's *Science and the Modern*

World (1925), the development of systems ideas reached its greatest intensity in the 1960s in the work of Ashby (1960), Beer (1966), Forrester (1961, 1968) and others who created an extensive body of theory about the nature and behavior of physical and social systems. This work demonstrated that a few entities linked by interdependencies and feedback mechanisms compose a simple system that may nonetheless be capable of generating very complex behaviors. Studies of systems behaviors further established that systems with certain kinds of interrelationships and feedback mechanisms are more capable than others of maintaining "quasi-stable" internal conditions while adapting to changing environmental conditions. The effort to understand the properties of systems that can maintain quasi-stability while adapting to change is epitomized in the work of Miller (1978), who hypothesized and provided support for a set of general principles for robust (survivable) systems that can be applied at the levels of individual cells, organs, the human organism, groups of people, organizations, societies, and "supranational" systems.

Given the power of systems principles to suggest models capable of generating complex dynamic behaviors of many kinds, systems theory became a fundamental framework for scientific and engineering analyses of complex phenomena in the 1970s. Although systems concepts enjoyed a period of popularity in management theory and practice in the late 1970s and early 1980s (*e.g.,* Checkland, 1981), systems theory did not exercise a significant influence on the then-forming field of strategic management, which looked largely to industrial organization economics and its essentially static view of competition ("industry structures") for foundational concepts. Recent work applying systems concepts to organizational learning (Morecroft & Sterman, 1994; Senge, 1990; Vennix, 1996), however, may herald a revival of interest in systems thinking in strategic management studies.

The central concepts of what we now refer to as complexity theory emerged in the physical and biological sciences during the 1960s to 1980s. Complexity concepts began to reach a wider audience in the 1990s largely through Kaufman's (1993) *The Origins of Order,* and has recently begun to enter the domain of organization studies (for example, McKelvey, 1997). Complexity theory suggests that complex phenomena exhibiting "chaotic" behaviors result from the elements of a system whose interactions are capable of generating essentially unlimited variations in patterns of behavior. Occasionally, however, the elements of a system may interact in ways that tend to keep the elements of the system within a certain range of variation, and a system that is capable of generating chaotic behavior will then begin to exhibit unpredictable behaviors that are limited in their range of variation. The result is "quasi-stable" patterns of behavior that emerge in the midst of previously chaotic phenomena. Modes of interaction between system elements that cause the elements to remain within certain ranges of variation are termed "attractors" because they lead to patterns of quasi-stability in otherwise chaotic processes. Thus, embedded within at least some systems is the potential for "self-organizing" processes that can create periods of quasi-stability or "near order" in otherwise chaotic phenomena.

For example, various species with certain interdependencies may form an ecological subsystem with greater survivability for all members, creating patterns of quasi-stable behaviors in the midst of an otherwise highly unpredictable environment. Analogously, certain organizations may establish competitive and cooperative relationships and practices that act like attractors in creating a quasi-stable, more survivable pattern of behavior in an otherwise unpredictable competitive environment.

An important conceptual commonality in systems theory and complexity theory can be recognized by conceiving of the two theories as, in effect, looking at the same phenomena from two "mirror image" perspectives. From an "inside-out" perspective, systems theory tries to explain the ways in which interactions between the interdependent elements of a system can lead to stable (quasi-stable) or unstable (chaotic) behaviors. From an outside-in perspective, complexity theory tries to explain how both chaotic behaviors and periods of quasi-stability could result from the interactions of the entities composing a system. These differing perspectives, while focused on the same phenomena, lead to different research styles and methods. Systems theorists tend to build "mechanistic" systems models that are based on deterministic relationships between variables, but that are nevertheless capable of exhibiting complex patterns of behavior. Complexity theorists, on the other hand, tend to use advanced mathematical techniques to analyze complex phenomena in the hopes of inferring underlying relationships between the elements of a system that are capable of exhibiting quasi-stable behaviors. Although each theory has adopted its own vocabulary and imagery for conveying its insights into the "origins of order" (Kaufman, 1993) in complex phenomena, systems theory and complexity theory provide complementary and ultimately convergent insights into the composition, interrelationships, and dynamics of complex adaptive systems.

Systems and Complexity Concepts in the Competence Perspective

In an effort to "reinvent strategic management" (Sanchez & Heene, 1997), the movement to develop a theory of competence-based strategic management has proposed four corner-stones of an expanded theoretical foundation for strategic management. Each of these theoretical cornerstones reflects important systems and complexity concepts.

The first cornerstone of competence theory is the representation of the environment of an organization as *dynamic*, which is taken to mean that current market preferences can change, available technological and organizational means for serving those preferences can change, and even the existing institutions, infrastructures, and norms that constrain the ways organizations may function can change. Thus, the activities which an organization must be capable of performing in order to survive in its environment will change over time, as will the set of capabilities which are potential sources of competitive advantage. The dynamic complexity of both the external and internal environments of organizations, however, makes the exact nature of most future changes and their implications for future sources of competitive advantage unpredictable to a significant degree. As a result, the complexities organizations face lead to significant uncertainties or *causal ambiguities* (Lippman & Rumelt, 1982; Sanchez, Heene, & Thomas, 1996b) about the nature of the specific resources and capabilities an organization will need to respond effectively to necessities and opportunities arising in the future.

A second cornerstone of competence theory is the characterization of organizations as *open-systems* embedded in larger systems of resources (like industries and nations) which each organization must be able to access in order to survive (Sanchez & Heene, 1996). Competition between organizations is therefore characterized as competition for access to critical inputs (skills, information, knowledge, imagination), as well as competition in markets for outputs. The challenge to strategic managers of organizations embedded in environments with dynamic and complex interdependencies is to devise an open-system design capable of accessing and coordinating a changing array of input resources (some internal, but many external) that enable the creation of a changing array of outputs. Thus, the desired property of an organization in a dynamic, complex environment is a *robust open-system design* which gives the organization adequate *strategic flexibility* (Sanchez, 1993, 1995) to respond to a changing set of opportunities and necessities in markets for both inputs and outputs.

The third cornerstone of competence theory is the view that, given the complexity and dynamism of an organization's environment, the most fundamental demands placed on strategic managers in a dynamic and complex environment will be *cognitive*. Managers must meet the mental challenge of devising a *strategic logic* that identifies the competences which they believe will best enable their organization to achieve its goals in its evolving environment. In both theory and practice, however, the imperfect information available to managers and the bounded rationality (Simon, 1947) which they, like all humans, are subject to makes it unlikely that anyone could identify a single set of resources and capabilities which would bring a "sustainable competitive advantage" to an organization in a dynamic and complex environment. Competition between organizations can therefore be seen as an ongoing "contest between managerial cognitions" (Sanchez, Heene, & Thomas, 1996b) in devising processes for organizational sensemaking (Weick, 1992), for the development and exercise of a corporate imagination (Hamel & Prahalad, 1991), and for articulating new strategic logics for improving the adaptive capabilities of firms as open systems (Sanchez & Heene, 1996).

Competence theory's fourth cornerstone is the proposition that managers must have a *holistic* view of their organizations if they are to build firms that can function effectively as adaptive open systems. To be capable of systemic change, organizations must successfully mediate the interests of diverse constituencies of resource providers internal and external to the firm. Managing the creation of wealth for providers of financial resources (shareholders) is therefore only one aspect of managerial work. In the more complete competence view, strategic management is a process of creating and distributing wealth to a diverse and (often) changing set of providers of essential resources required by the firm as an evolving open system.

Through these four cornerstone notions of the dynamic, systemic, cognitive, and holistic nature of the internal and external environments of organizations, the systems and complexity concepts incorporated in the competence perspective lead to a new view of the fundamental nature of the strategic management task. In this view, strategic management becomes an effort to reduce the impact of environmental complexity and uncertainty on organizations by devising a set of relatively simple rules for ordering organizational processes in ways capable of maintaining quasi-stability while an organization adapts to a complex dynamic environment. The next section considers several ways in which this view of *strategic management as adaptive system design* expands the traditional theory base in strategy and leads to new concepts for the practice of strategic management.

Expanding the Conceptual Base of Strategic Management

When organizations are viewed as open systems whose interactions with complex environments create dynamic webs of uncertainty, many traditional strategic management concepts about firms and their competitive interactions can be seen as rather special cases in a broader set of possibilities. The following discussion suggests some resulting reinterpretations of traditional strategy concepts and principles and places them in a conceptually expanded set of possibilities recognized in the competence perspective.

From "Content" to "Process" Explanatory Variables. Traditional strategy theory tries to provide a framework for identifying the "content variables" that are the sources of competitive advantage and resulting superior performance — for example, possession of a major position in an industry structure or of some strategically valuable resources. From the competence view, however, this sort of *ex post* strategic content analysis can be seen as relevant to the special case of environments in which the sources of competitive advantage are essentially static. When competitive environments are assumed to be capable of changing in ways that are imperfectly predictable, the usefulness of the findings of *ex post* content analyses of successful strategies for *ex ante* strategic decision making becomes unclear.

The inherent limitations of *ex post* content analyses of sources of competitive advantage are evident in the resource-base view in strategy theory. In the resource-base view, to identify specific strategically important resources, one studies successful firms *ex post* to discern their endowments of unique, difficult to imitate, non-substitutable, and valuable resources (Barney, 1991). Such resources are then said to be responsible for the firm's success. This essentially tautological analysis may be useful to strategic managers in the special case in which the resources that can be sources of competitive advantage are not changing. If new kinds of resources are being created or new kinds of market requirements are evolving, however, the resources that have been strategically valuable in the past may be different from those that will prove to be strategically valuable in the future. Thus, both the conceptual relevance and practical usefulness of *ex post* resource-base analysis to *ex ante* strategizing is limited to those environmental contexts with static sources of competitive advantage.

To respond conceptually to the more general case in which environments and the resources which can be sources of competitive advantage may change over time, the competence perspective shifts the focus of strategic analysis from the specific content of the "firm as an open system" at a given point in time to the dynamic processes by which a firm identifies and develops strategic resources on an ongoing basis. Thus, the competence perspective analyzes *processes* in organizations for sensemaking in a changing environment, for developing new internal resources and capabilities, for accessing new external resources, for defining new organizational goals, and for coordinating available resources and capabilities in the pursuit of an evolving set of strategic goals. When the resources that may be sources of competitive advantage in the future are uncertain, understanding the process capabilities that enable an organization to develop or access resources becomes essential to the strategic management task of developing better adaptive system designs.

Thus, in a dynamic and uncertain environment, studying organizational processes for adaptive change — *i.e.,* for identifying, accessing, and coordinating changing arrays of strategically important resources — becomes essential to developing theory that can improve *ex ante* strategic decision making.

From Industry Structures to Cognitive Processes. A traditional view in strategic management takes industry structures as both given (exogenously determined) and static. Taking the view that the competitive environment is a complex evolving system in which various quasi-stable conditions may emerge, however, firm strategies may be seen as efforts to discover and put in place asset structures that, like attractors in complexity theory, create quasi-stable, survivable conditions for a firm or group of firms in a complex environment. In this sense, the competence perspective views current industry asset structures as products of past managerial cognitive processes (Gorman, Thomas, & Sanchez, 1996). Because managerial perceptions of assets that may be potential new sources of profitable quasi-stability can lead to development of new firm-level assets that collectively comprise new industry asset structures, within the competence perspective *industry structure* is seen as both dynamic and determined by evolving managerial cognitions. Thus, the competence view endogenizes the cognitive processes of managers whose strategic goals (Sanchez & Thomas, 1996) are seen as eventually leading to new industry asset structures.

Further, in contrast to the traditional focus on tangible assets like production capacity in strategic analysis of industry structures, the competence perspective also recognizes the "structural" importance of intangible assets like knowledge and capabilities that are needed to use tangible assets effectively. Competence theory presumes that it is generally more difficult and time-consuming to change the *ideas* that organizations use than the *things* that organizations use. As a result, the concept of industry structure and its impact on competition is expanded to include not just firm endowments of tangible assets and their associated recurring costs, but also firm endowments of intangible assets and the cognitive difficulties which must be overcome to change a firm's stock of intangible assets (Dierickx & Cool, 1989). Thus, a firm may be seen as a sensemaking system that creates a cognitive structure that determines how it uses the assets it possesses. Industry level "competence groups" are formed when firms with similar cognitive structures follow convergent, quasi-stable patterns in their creation and use of tangible assets and capabilities. In this way, competence theory also extends the traditional strategy concept of strategic groups within an industry to include groups based on shared cognitive structures (Porac, Thomas, & Baden-Fuller, 1989).

From Strategic Commitment to Strategic Flexibility. Traditional strategy theory has often asserted the importance of creating organizational commitment to specific strategic goals as essential to effective strategic management. Usually this assertion is supported by examples of firms that enjoyed competitive success in pursuing a course of action that was preceded by a significant organizational commitment to that course of action (Sanchez, 1994). Within the competence perspective, however, commitment is seen as only a final step in a strategic process of creating competences that ultimately give an organization *strategic options* to commit to alternative courses of action (Sanchez, 1993, 1995).

Further, while strategic commitment may appear courageous when followed by success, commitment may also lead to significant negative consequences or even organizational calamity when the uncertainties of a dynamic complex environment make it impossible for managers to discern a clearly optimal course of action. In a dynamic and complex environment, organizational survival may depend on an organization's ability to maintain the strategic flexibility to alter a course of action when evolving circumstances indicate a need for change. Thus, competence theory places the traditional strategy notions of contingency and strategic fit in a dynamic context in which managers must solve an evolving "situational puzzle" (Martens, Bogaert, & Van Cauwenbergh, 1994) to achieve strategic fit with changing circumstances and new contingencies. In effect, competence theory proposes that the dominant strategy for surviving the evolving uncertainties of a complex environment is less likely to be making major strategic commitments to specific courses of action, and more likely to be developing the firm as a strategically flexible open system capable of redeploying its resources and capabilities when it is advantageous to do so.

From "Decide and Control" Strategic Management to the Design of Self-Managing Systems. Much traditional theory characterizes strategic management as a process of top-level decision making, formulating strategic plans, and implementing controls to be sure plans are carried out as intended. Competence theory, in addition to recognizing the cognitive limits of even the most brilliant managers facing dynamic and complex competitive environments, presumes that top managers simply do not have the information, expertise, or time needed to make detailed strategic decisions, to draft plans for implementing their decisions, and to monitor full compliance with plans.

As a result, the competence perspective recasts the role of strategic managers as one of designing adaptive organizational systems in which decision making is widely distributed so that it can be brought into alignment with the information, expertise, and other resources needed to make good decisions at various levels of complexity in the decision making process. In essence, to reduce complexity in decision making and avoid cognitive overload for the top managers of organizations, the competence perspective suggests that the content of much traditionally top-level strategic decision making must be devolved to other levels and entities in an organization where more fully informed decisions can be made. When strategic managers are successful in designing organizations with better alignments of decision making with the information, expertise, and resources needed to make good decisions, the result is not just a much "flatter" or decentralized organization structure. The result is a *system design* composed of largely *self-managing processes,* usually vested in "empowered" teams. This new form of organization design, through which an organization may take on many of the properties of a *self-organizing system,* is contrasted with the traditional strategy model of hierarchical decision making in Figure 1.

Strategic managers who are successful in creating largely self-managing system designs can shift their cognitive and decision making activities to the more conceptual task of defining *strategic boundaries* that will give strategic direction and guidelines to self-managing processes within an organization. Strategic managers may then monitor the progress of self-managing teams in meeting broad milestones agreed between strategic managers and self-managing teams, as well as taking responsibility for providing the agreed-on resources that self-managing teams need to carry out their processes and meet

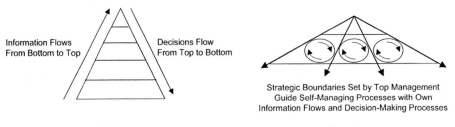

Figure 1:   Information and Decision Flows in Organizations with Traditional Management
Hierarchy *versus* System Design with Self-managing Processes.

their milestones. Key aspects of this new way of strategically managing a firm composed
of largely self-managing processes are apparent in the relationship between Chrysler
Corporation's strategic managers and its largely self-managing "platform teams" for new
car development (Sanchez, 1996).

Another important approach to creating self-managing organizational processes is the
creation of *modular product and process architectures*. Modular architectures establish
information structures that provide "embedded coordination" of distributed, self-managing
development and production processes (Sanchez & Mahoney, 1996). Many of the
networks of "modular organizations" gaining prominence today use modular product and
process architectures and common computer platforms as frameworks for creating self-
managing interorganizational processes (Sanchez, 1996).

Whether self-managing processes are wholly internal to an organization or extend into
a network of available resources, the devolution of much traditional management work
to self-managing processes within an organization greatly reduces the complexity of the
strategic management task, allowing strategic managers to attend to improving their
cognitive processes for discerning promising strategic directions in their evolving
environments.

Conclusions

Creating a design for a firm as an adaptive system in a complex environment is perhaps
one of the most intellectually challenging tasks one can undertake. Managers and
management theorists drawn to this challenge may find it useful to contrast the search for
an optimal organization design that infuses much traditional strategic management
thinking with the properties of attractors in complexity theory. Attractors are patterns of
interactions between entities in a complex system that lead to islands of "near-order" or
"quasi-stability" in the midst of otherwise chaotic environments. In at least a metaphor-
ical sense within the competence view, different strategies may be thought of as
alternative adaptive system designs that compete to attract critical resources from

providers of inputs and from customers for outputs by providing alternative quasi-stable relationships amidst the chaos of complex economic competition. Within this metaphor, competence-based strategic management may be thought of as a cognitive search for some relatively "simple rules" for ordering complex stocks and flows of resources in ways that act as attractors capable of forming quasi-stable relationships within and between adaptive open systems. The continuing commercial success of popular management books offering some version of the "seven secrets of competitive success" or the like may be indicative of a genuine need of managers today for "simple rules" that reduce the complexity of the management task to more manageable proportions. The intent of such books should challenge strategic management researchers to search for "simple rules" or principles for strategic organizing that may be capable of creating quasi-stability and survivability for firms in different kinds of complex competitive environments (Sanchez, 1996).

Competence-based strategic management as a "contest between managerial cognitions" may consist, in its most fundamental respects, of a search by managers for the most *understandable* system designs for ordering relationships in their complex organizations and environments. In this regard, the principle of creating system designs that devolve much decision making activity to largely self-managing processes may be seen as an important step towards defining a simple rule of system design for improving the adaptive capability of organizations in complex environments. This principle may be only a first step in an eventual evolution — in both strategic management theory and practice — from conceiving of management as a system for controlling organizational processes to conceiving of management as a process for creating self-organizing systems.

A growing number of contemporary organizations appear to be adopting various forms of system designs for creating and leveraging competences through self-managing processes (Sanchez & Mahoney, 1996). In effect, what we may now be witnessing is the realization in practice of contemporary versions of Ashby's (1960) and Beer's (1966) early designs for "the firm as a brain" — *i.e.,* intended system designs with distributed, self-managing interpretation and action-taking processes carried out within a broad strategic framework guided by top managers. If this is a correct characterization of the changes many organizations are undergoing today, we may also be entering an era in which we will witness the achievement of new levels of organizational competence and performance, because such organizations may at last be overcoming the "cognitive bottleneck" of concentrated decision making and control at the top that limits the ability of traditional hierarchical management structures to interpret and respond effectively to the complexity of their organizations' internal and external environments.

If this interpretation of the new organizational forms and their strategies for managing dynamic complexity is correct, we can expect to see both growing success and wider adoption of these more cognizant, adaptive, and thus robust system designs for organizations. Designing organizations as largely self-managing systems for creating and leveraging competences may therefore represent a new dominant logic (Prahalad & Bettis, 1986; Sanchez, 1995) for strategic management in complex dynamic environments.

References

Ashby, W. R. (1960). *Design for a Brain: The Origin of Adaptive Behavior.* London: Chapman and Hall.

Barney, J. (1991). Firm resources and sustained competitive advantage. *Journal of Management, 17,* 99–120.

Beer, S. (1966). *Decision and Control.* New York: John Wiley & Sons.

Checkland, P. (1981). *Systems Thinking, Systems Practice.* Chichester: John Wiley & Sons.

Dierickx, I., & Cool, K. (1989). Asset stock accumulation and sustainability of competitive advantage. *Management Science, 35,* 1504–1511.

Forrester, J. W. (1961). *Industrial Dynamics.* Cambridge, MA.: MIT Press.

Forrester, J. W. (1968). *Principles of Systems.* Cambridge, MA: MIT Press.

Ghemawat, P. (1991). *Commitment: The Dynamic of Strategy.* New York: Free Press.

Gorman, P., Thomas, H., & Sanchez, R. (1996). Industry dynamics in competence-based competition. In R. Sanchez, A. Heene, & H. Thomas (eds) *Dynamics of Competence-Based Competition* (pp. 85–98). Oxford: Elsevier.

Hamel, G., & Prahalad, C. K. (1991). Corporate imagination and expeditionary marketing. *Harvard Business Review, 69(4),* 81–92.

Heene, A., & Sanchez, R. (eds) (1997). *Competence-Based Strategic Management.* Chichester: John Wiley & Sons.

Kaufman, S. (1993). *The Origins of Order.* Oxford: Oxford University Press.

Lippman, S. A., & Rumelt, R. P. (1982). Uncertain imitability: An analysis of interfirm differences in efficiency under uncertainty. *Bell Journal of Economics 13,* 418–438.

Martens, R., Bogaert, I., & Van Cauwenbergh, A. (1994). Strategy as a situational puzzle: The fit of components. In G. Hamel & A. Heene (eds) *Competence-Based Competition* (pp. 57–76). Chichester: John Wiley & Co.

McKelvey, B. (1997). Quasi-natural organization science. *Organization Science, 8(4),* 352–380.

Miller, J. G. (1978). *Living Systems.* New York: McGraw-Hill.

Morecroft, J., & Sterman, J. (1994). *Modeling for Learning Organizations.* Portland, Oregon: Productivity Press.

Porac, J., Thomas, H., & Baden-Fuller, C. (1989). Competitive groups as cognitive communities: The case of the Scottish Knitwear manufacturers. *Journal of Management Studies, 26,* 397–416.

Prahalad, C. K. & Bettis, R. A. (1986). The dominant logic: A new linkage between diversity and performance. *Strategic Management Journal, 7(6),* 485–501.

Sanchez, R. (1993). Strategic flexibility, firm organization, and managerial work in dynamic markets: A strategic options perspective. *Advances in Strategic Management, 9,* 251–291.

Sanchez, R. (1994). Higher-order organization and commitment in strategic options theory: A reply to Christopher Bartlett. *Advances in Strategic Management, 10B,* 299–307.

Sanchez, R. (1995). Strategic flexibility in product competition. *Strategic Management Journal 16* (summer special issue), 135–159.

Sanchez, R. (1996). Strategic product creation: Managing new interactions of technologies, markets, and organizations. *European Management Journal, 14(2),* 121–138.

Sanchez, R., & Heene, A. (1996). A systems view of the firm in competence-based competition. In R. Sanchez, A. Heene, & H. Thomas (eds) *Dynamics of Competence-Based Competition* (pp. 39–62). Oxford: Elsevier.

Sanchez, R., & Heene, A. (1997). Competence-based strategic management: Concepts and issues for theory, research, and practice. In A. Heene & R. Sanchez. (eds) *Competence-Based Strategic Management* (pp. 3–42). Chichester: John Wiley & Sons.

Sanchez, R., Heene, A., & Thomas, H. (1996a). *Dynamics of Competence-Based Competition.* Oxford: Elsevier Pergamon.

Sanchez, R., Heene, A., & Thomas, H. (1996b). Towards the theory and practice of competence-based competition. In R. Sanchez, A. Heene, & H. Thomas (eds) *Dynamics of Competence-Based Competition* (pp. 1–36).Oxford: Elsevier Pergamon.

Sanchez, R., & Mahoney, J. T. (1996). Modularity, flexibility, and knowledge management in product and organization design. *Strategic Management Journal, 17* (Winter Special Issue), 63–76.

Sanchez, R., & Thomas, H. (1996). Strategic Goals. In R. Sanchez, A. Heene, & H. Thomas (eds) *Dynamics of Competence-Based Competition.* Oxford: Elsevier.

Senge, P. (1990). *The Fifth Discipline.* New York: Doubleday.

Simon, H. A. (1947). *Administrative Behavior.* New York: MacMillan.

Vennix, J. (1996). *Group Model Building: Facilitating Team Learning Using Systems Dynamics.* Chichester: John Wiley & Sons.

Weick, K. (1992). *Sensemaking in Organizations.* Thousand Oaks: Sage Publications.

Wernerfelt, B. (1984). A resource-based view of the firm. *Strategic Management Journal, 5(2),* 171–180.

Whitehead, A. N. (1925). *Science and the Modern World.* New York: Macmillan.

Index